Aviation Ground Operation

Safety Handbook ▪ Fourth Edition

Aviation Ground Operation

Safety Handbook ▪ Fourth Edition

GREEN CROSS FOR SAFETY ® National Safety Council

Project Editors: Janet K. Battiste
Patricia M. Laing
Technical Adviser: Barbra Jean Dembski
Cover and Interior Design: Steve Hamann
Composition: Media Graphics Corporation
Cover Photos: Upper left: courtesy United Airlines; upper right: courtesy Air Canada; bottom: courtesy United Airlines, photo by Mike Sroka.

Printed in the United States of America.
93 92 91 90 89 88 5 4 3 2 1

Library of Congress Cataloging in Publication Data
National Safety Council.
Aviation Ground Operation Safety Handbook
International Standard Book Number: 0-87912-138-6
Library of Congress Catalog Card Number: 87-063466
1M688 Product Number 129.63

CONTENTS

INTRODUCTION

Safety in aviation ground operations is an integral part of maintaining safe, reliable, economical airline service. Safety practices in the shop, hangar, on grounds and ramps, and in the terminal may very well determine the safety of passengers in the air. This handbook suggests practices and programs that will improve ground safety.

ECONOMIC IMPACT OF ACCIDENTS

The employee, family, and society suffer as a result of an accident. There is also significant economic effect on a company's profits. Many line management personnel are under the false impression that all losses resulting from an accident are covered by insurance. In fact, the indirect and usually noninsurable costs can be many times higher than the direct costs. Some of the indirect costs are these: the cost of overtime or additional wages to replace an employee; the cost of time spent by supervisory personnel in investigation and preparing required accident reports; the cost of selecting and training a replacement employee. If an aircraft is damaged, costs may increase because of loss of passenger revenue, ferry expenses, flight crew salaries, and so on. Insurance premiums are usually based on past accident experience and also increase as the losses increase.

Safety Policy

Management's responsibility for preventing accidents is the same as its responsibility for administering any other business function. A high accident frequency is an indication of inadequate management policies and safety programs. Supervisors must be held responsible for accidents in the same manner as for on-time performance and cost control.

A statement of the safety policy that clearly defines the responsibilities of management and employees in maintaining a safe working environment should be published and enforced.

EFFECTIVE GROUND SAFETY ADMINISTRATION

The administration of an accident prevention program may be delegated to one person, preferably a qualified health and safety professional; however, the ultimate responsibility for preventing accidents still rests squarely with management.

The person selected to administer an accident prevention program should report to a top executive officer in the company. In this position, the safety administrator will be able to advise and to represent management. Details regarding the responsibilities of safety administrators or those designated as safety professionals are discussed in Chapter 11, Safety Program Organization.

Companies that do not have an assigned individual for administering the accident prevention program should seek assistance from their insurance carriers, the National Safety Council, and the appropriate governmental agencies.

HANDBOOK SCOPE

This handbook is designed to guide the user in the prevention of accidents that may result in injuries to employees and the general public, and in damage or other loss to customers' and company property or equipment.

This handbook sets forth the guidelines for safely accomplishing most ground operations associated with aircraft. Such guidelines are applicable (but not limited) to the following:

- All air carriers
- Fixed base operators
- Corporate fleet operators
- Airport operators
- Aircraft service contractors.

In addition to the material in the text, the Reference sections at the end of each chapter list many codes or standards. This Handbook uses United States of America standards. Other standards may apply outside the United States. It is strongly recommended that readers refer to these codes or standards in their jurisdiction to obtain more information.

FOURTH EDITION

This fourth edition is an updating by the Executive

Committee of the International Air Transport Section of the National Safety Council. Its express purpose is to give practical guidelines that will help reduce ground accidents within the industry. The contents are not regulations but suggested good practices. Where any conflict exists between these suggested practices and the legislation in the country where they are to be applied, the legislation will, of course, take precedence.

In this edition, an extensive discussion of fuel tank entry procedures has been added to Chapter 5, Hangar and Shop Operations.

While the information and recommendations contained in this publication have been compiled from sources believed to be reliable, the National Safety Council makes no guaranty as to, and assumes no responsibility for, the correctness, sufficiency, or completeness of such information or recommendations. Other or additional safety measures may be required under particular circumstances.

The Fourth Edition was prepared with the assistance and cooperation of the International Air Transport Section Executive Committee of the Industrial Division of the National Safety Council, including the following members and honorary members:

Air Canada
Aircraft Service International, Inc.
Air New Zealand
Alexander & Alexander, Inc.
Alitalia
American Airlines
American West Airlines
Ansett Airlines of Australia
Applegate, William
ARA Services
Australian Airlines
British Airways
British Caledonian Airways, Ltd.
Boeing Commercial Airplane Co.
Canadian Air
Chouinard, Richard
Christoffel, N. L. Chris
Consolidated Freightways, Inc.
Continental Airlines, Inc.
Dee, Ralph J.
Dobbs Hause, Inc.
Eastern Airlines
Federal Express Corp.
Fitzpatrick, William J.
Flying Tiger Line, Inc.
Frank B. Hall Co.
The Hartford Insurance Group
Horn, Ronald A.
Hudson General Aviation Services, Inc.
Hudson General Corporation
Johnson & Higgins, Inc.
KLM Royal Dutch Airlines
Lockheed Georgia
Lufthansa German Airlines
M & M Protection Consultants
McCarran International Airport
Machinists Union
Marriott Corp.
Midwest Express Airlines
Moore & Sons, Inc.
Nasr, Malhab
Northwest Airlines, Inc.
Norton Air Force Base
OCCU-TEC, Inc.
O'Donnell, Joseph
Orion Air, Inc.
Pan American World Airways, Inc.
Piedmont Airlines
Port Authority of New York and New Jersey
Quantas Airways Limited
Rollins Burdick Hunter Co.
Saudi Arabian Airlines
Scandinavian Airlines System
Snider, Bruce
Svahn, Albert R.
Swissair
Trans World Airlines, Inc.
Trinidad & Tobago BWIA International Airways Corp.
United Airlines Inc.
United Parcel Service
University of Tennessee
U.S. Air
U.S. Aviation Underwriters, Inc.

We extend special thanks to the following people for their assistance in obtaining photographs: Chicago Fire Department, Rescue Station No. 1, O'Hare International Airport: Chief David J. Lozeau, Captain A. Rosenquist, Engineer J. Neary, Fire fighters A. Prendergast and R. Moser; Jerry Lawrence, Director of Media Affairs, Chicago Fire Department; Kathy O'Malley, Department of Aviation, City of Chicago; Dr. Willard Wells, Director Ground Safety, United Airlines; Joseph Hopkins, Corporation Communications Manager, United Airlines; John J. O'Reilly, Sr., Safety Engineer, Port Authority of New York and New Jersey; Joseph G. Svadlenka, Sr. Manager, Safety, Health and Fire Prevention, Federal Express; Mick Paice, Sr. Ground Safety Advisor, British Airways; Anthony Walsh, Airport Operations Services Manager, Air Canada; Robert Mackey, Assistant Vice President, U. S. Aviation Insurance Group; John F. Montgomery, Ph.D., Manager, Ground Safety, American Airlines; Joy Prescott-Church, Manager, Ground Safety/Loss Control, Continental Airlines; and William Simpson, Piedmont Airlines. Thanks also to Nancy Krynski, Johnson & Higgins, and Margaret Neumeier, U. S. Aviation Underwriters, Inc.

Customer Service Center
Gates C19-C32
Concourse
Baggage Claim
Terminal
Rapid Transit To City
C18a

CHAPTER 1

Airport Buildings and Fixed Facilities

Top: Prominently displayed, easy-to-read signs help the public locate and proceed to destinations more quickly. Note that these signs are near the ceiling and pose no impediment to traffic flow.

Bottom left: Dual-level ramps with one-way traffic flow promote safe and efficient use.

Bottom right: The control tower directs all traffic on the ramps and in the airspace around the airport.

Courtesy United Airlines; photos by Mike Sroka.

Buildings and facilities at an airport affect the operation of the airlines and influence the attitude of the public toward air travel. Safe and attractive fixed facilities help speed the movement of passengers and the work of airline employees. In addition, pleasant, efficient surroundings can contribute to a positive attitude of the public toward air travel (Figure 1-1).

The safety and health requirements needed to maintain airport buildings, hangars, and fixed facilities safely will be discussed in this chapter.

AIRPORT TERMINALS

The design of airport facilities is of concern to safety personnel. Proper layout and construction can help control injuries, fires, and hindrances to operations. Ample size of facilities is desirable; otherwise, airport overcrowding can lead to accidents and injuries.

Building codes prescribe proper construction materials, adequate fire protection, and satisfactory building egress. Before construction of a new building or transfer to an existing one, the structure should be checked to determine how well it complies with building codes. Any required changes should be made to ensure compliance with the applicable codes. The usual sources of building codes and standards are the local city and state governments, federal and state regulatory agencies, the National Fire Protection Association (NFPA), and the American National Standards Institute (ANSI). (See References at the end of this chapter.)

Passenger terminals are generally laid out to provide the least possible delay to passengers from the time they arrive at the airport until they board their flights. The construction of the facilities should minimize hazards that cause falls and protect people from harmful contact with machinery. Facilities also minimize the necessity for people to handle baggage manually.

Throughout the terminal complex, in the terminal building, and in hangars and shops, falls suffered on stairs are one of the most common of all accidents. Falls are usually caused by undue haste, poor illumination of stairs, or defective or poorly designed steps.

Lighting in entrance areas, in stairwells, and in all other areas of a terminal building should be adequate to provide easy visibility by night. Suggested illumination levels for many operations are listed in the Illuminating Engineering Society of North America (IES) *Lighting Handbook.* (See References.)

Entrance doors should be automatic to eliminate any impediment to handicapped people or people with baggage. Railings should separate the entranceways to doors. Glass doors should have an eye-catching strip across them. Doors should open away from the person going through. Exits should be treated in the same manner as entrances.

Emergency egress should conform to the *Life Safety Code,* NFPA 101. (See References.) Emergency exits discharging directly onto an airport ramp should be clearly identified with EMERGENCY EXIT ONLY signs, with lettering a minimum of two inches high. *Exits of this type should be locked and must be equipped with panic hardware to allow the door to be opened in an emergency.*

Courtesy United Airlines.

Figure 1-1. Terminal buildings provide safe, attractive, and efficient surroundings for passengers and airport employees.

Escalators have been a common source of injury (Figure 1-2). These, as well as elevators and moving walks, should be installed in accordance with the applicable ANSI standards. (See References. Other standards might apply outside the United States.) One extra precaution is recommended, however. The ANSI standard for escalators permits a maximum speed of 0.64 m/s (meter per second) (125 fpm [feet per minute]), but because of the heavy traffic and the wide range of age among passengers, the escalator should travel less than 0.4 m/s (90 fpm).

Ticket counters should be placed as near to the terminal entrance as practical to minimize the distance passengers must travel with baggage. However, ample room for traffic on the concourse should be allowed. Ticket and baggage check-in counters should be conspicuously identified to prevent confusion which might lead to collisions and falls. Counter surfaces should be free of sharp edges or corners.

Weight scales with rounded corners and no jagged edges should be installed as close to floor level as practical, and entrances to the scales should be left free so that baggage can slide on easily. Post weigh-in baggage conveyor systems, when used, should be installed as near to the floor as possible, to minimize lifting. Nonpublic conveyor installation should conform to applicable codes, and conveyors should be located so that the public does not have access to them. All pinch points on conveyors should be enclosed, and the conveyors guarded from contact by personnel, except opposite the weight-scale passage.

Power services should be installed, maintained, and inspected according to the *National Electrical Code* (NFPA 70; see References) or the electrical code of the local governing body. Power panels and outlets should be guarded from access by unauthorized personnel. Power outlets on floors should be placed where they present no tripping hazard.

Fire extinguishers and sprinkler systems should be located throughout the airport terminal building. Their placement and type should be in accord with NFPA 10, *Portable Fire Extinguishers* and NFPA 13, *Installation of Sprinkler Systems.* (See References.)

Observation decks are common facilities at most airports. In addition to helping relieve congestion within the terminal, they can provide the airport with a source of income if the public is charged admission to them. Terminals built after the advent of the jet aircraft were constructed with the jet blast hazard in mind. However, older facilities did not have provisions for jet blast, and, as a result, the public on observation decks can be exposed to a serious hazard. Before jet operations

Courtesy United Airlines.

Figure 1-2. Escalators in air terminals should be easy to find and prominently marked. Escalators should travel less than 0.45 m/s (90 fpm).

are introduced into older air terminals, blast tests should be conducted in order to determine the hazard involved in continuing to permit the public on an observation deck. If tests disclose undesirable conditions, observation areas should be closed or protected to control the hazard.

HANGARS, SHOPS, AND FREIGHT TERMINALS

Hangars

The construction of hangars is covered by federal, state, and local building codes, as well as many National Fire Protection Association (NFPA) standards. (See References.)

Hangars should be designed so that aircraft can be rapidly removed in an emergency. Nesting, or heavy interlocking of aircraft, should not be permitted. Adequate aisle space and access to fire extinguishers, hoses, sprinkler-control valves, and fire alarm stations should be maintained.

Valuable aircraft parts, engines, instruments, fixtures, and other materials should be stored in a separate building. If they are stored in the hangar, they should be physically separated from the repair or service areas. A barrier should be constructed of materials having a minimum fire rating of one hour. If the hangar is equipped with sprinklers, the storage area should be similarly equipped, but supplied by a separate system. The roof of the storage area should be watertight in order to prevent damage to stock if the hangar system deluge equipment or sprinklers go into operation.

Work Docks. Work docks and stands in hangars should be constructed of fire-resistive material and should be provided with handrails, guardrails, and toeboards (Figure 1-3). The deck of these units should be of a material that offers a firm footing or be provided with skid-resistant coverings. Electrical service outlets should be provided on stands and docks as required. They should conform to the *National Electrical Code* (NFPA 70; see References). Large metal complexes such as aircraft docks should be permanently bonded and grounded.

The maintenance requirements of T-tailed aircraft have resulted in the construction of large, complex, movable tail docks. The height of the aircraft has required the installation of a lifting device or cage similar to an elevator within the superstructure of the work dock.

The classification of such a hoisting unit is a code problem in some states or municipalities, and the matter should be resolved prior to construc-

Courtesy Air Canada.

Figure 1-3. Work docks and stands should offer firm footing and be protected by guardrails. Their decks should provide a firm footing or be provided with skid-resistant coverings. Workers at elevated heights must wear safety harnesses and lines when required to do so by the specific exposure or by company policy.

tion. Minimum safety requirements should be established whether or not a code is applicable. It is advisable to construct the unit as close to code compliance as possible. In addition, the dock load capacity should be posted.

Large tail docks require extensive electrical systems for power movement of the dock and hoist and for the outlets of maintenance equipment. The dock electrical system as well as that of the complete hangar should comply with the *National Electrical Code* (NFPA 70; see References).

Electrical Systems. Primary sources of electrical power to hangars should be approved for the location according to the *National Electrical Code,* NFPA 70, and *Aircraft Hangars,* NFPA 409. (See References.) Outdoor power outlets should also be code-approved, and all outlets should be the three-pole locking type for use with hand-held lighting equipment. Hangars should have grounding plugs for aircraft.

Lighting. The lighting should be adequate for the task performed in each hangar location. Extension lights should be vaportight and equipped with suitable guards. Mobile lighting for use in and around aircraft should be of explosion-proof design.

Heating Systems. The standards for heating systems and their location in hangars should be in accordance with NFPA 409. (See References.) Unit heaters approved for the area must not create a forced draft in the immediate vicinity of aircraft dockage. Heating systems should be maintained to comply with manufacturer's standards. Coils, heat exchangers, and other parts that are within casual reach of employees should be guarded.

Ventilation Systems. These should be installed in accordance with NFPA 409, or equivalent, and should use power machinery suitable to the location. (See References.) Ventilation should be adequate to the conditions of climate and be installed to eliminate forced draft in any area of the hangar in which work is being performed on aircraft.

Safety Measures. Compressed gases such as nitrogen, carbon dioxide, acetylene, helium, oxygen, and hydrogen should be stored in a designated area, and separated accordingly. Cylinders should be stored in a rack or secured by chains. Protective valve caps should be in place. (See Compressed Gas Association pamphlets C-6, C-8, and P-1, which are listed in the References.)

Bulk storage of flammable materials should be in a fire-resistive enclosure. The area should be provided with an explosion-proof electrical system and automatic fire protection. To protect against static buildup, all flammable containers should be provided with a grounding and bonding wire.

Fire protection, automatic and portable type, should conform to the requirements in NFPA 409 and NFPA 10. (See References.)

Emergency eyebaths and showers should be provided for the immediate use of personnel who may accidentally contact aviation fuels or any other materials hazardous to the eyes or body.

Shops

The construction of automotive maintenance buildings should conform to the building codes required for automotive repair garages. Fire protection should conform to NFPA 10 and 13. (See References.) Automotive hoists should meet the applicable code requirements and be provided with safety bars. Hoist capacities should be displayed prominently.

Designated areas for welding operations should be established and the necessary equipment provided. A work-permit system should be set up for performing welding operations away from designated areas. Physical separation of welding from other operations is mandatory. Adequate ventilation should be provided in welding areas; in new buildings, fixed exhaust ducts should be incorporated into design plans.

Spray painting must be done in a physically separated painting room. The spray booth and spray methods should conform to the requirements of NFPA 33, *Spray Application.* (See References.) Paints, thinners, reducers, and other flammables should be stored in approved cans which are kept in metal lockers or wall cabinets.

Freight Terminals

A great deal of airfreight is handled in old buildings that were intended for other uses and were vacated when new structures were built. Freight is usually handled manually and with lift trucks and carts. Power conveyors and automatic handling systems are rare. Efficiency is maintained by good supervision and tight scheduling, along with excellent housekeeping.

Satisfactory airfreight terminals can be constructed similar to a commercial warehouse or motor freight terminal. Construction should comply with the applicable building codes and the NFPA standards. (See References.)

The layout of the buildings should expedite the handling of both inbound and outbound freight. Power conveyors should be utilized where possible. The system should be designed to eliminate multiple handling of freight.

Aisles and separations in airfreight terminals should be sufficiently wide to increase the possibility of containing a fire within a small area. Dividing racks into smaller segments by means of fire partitions is another method of limiting a fire to a small area. It should also be noted that the height of stored material should be kept as low as practical within the limitations of automatic or manual fire-extinguishing provisions. Using noncombustible materials for racks, shelving, and pallets will reduce the fuel that could feed a fire and thus increase the possibility that stored material could be removed in an emergency.

Sprinkler protection can be effective in controlling ceiling temperatures and preserving structural integrity, if selected on the basis of hazard classification and the vulnerability of the roof or ceiling construction. (High-expansion-type foams are finding increased acceptance in warehouses and airfreight terminals.)

The type of fire protection system required is dependent upon the type of material stored, the height and density of stored materials, aisle width, and construction material of racks and pallets, etc. *Rack Storage of Materials,* NFPA 231C, applies to a broad range of combustibles stored over 3.6 m (12 ft) in height on racks. Storage on plastic pallets or plastic shelves, bin storage, or shelf storage is not covered. Nor is storage of high hazard materials, such as tires, roll paper, or flammable liquids. For storage on less than 3.6 m racks, see *Installation of Sprinkler Systems,* NFPA 13 (see References and Chapter 7).

Standard docks should be provided for both inbound and outbound freight. Spring-loaded dock plates should be built-in so that material-handling equipment can move in and out of trailers and trucks with minimum restrictions. If standard dock plates are used, they should have cleats or pins that ensure proper locking.

The ideal facility provides a dock that permits transfer of freight to and from truck beds at the same level as the terminal floor. Arrangements should be provided for station-wagon and pickup-truck heights as well as for the higher wheels-under-bed trailers. Truck wells or dock levelers can fill this function.

Forklifts or similar removal equipment must not enter a docked vehicle unless the wheels on the vehicle are chocked to prevent movement.

The area in front of the dock should be kept clean and free of any broken boxes or cartons. Adequate lighting is required to enable the truckers to back into a position without hitting adjacent trucks or people.

Overhead doors in the freight terminal should be counterbalanced to facilitate opening.

Adequate ventilation should be provided to dispel fumes generated by combustion-engine equipment moving in and out of the facility. Consideration should be given to the use of electrically operated material-handling equipment in a freight terminal rather than engine-driven.

Stacking pallets of freight for cargoliners requires a hoist or platform to build up the pallet stack. The hoists, though excluded from the ANSI standard for elevators, A17.1 (see References), do come under local or state codes in some instances. Before the hoist or platform is installed, the appropriate code should be checked and any compliance requirements met. The main issue with pallet-buildup hoists involves the requirement of a

Courtesy United Airlines; photo by Mike Sroka.

Figure 1-4. Covers for service facility pits should be of lightweight metal and should require no more than 130 newtons (30 lb) to lift.

skirt guard to enclose the unit fully while it is raised to its uppermost position.

Smoking should be prohibited in the general air-freight building. Specific areas should be designated where smoking is permitted; these should be restricted to ready rooms or lunch areas.

For information on procedures for handling freight in dock areas, see Chapter 6, Air Cargo Operations.

RAMP SERVICE FACILITIES

Aircraft service facilities located in ramp pits are becoming common both at existing airports and at new facilities. These pits do much to improve the efficiency of the general ramp operation by eliminating the need for mobile ground equipment.

The pits should be located as near to the aircraft service connections as possible. Proper planning will eliminate the necessity for cables or hoses to be lying on a ramp (Figure 1-4).

Periodic checks of the pits should be established in order to determine and control possible fuel or fume accumulation.

Electrical power pits in ramps should have a stationary motor-generator. Mobile ground power units should not be permitted. The motor-generator should be located alongside the terminal concourse. Maximum voltage is 220. Warning signs must be posted [see *National Electrical Code 1987 Handbook,* section 110-17(c)]. Electrical wiring should conform to *National Electrical Code,* NFPA 70, for Class I, Group D, Division I hazardous locations. (See References.)

Fuel pits should be located a minimum of 15 m (50 ft) away from a terminal building or concourse (Figure 1-5).

The flow of more than one fuel through a single line is prohibited. Separate pumps, single lines, and standard couplings will be utilized for each type of fuel. Color codes should be mandatory and should comply with the accepted standard.

The compressor, air conditioning, and heating units for the ramp pits should be located in the concourse structure. Their installation should comply with applicable codes.

The connector on the air starter should be

Courtesy United Airlines; photo by Mike Sroka.

Figure 1-5. Fuel pits should be located at least 15 m (50 ft) away from the terminal building or concourse.

designed to eliminate the possibility of an accidental disconnect during start-up.

CONSTRUCTION SAFETY

Contractors engaged in new construction, major alterations, or demolition of buildings should be required by contract to operate in a safe and controlled manner. Requirements should be based on established work practices, the Associated General Contractors of America *Manual on Accident Prevention in Construction,* and NFPA 241, *Safeguarding Building Construction, and Demolition Operations.* (See References.)

Contractors should be advised of the problems associated with prop and jet blast, both personal exposure and property damage hazards. They should be given assistance in developing a program for materials handling, general cleanup and housekeeping, and fire protection.

Prior to the start of construction, the site should be inspected to determine the requirements for public protection. Providing barricades and overhead protection should be the responsibility of the contractor. Constant monitoring of construction areas should also be provided to ensure that safety standards are being met.

Construction offices and storage sheds should be of noncombustible materials. Heaters should be of the approved type only, and installations should comply with applicable codes. L-P gas interior heater and temporary outside heaters should comply with NFPA 58 *Liquefied Petroleum Gases.* (See References.)

Contracts should reserve the right to require all of the contractors' and subcontractors' employees to operate in accordance with the contract.

Temporary Structures

Temporary structures anywhere at the airport should be of sound and substantial construction. Illumination, heating, and fire protection should conform to applicable standards. Temporary structures, for the most part, are of materials with low fire-resistive ratings. As a result of their potential fire hazards, they should not be constructed near facilities housing high-value merchandise, aircraft, or important operations.

Temporary structures should be removed as soon as they are no longer needed in order to eliminate unnecessary ramp or gate congestion.

MAINTENANCE OF OPERATIONAL FACILITIES

All buildings are subject to deterioration; therefore, procedures should be established so that any evidence of structural failure or deterioration is reported at once and repairs made immediately. Responsible personnel should make continuous surveys of facilities to detect unsafe conditions or hazards, and a preventive maintenance program should be in effect.

Building Maintenance

Roofs should be inspected annually, as well as after violent storms. It is important to look for signs of excessive movement, strain, or overloading in the structural members of roofs, framing, trusses, and floor joists.

All building doors should open outward. Exits should be well lighted and marked. Illuminated exit signs should be installed for all emergency exits and passageways, as required by NFPA and local building codes. Panic hardware should be installed on the exterior doors used for emergency exits. Exit doors should be kept unobstructed and unlocked in the direction of egress. Doors should not open immediately onto a flight of stairs, but onto a landing at least the width of the door. Emergency evacuation plans should be posted in all buildings.

Windows designed to be opened should be kept in good operating condition to prevent sticking. Broken windows and screens should be replaced or repaired as soon as possible.

Bolts used for attaching window washers' belts should be fastened to reinforced window frames, not to exterior walls. These bolts should be installed on all windows above the ground floor, unless the windows can be safely cleaned from the inside without the window washer having to lean out. When working above the ground floors, window washers should wear safety belts. All belts should be checked periodically for defects, and should be stored and maintained in good condition.

A sufficient number of approved fire extinguishers should be located in all buildings. They should be easy to reach in case of fire. A clear access passage of at least 0.9 m (3 ft) wide should be maintained for them at all times. Extinguishers should be serviced according to NFPA codes.

Stairs, Ladders, and Ramps

To reduce the possibility of accidents, stairs and steps should be kept clean and free of obstacles or slippery substances at all times. Stair surfaces should be kept in good repair. Loose boards, insecure treads, protruding nails, and torn or worn stair treads should be repaired or replaced immediately upon detection.

The use of open risers should be avoided whenever possible. Slippery treads should either be replaced or coated with slip-resistant surfacing materials. Stair nosings should be securely fastened and rounded or beveled to prevent people from catching their heels on the treads.

Where there is less than 2.1 m (7 ft) of headroom over stairs, the obstruction should be padded, suitable warning signs posted, or the overhead obstacle clearly painted in contrasting colors.

Both interior and exterior stairways should be sufficiently lighted so that all treads and landings are clearly visible. For indoor stairs lights, there should be three-way switches at both the top and the bottom landings.

Floors

Cracks, holes, bumps, and other defects in floors can endanger safe handling of materials and cause injury to employees. Therefore, floors should be kept in good repair. To reduce the chance of falls, floors should be cleaned with slip-resistant substances or covered with slip-resistant materials.

When floors are misused, they will wear excessively. Here are some misuses or abuses that should be avoided:

- Use of heavy equipment or storage of heavy materials may overstress or weaken floors.
- Spilling acid or oil on nonresistant floors can damage their surface.
- Dropping heavy or sharp articles, such as aircraft towbars, can cause floors to spall or crack.

The maximum allowable loading per square foot of floor should be prominently displayed in all storage areas. In cases of unusually heavy, concentrated loads, such as safes, a structural engineer should analyze the condition and determine if floors are strong enough. The engineer should recommend means of additional support, if necessary, or alternate storage areas. Recommended load limits should never be exceeded, and heavy loads should be spread over large areas instead of being concentrated in one location. The weights of hoists and other equipment suspended under the floor should be considered in determining the floor's safe load limit.

Joists, beams, or subflooring in old structures may have deteriorated to such an extent that the original maximum load limits are no longer valid. Where there is evidence of deterioration, a structural engineer should determine the safe load limit or the need for repairs.

Floor openings should be guarded by railings and toeboards unless they are fully protected by other means. After dark, floor openings should be adequately illuminated to prevent anyone from falling through. Any telephone and electric conduit inspection plates should be kept in safe condition to prevent tripping.

Floors and stairways should not be waxed if this causes a slipping hazard. Appropriate slip-resistant waxes or other finishing compounds should be used for floor protection. The primary reasons for waxed floors becoming slippery are too much wax, excessive buffing or polishing of newly waxed floors, and accumulations of liquids or other slippery substances.

MAINTENANCE OF EXTERIORS AND GROUNDS

Exteriors

Metal chimneys or stacks should be frequently checked for corrosion and other defects that could possibly cause them to collapse. Steel guy wires, used to brace stacks, should also be checked periodically for defects.

Wire braces and guys should be properly placed and kept under proper tension. In areas where vehicles will pass under guys, the wires should be kept at least 3.5 m (12 ft) above the ground by means of posts. This gives sufficient clearance to prevent vehicles from catching the guys and toppling the chimney.

All chimneys and stacks should be fitted with spark arrestors if located in areas where flying sparks may be a fire hazard. Adequate lightning protection systems, connected to low-resistance grounds, should be provided on all high objects.

Chimneys, water towers, and other high obstructions should be painted in a proper safety color-code as required by the authority having jurisdiction. They should be equipped with appropriate warning lights for after-dark identification.

Grounds

The grounds, particularly around buildings and flammable or explosive storage areas, should be well guarded and kept free of nonessential flammable materials.

All construction work on grounds should be clearly identified by signs. Construction areas should be protected by barriers suitably marked with reflective materials or illuminated—or both—for easy visibility after dark.

Roads and walkways should be kept clear and in good repair. They should be defined. They should be adequately lighted at night to ensure pedestrian and vehicle safety.

During winter months, snow and ice removal equipment and materials should be kept immediately available. Sand, cinders, ashes, or sodium or calcium chloride should be used to cover icy roads and other slippery surfaces. Icicles should be removed from above doorways. Those doing the task should take precautions to avoid being hit by falling icicles.

Lines, wires, and similar obstructions strung less than 2.1 m (7 ft) above the ground should be clearly marked. Normally, low-hanging wires should not be located over roads or sidewalks, but where necessary, particular care should be taken to avoid contact by passing vehicles or people. Electrical lines must be either elevated enough to clear traffic or buried underground.

Open drainage ditches should be guarded by

fences, barricades, or other protection when there is danger of persons falling in. Closed drainage is preferred and should be provided whenever possible. All open ditches which present any kind of hazard should be effectively illuminated at night, identified by day, or suitably guarded.

Power Mower Safety

During the spring, summer, and fall, frequent lawn mowing is necessary to keep grounds attractive and in good condition. For convenience and efficiency, power mowers are typically used.

Before a power mower is used, it should be inspected for safe operating condition. Only mowers that conform to ANSI standards should be used. (See References.) Mowers in need of repair should not be used until repairs are made. They should be tagged as unserviceable and routed to the proper authority for repair or disposal. No adjustments or repairs should be attempted by the operator or maintenance personnel while the mower is running.

Only trained workers should be permitted to operate power mowers without supervision. Mower blade height should be adjusted in accordance with manufacturer's recommendations. Mower blades should never be set lower than 4 cm (1½ in.) above the ground.

Power mower operators should wear ear protection, eye protection, and safety toe shoes or metal toe guards.

Mowers should be fueled outside buildings after the motor has had time to cool sufficiently. All sources of ignition should be kept clear during fueling. Workers are not to smoke while pouring gasoline into lawn mowers. The fuel container and fuel tank should be effectively bonded.

Operators attempting adjustments or repairs should take precautions to avoid starting mower engines accidentally. Ignition wires should be disconnected because the engine may start if the blades are rotated while the engine is hot. On rotary mowers, the cutting bars operate at 2,500 to 3,500 revolutions per minute. No liberties should be taken with equipment and guards *must* remain in place. If the mower is not equipped with adequate safety skirts around the blades, it should not be used until suitably modified.

The mowing area should be kept clear of all debris. Because of the clearance needed between the mower housing and the ground for satisfactory operation, the suction effect caused by the blades is sufficient to pick up debris and hurl it outward with enough force to cause serious injuries.

Mowers with "deadman" safety stop devices should be tested by releasing the handle of a standing, idling mower at least once each time the mower is started. If the safety stop is not functioning or if doubt exists about whether it is properly functioning, operators should check with maintenance for adjustments or repair.

Operators should mow in a forward direction at all times. When it is necessary to mow backward, operators should not lift the rear of the mower because they might set the mower down on their toes or their feet may slip underneath the housing. Operators must be particularly cautious when mowing over uneven ground. On rolling terrain, they should never mow uphill or downhill. The preferred method is to mow across the hill or slope.

Electric lawn mowers should be plugged into a ground fault circuit interrupter (GFCI) when possible. If a GFCI is not available, a three-prong electric adapter should be used. If an extension cord is used, be sure it is approved for outdoor use. Electric mowers should not be used when the ground is wet or damp, nor should they be stored in damp areas.

REFERENCES

American National Standards Institute, 1430 Broadway, New York, NY 10018.

Elevators, Escalators, and Moving Walks, ANSI A17.1-1984.

Marking Physical Hazards, Safety Color Code for, ANSI Z53.1-1979.

Turf Care Equipment—Power Lawn Mowers, Lawn and Garden Tractors—Safety Specifications, ANSI/OPEI B71.1-1986.

Associated General Contractors of America, Inc., 1957 E St., NW, Washington, D.C. 20006.

Manual of Accident Prevention in Construction, 1977.

Compressed Gas Association, 1235 Jefferson Davis Hwy., Arlington, VA 22202.

Requalification of DOT-3HT Seamless Steel Cylinders, CGA C-8-85.

Safe Handling of Compressed Gases in Containers, CGA P-1-84.

Visual Inspection of Steel Compressed Gas Cylinders, CGA C-6-84.

Illuminating Engineering Society of North America, 345 E. 47th St., New York, NY 10017.

IES Lighting Handbook.

National Fire Protection Association, Batterymarch Park, Quincy, MA 02269.

Aircraft Fuel Servicing, NFPA 407, 1985.

Aircraft Fueling Ramp Drainage, NFPA 415, 1983.

Aircraft Hangars, NFPA 409, 1985.

Aircraft Maintenance, NFPA 410, 1980.

Aircraft Rescue and Fire Fighting Vehicles, NFPA 414, 1984.

Construction and Protection of Aircraft Loading Walkways, NFPA 417, 1985.

Construction and Protection of Airport Terminal Buildings, NFPA 416, 1983.

Evaluating Foam Fire Fighting Equipment on Aircraft Rescue and Fire Fighting Vehicles, NFPA 412, 1974.

Installation of Sprinkler Systems, NFPA 13, 1987.

Life Safety Code, NFPA 101, 1985.

Liquefied Petroleum Gases, Storage and Handling of, NFPA 58, 1986.

Motor Freight Terminals, NFPA 513, 1984.

National Electrical Code, NFPA 70.

Portable Fire Extinguishers, NFPA 10, 1984.

Rack Storage of Materials, NFPA 231C, 1986.

Safeguarding Building Construction and Demolition Operations, NFPA 241, 1986.

Spray Application Using Flammable and Combustible Materials, NFPA 33, 1985.

National Safety Council, 444 N. Michigan Ave., Chicago, IL 60611.

Power Lawn Mowers, 464.

FLIGHT
ARRIVAL
INFORMATION

Handicap
Pick-up/
Drop-off

THIS AREA RESERVED
FOR PASSENGERS
REQUIRING SPECIAL SERVICES

CHAPTER 2

Safeguarding Passengers in Terminals

Top: Providing vital flight information on easily accessible boards helps prevent accidents caused by haste, crowding, or confusion.

Bottom: Areas reserved for people requiring special services reduce the accident potential and enable airport personnel to more efficiently serve these passengers.

Top and lower right: courtesy United Airlines, photos by Mike Sroka; lower left: courtesy City of Chicago, Department of Aviation.

A passenger terminal may be as simple and unpretentious as a room next to the hangar or a hangar annex used by the fixed-based operator as a gathering point for clients and customers. In a small community, a local service terminal building of modest size with adjacent ramp area may be used to process and board passengers. However, the great majority of air travelers pass through the extensive building and ramp complexes of the the major air terminal.

The material in this chapter can be applied in both small and large terminals. In either, there is a tremendous potential for loss if systems fail or a major disaster occurs.

PUBLIC AREAS

To prevent injuries to the public in terminals, these basic principles and considerations apply:

- No hazards should impede the flow of passengers from the street to the aircraft. This is important since most injuries are caused by falls.
- Facilities should be clean and well maintained to eliminate hazards that deterioration of facilities or poor housekeeping can cause.
- Efficient handling of passengers is essential. Otherwise, crowding will pose an accident hazard.
- The fact that people of all ages—from infants to the elderly—use air terminals must be considered in their design. Many people are new to air travel, and others may be confused when facilities at a strange terminal differ from those with which they are familiar. Also, airport sightseers,

Courtesy City of Chicago, Department of Aviation.

Figure 2-1. Crowds of sightseers and well-wishers, as well as passengers, must be safeguarded from injury in airport terminals.

of which there may be fairly large numbers, need protection from personal injury (Figure 2-1).

- In designing the airport, remember that rapid travel upsets people's routine and often is fatiguing. Therefore, terminals should be built to allow for reduced awareness on the part of the users. For example, consideration should be given to providing more foot candles of illumination than comparable areas in other kinds of facilities would require. The decor of air terminals should incorporate as much bright, distinctive color as possible, particularly on stairs, at exits, and in corridors. Signs should be easy to notice and to read (Figure 2-2).

Parking and Vehicle-Access Areas

Public parking areas around airport terminal buildings should be situated as close to the terminal entrances and exits as is consistent with the general plan. Parking lots should be well surfaced, drained, and lighted. They should have pedestrian walkways and car parking lines that are conspicuously marked and maintained (Figure 2-3). Parking areas should be kept free of debris. Snow and ice should be cleared as they build up during a storm. Parking areas should be patrolled to detect unsafe conditions and to discourage vandalism.

Where multistory parking facilities are needed, care should be taken to ensure that the direction of traffic flow is obvious. Adequate illumination must be provided in multistory parking lots; it is possible that interfloor illumination will be required 24 hours a day.

Traffic patterns in and near parking areas should be circular. The entrances and the exits should be on opposite sides of the lot. Traffic should flow in accord with designed patterns to avoid collision possibility and pedestrian injury. Pedestrian exits from parking lots and walkways to terminal entrances and exits should be controlled by traffic signals during peak hours of traffic.

For vehicles approaching the terminals, dual ramps—one for arrivals and one for departures—help prevent accidents. The traffic on the ramps should be circular (Figure 2-4).

Cab ranks should be maintained as near to the exit of the terminal as is compatible with general congestion in the area. It may be necessary that there be a holding area at some distance from the terminal building and that cabs be called up as required with the aid of shortwave radios operated by traffic marshals.

Passenger-Access Areas

It is essential that no impediment be placed in the path of passengers entering the terminal building. Porter locations, benches, dolly carts, dispatcher locations, and other obstacles must be kept clear of terminal entrances. There should be unimpeded access to the terminal entrance *at all times.*

Pads or mats for automatic door-opening devices should be well maintained to reduce the possibility

Courtesy United Airlines; photo by Mike Sroka.

Figure 2-2. Signs that guide passengers should be prominently displayed.

Figure 2-3. Public parking lots should be as close to the terminal as possible. Parking lots should be well lighted; they should have easy-to-follow identifying systems.

Courtesy City of Chicago, Department of Aviation.

Figure 2-4. Dual ramps with circular traffic patterns produce a regular traffic flow and help prevent accidents. Here departing passengers use the upper ramp; arriving passengers, the lower.

of tripping. Most floors become very slippery when wet. Therefore, runners or floor mats may be advisable during inclement weather. Floors should be finished with slip-resistant floor wax, as tested and classified by Underwriters Laboratories (UL) or similar agencies.

Corridors, stairs, escalators, and moving sidewalks leading from the ticketing area to the aircraft boarding area should be kept as clear and orderly as practical. Baggage carts, folded invalid chairs, lounges, ashtrays, refuse containers, planters, and other furniture awaiting use should be out of the way, positioned along corridor walls (Figure 2-5).

Areas where no-smoking ordinances apply must be clearly designated with adequate signs.

An adequate number of ashtrays and refuse containers should be placed throughout the passenger area. Rubbish containers should be identified with FOR TRASH ONLY signs. Ashtrays should incorporate an extinguishing feature; they should be fastened to a substantial base that will prevent tipping if they are accidentally bumped. Self-closing cigarette containers or standard sand buckets are recommended. These conveniences must be kept in good condition.

Stairways should be covered with slip-resistant material, and handrails must be maintained in good condition. Escalators should be maintained to manufacturer's standards. They should be suitably guarded and posted with signs indicating the location of emergency stop buttons and the correct method of using them. Similar precautions apply to moving sidewalks. Load limits should be posted on elevators and escalators. Wheeled vehicles, such as baby carriages and wheelchairs, should be prohibited from escalators. (See ANSI standard in References.)

Escalators may pose a hazard to young children and senior citizens; special arrangements should be made for these two groups. Signs may redirect them and the people accompanying them to elevators. In larger terminals, passenger service carts may be made available from the traffic staff department; signs in the terminal should indicate the availability of this service.

Lighting in all areas of a terminal building should be well maintained. An emergency lighting system should be installed as a precaution if a primary power failure occurs.

Warning signs and barricades should be placed around areas where remodeling or other construction work is taking place.

Baggage-Handling Areas

Baggage weigh-in facilities should minimize the need for passengers and employees to lift and handle bags (Figure 2-6). Where fully automated combined check-weigh conveyors are used, consideration should be given to locating the baggage-height gauge at the front of the check-in desk. A split curtain or screen should be installed to discourage youngsters from climbing onto the mechanized handling system.

In baggage claim areas, the carousels, conveyors, and dispensers should have emergency shutoffs, be inaccessible to children, and have built-in guards that prevent any hazard to passengers or workers.

Baggage claim areas should be patrolled by company personnel. If a "hang-up" occurs to baggage, passengers should not be allowed to scramble over a moving carousel or other conveyor to retrieve baggage that has stopped moving. Power equipment for the baggage conveyor systems should be positioned and guarded to minimize passenger hazards.

Arriving passengers are often accompanied by relatives and other greeters, so the baggage pickup area can become quite congested. Security officers may be warranted to verify bag ownership and encourage safe passenger flow. Easy access to and egress from the baggage areas must strike a balance with security considerations.

Exits from the baggage pickup area should be automatic, and rail guards should lead to the doors. Canopied areas should be well lighted and protected. Stairs to the street level should be slip-resistant and provided with handrails. Direction signs should be illuminated at all times, and pedestrian walkways should be indicated, outlined, and controlled. Luminous signs, which remain visible in the dark, may be advantageous if a power failure occurs.

Public Service Areas

Terminal buildings are designed to facilitate the movement of passengers on and off aircraft, speeding them on their way but also catering to their needs in the process. Extensive service areas are a necessary part of this process.

Service areas usually include restaurants and cocktail bars, observation decks, lounges, rest rooms, nurseries, shops, and kiosks. The public areas around them should be well maintained.

Standard railings should be considered for protecting glassed areas from damage by carts, baggage, or pressing crowds. It is important that glass doors and walls be noticeable so that pedestrians do not accidentally collide with them.

Where national or local government regulations apply to public areas, the owner, landlord, tenant, or concessionaire should see that such regulations are enforced. These areas include restaurants, cocktail lounges, kitchens, passenger elevators, and escalators. Regulations often require controlling maximum seating capacity, providing an adequate number of exits and free egress from those exits, and marking aisleways, routing, and electrical wiring maintenance. Often regulations call for regular inspection or certification.

Lounges, washrooms, and nurseries should be kept clean and be furnished with ample supplies.

Ideally, lounges should be well away from crowded corridors and ticketing areas, because their prime function is to provide a rest area for passengers. However, rest rooms should be in high-traffic areas and well lighted in order to discourage vandalism and harrassment of users. Nurseries should be in well-controlled, high-security areas.

Courtesy United Airlines.

Figure 2-5. Traffic areas should be kept clear and orderly. Floors should be finished with slip-resistant preparations and kept free of all impediments to passenger movement.

Courtesy United Airlines; photo by Mike Sroka.

Figure 2-6. Weigh-in facilities located at check-in counters reduce the need for passengers to handle and lift baggage. Guards and emergency shut-off prevent any hazards to workers.

OPERATING AREAS

Airport personnel should be aware of special safety precautions to be followed when guiding passengers to and from aircraft. Weather conditions may also require special safeguarding practices.

Gate Positions and Holding Areas

Potential accident situations at gate positions must be identified and avoided. For example, once a flight has been announced, passengers may crowd at the ramp entrance. Procedures should be established to reduce such hazards, and employees should exercise judgment in handling passengers.

Signs designating gate areas should be prominent. In order to provide adequate control and accommodation in holding rooms, occupancy should be limited to passengers only.

Signs designating NO SMOKING BEYOND THIS POINT should be located at doors leading to ramps or to aircraft loading walkways and supplemented by pictograph symbols and broadcast messages in languages appropriate to the terminal.

When practicable, there should be no steps from the holding room to the tarmac, but rather a gradual incline. Furnishings within the holding area should be solid, but positioned out of the traffic path leading from the plane. Floor coverings should be slip-resistant, even when wet. Carpeting is one solution.

Aircraft Loading Ramps

Aircraft loading walkway construction should be in accord with local legislation or authority. As an example, NFPA 417 (see References) applies in the United States.

Because of the large number of moving vehicles on them, ramps or aprons are potential sources of passenger injury. For this reason, it is essential to position equipment around aircraft so that passenger walkways are completely unobstructed. Walkways should be marked with movable tapes or otherwise defined to keep passengers clear of the aircraft and support equipment. This is particularly important with propeller-engine or rotary-winged aircraft. Walkways should not lead over tripping hazards or low-lying portions of the ramp where puddles may have accumulated.

Passenger pathways on the tarmac should not pass under aircraft wings where engines and other pendants might cause head injuries. Wheel chocks, fire extinguishers, and other impediments should be kept well clear of pedestrian pathways. Service vehicles should not cross tarmac-level boarding and disembarking routes. Passengers must be protected against jet engine blast (Figure 2-7).

Equipment not in use at an aircraft should be parked against a building, finger, or wall, or it should be cordoned off. In either case, it should be out of the way of passenger and vehicular traffic.

Ramp areas adjacent to parked aircraft should be well lighted by glare-resistant lamps to allow disembarking passengers to identify the appropriate entrances. Such lamps should be positioned as high as practical. Lighting provided by floodlights mounted on the terminal building would be preferable to avoid obstruction hazards presented by pole- or standard-mounted lights.

Weather Factors

Roadways, walkways, and exitways should be protected from the elements, insofar as practical.

Ramps, parking lots, and areas of vehicular congestion should be constructed and surfaced to drain rapidly. They should be kept free of any obstruction to the free flow of traffic or to snow removal equipment. Ice and snow removal should continue as a storm progresses, so that no areas become blocked. During snowstorms, ramps should be cleared, and icy patches sanded or chemically treated before passengers are allowed to pass to or from an aircraft. If responsibility for snow and ice clearance rests with an airport or a local government authority, conveniently located containers of salt or sand mix might be provided for airline staff use during weekends or nights, when it is often difficult to alert the responsible authorities.

During high winds or when they are forecast, it is advisable to park aircraft to the windward side of the terminal finger, whenever possible. This helps ensure that any gravel blowing off the roof will not injure passengers and workers. (In extreme cases, part of the roof might peel off and cause serious injury.) In addition, parking aircraft upwind of the holding room will have the added advantage of protecting passengers while they are embarking.

Operations should be suspended while an electrical storm is in the immediate area of a ramp. High projections, preferably metal structures, designed to conduct electrical discharge to the ground can help reduce personal injury, equipment damage, and fire exposure. Electronic equipment is available that measures the probability of lightning strikes within various distances of the terminal.

MEDICAL FACILITIES

The extent to which medical or first aid services will be provided depends on terminal size, passenger traffic, and resources available outside the airport.

Smaller airfields must make arrangements with a local medical authority for support in case of serious accident or illness. In larger airports, permanent facilities, staffed with fully qualified medical personnel, might be provided. Services to passengers can include not only first aid and emergency medical treatment, but also, in the case of international passengers, inoculation, and issuance of medical certificates.

In most major domestic and international airports with high traffic frequency, a comprehensive medical center would be an integral feature of the airport plan to provide an immediate response to an airfield crash.

Airports served by airlines must have a medical plan to deal with emergencies involving the largest aircraft that might land there. In the United States, the Federal Aviation Administration requires plans that detail the capabilities of medical facilities, rescue units, available safety-security-military personnel, and nearby shelter areas.

Every airline must also develop methods "appropriate to its own operations and aircraft" for transporting physically handicapped people, as well as for getting them out of a plane in an emergency.

SECURITY

Airports and airline operators have been a target of both political malcontents and thieves. Aircraft have been hijacked and destroyed, passengers held hostage and killed, both in aircraft and in airport lounges.

Security Measures

Measures adopted to counter threats to passenger safety have varied widely: some are publicized; others, for security reasons, kept secret. Protection includes:

- Laminated bullet-resistant glass for check-in points
- Treated-surface glass, which reduces flying glass following a bomb blast
- Closed circuit TV to monitor movement in critical areas

Courtesy United Airlines; photo by Mike Sroka.

Figure 2-7. Loading bridges protect passengers from the environment, aircraft, and operational equipment.

- Physical searches of passengers, hand baggage, and checked baggage.

NOTE: Combined magnetic field doorways, TV apparatus, and vapor detectors have been developed to assist in search processes. With such equipment, staff operators must be provided with the usual film badges to measure their exposure to x-radiation.

There are both financial and social constraints on the degree of security possible. For example, it may be unacceptable to restrict access to airfields to ticket-holding passengers only.

The extent to which a terminal operator should develop security measures is dictated by finances, degree of exposure, and incident experience. Specialist advice can be obtained from local and federal law enforcement agencies, which could also provide backup support.

It is essential that all airport personnel be familiar with procedures for evacuating terminals, even when it is difficult to hold actual rehearsals because of the presence of passengers.

Airport Baggage Inspection Systems

As a result of increased armed hijackings and attempted bombings of commercial airlines in the early 1970s, the United States Federal Aviation Administration required that all passengers and carry-on baggage be subject to a preboarding security examination. (Figure 2-8.)

Specially enclosed, pulsed x-ray fluoroscopic examination systems were developed to increase the speed of baggage inspection, minimize cost, and help ensure passenger acceptance. In general, the system consists of an x-ray generator and an electronic radiation dectector on opposite sides of a chamber, onto which baggage is placed. Signals from the detector generate a video display of baggage contents.

All systems use some form of image amplification to minimize the radiation intensity required to produce a suitable display. To protect both employees and the public, systems are shielded to reduce x-ray emission. Interlocks prevent the system from operating if shielding is not in the proper position.

The system requires at least two people—one to load baggage and the other to monitor the video display. If traffic volume is high enough, as many as five additional employees may work with a single unit.

Baggage inspection units present an unusual occupational radiation exposure because units are operated by security people rather than by trained radiation workers. Personnel working with these units are required to wear a whole-body monitoring device, such as a film badge or a thermolumines-

Courtesy City of Chicago, Department of Aviation.

Figure 2-8. X-ray fluoroscopic baggage examination systems quickly scan all carry-on baggage to protect passengers from armed hijackings and bombing attempts.

cent dosimeter.

Two radiation protection standards are applicable to radiation exposure levels from x-ray baggage units. The Food and Drug Administration (FDA) standard states that radiation exposure from a baggage x-ray inspection system shall not exceed 0.5 mR (millirems) in one hour at a distance of 5 cm (2 in.) from any external surface. The Occupational Safety and Health Administration (OSHA) standard limits an employee's exposure to not more than 5,000 mR in any one quarter year.

A study conducted by the Air Transport Association and the National Institute for Occupational Safety and Health (NIOSH) at five U.S. airports showed the maximum documented whole-body x-ray exposure recorded to be 10.8 mR biweekly; the level represents an annual value of 270 mR, which is considerably lower than either the FDA or OSHA regulation. This figure assumes continuous operation (24 hours per day), and, therefore, any individual employee would not be exposed to more than one third this level.

NIOSH recommends that periodic maintenance programs be instituted to check the effectiveness of the shielding on the baggage inspection systems.

REFERENCES

American National Standards Institute, 1430 Broadway, New York, NY 10018.

Industrial Lighting, Practice for, ANSI/IES RP7-1983.

Elevators, Escalators, and Moving Walks, ANSI/ASME A17.1-1984.

National Fire Protection Association, Batterymarch Park, Quincy, MA 02269.

Construction and Protection of Aircraft Loading Walkways, NFPA 417, 1985.

U.S. Department of Health and Human Resources, National Institute for Occupational Safety and Health (NIOSH), Cincinnati, OH 45226.

"Documented Personnel Exposures from Airport Baggage Inspection Systems." October 1976. Publication #77-105. Available from National Technical Information Service, Springfield, VA 22161; Stock No. PB 274-202.

KE 43
UNITED
JET A
KE43
UNITED
FLAMMABLE

529

CHAPTER 3

Ramp Operations at Passenger Terminals

Top and lower right: A worker connects an underwing fueling hose and observes carefully while the operation is in process.

Lower left: A worker in an aerial basket carries out a deicing operation. He is wearing ear protection and a fall protection harness.

Top and lower right: courtesy United Airlines, photos by Mike Sroka; lower left: courtesy British Airways.

Whether hundreds of passengers and tons of cargo or only one passenger and his or her luggage are to be loaded, the principles are the same for safe operation at passenger terminal ramps. The discussion in this chapter is intended to help minimize accident exposure to passengers and employees and damage exposure to aircraft, ground support equipment, and facilities in the ramp areas of passenger terminals.

PARKING AND MOVING AIRCRAFT

Factors that determine parking position of aircraft are:

- Position of fueling or other fixed services
- Position of the jet bridge for passenger disembarking
- Positions of passenger gates and boarding and disembarking paths
- Position designated for adjacent parked aircraft
- Access and working positions for aircraft service, passenger service, and cargo-handling vehicles and equipment.

One variable factor that affects the parking position of aircraft is the wind. Both the direction and the velocity of the wind should be taken into account.

At times, such factors as heavier-than-normal ramp traffic, repairs on ramps or terminals, construction operations, or snow and ice accumulation make it necessary to park aircraft in less than desirable areas. In such instances, special care and alertness are required of ramp crews. Some precautionary measures to use are temporary lighting, roped or taped walkways, and additional staff to direct passengers around or clear of the hazardous areas.

The principal hazards to be guarded against while moving aircraft on ramps are collision and prop wash or jet blast. Whether aircraft are taxiing or being towed, their wing tip, tail, and nose positions should be closely watched so that warning can be given against impending collision with other aircraft, fixed installations, or ground equipment. (See Communications section, near the end of this chapter, for further details.)

When aircraft are taxiing, prop wash or jet blast hazards are to be guarded against. Wash or blast can slam doors closed, knock people down, and cause turboprop propellers to rotate. The strong turbulence can also cause unsecured equipment to roll or blow over or cause debris to be blown into the engines of other running aircraft or onto people in the area. Such occurrences can result in injured people and damaged equipment. Prevention requires well-planned operating procedures executed by trained and disciplined ramp crews.

Engine Starting

During engine start at a ramp, alertness on the part of ground and flight crews and precise operation are required to ensure the safety of passengers, employees, and equipment.

At all times, the engine-start sequence should be supervised by a capable and reliable person. It is the duty of this person to make sure that all personnel are clear of danger areas. Further, all unnecessary ground support equipment is to be removed from the vicinity of the aircraft. The person in charge must maintain close watch of the aircraft and its vicinity to make sure no one enters the danger areas once the start sequence has commenced. This person must also watch for boarding or disembarking passengers at other aircraft in the vicinity, particularly those behind the one being started. Jet blast or prop wash could injure passengers or employees in the area.

Before the actual engine-start sequence begins, the person controlling the start procedure must ascertain that all of the following are properly secured: passenger entrances, galley service doors, cargo compartment doors, and access and service panels.

A common method of communicating with the flight captain is hand signaling and voice. It is essential that standard authorized signaling procedures be followed (Figure 3-1). The flight deck crew and ground employees controlling the start sequence should have a firm knowledge of the signals, particularly those used to indicate the presence of an emergency or a hazardous condition. Signals must be executed in a clear, sharp manner that precludes confusion between signals. Ramp workers must avoid lazy half-motions. They also should refrain from making any motions such as adjusting their head cover or rubbing their nose or face because such gestures may be misconstrued as a signal. (Interphones for direct contact between the ground and the flight crew may also be used.)

Communications between an aircraft and ground often require telephone or radio communication sets. It is a prime requisite that such sets be maintained in good working order and that all personnel responsible for their use understand both their operation and the procedures laid down for their use. Unnecessary conversation during the start sequence must be avoided since it could cause misunderstanding of important commands or acknowledgments. (See the Communications section, later in this chapter.)

Workers charged with the responsiblity for engine starting should have full knowledge of all procedures and regulations necessary to accomplish the procedure under unusual, as well as usual, conditions. (Unusual conditions might be starting engines with passenger stands positioned at an aircraft, with the jetway extended to the aircraft, or with the aircraft integral stairway extended.)

All nose gear pins, main gear locks, pitot covers, control locks, wheel chocks, static ground wires, and power leads must be removed from the aircraft prior to departure.

As protection against fire, there should be fire extinguishing equipment in the area during every aircraft start. The size and type of equipment will vary with aircraft type and size. These units must be maintained in good working order, and all workers likely to be called on to operate them should be thoroughly trained in their use.

AIRCRAFT LOADING AND UNLOADING

The well-being of passengers at the terminal ramp is of primary importance. The most common hazards for people in the ramp area are falling, tripping, and being struck by moving ramp equipment. In addition, bad weather causes hazards. The essential points in protecting passengers, as well as ramp personnel, are discussed in this section.

Passenger Loading

The following specific points should help ensure passenger safety during boarding and disembarking:

- Passenger stands or loading bridges should be properly positioned so that there is no gap between them and an aircraft (Figure 3-2).
- After the passenger stand or loading bridge has been positioned, the brakes and position locks should be set to prevent movement. The stand should also be properly set to prevent it from wobbling, bouncing, or sagging.
- The maximum load capacity for passenger stands should not be exceeded. The load should be checked especially when the stand is used for group photos.

Courtesy United Airlines, photo by Mike Sroka.

Figure 3-1. Those using hand signals to communicate with the flight crew should execute the signals in a clear, precise manner.

Courtesy British Airways.

Figure 3-2. Passenger stands should be positioned so that there is no gap between them and the aircraft.

- Obstacles in the passengers' pathway from the plane to the gate should also be checked. (For example, check fueling hoses, ground wires, power cables, patches of ice or snow, oil or grease slicks, or water puddles. In addition, vehicles must be restricted from crossing the loading path during passenger boarding and disembarking.)
- The movement of other aircraft in the area should be checked before passengers board or disembark.
- Passengers should not be permitted on ramps while there is a danger of prop wash or jet blast.
- Movements of passengers should always be under control; passengers must not be allowed to roam free for both safety and security reasons.
- All employees should make sure that there is no smoking on the ramp—either by passengers or any airport or airline employee.

Courtesy United Airlines, photo by Mike Sroka.

Figure 3-3. Efficient planning of the loading operation allows large amounts of cargo to be moved quickly and safely.

Employee Procedures at Ramps

Because service employees are acutely conscious of meeting schedules, they may use undue haste during loading or unloading operations at a terminal ramp. Rapid, efficient work can be done safely, provided each member of the team does his or her job and uses proper methods and equipment. Any attempt to take shortcuts could result in delay, damage, or injury.

The following employee guidelines should help to achieve a safe on-time operation.

- Each employee should understand and know how to carry out his or her particular function.
- Each employee should know the layout, function, and location of each section of the aircraft on which he or she works.
- It is important that only experienced operators be allowed to operate mobile ground equipment.
- A preplanned method of working on each specific aircraft will prevent confusion, mishandlings, and unnecessary rushing, all of which could lead to accidents and injuries.
- If an employee is in doubt as to how to perform a particular function, the employee should be encouraged to apply the maxim, "Don't guess. Ask someone who knows."
- Horseplay is a frequent cause of accidents. There is no room for clowning either on an airport ramp or in the vicinity of an aircraft. Such behavior *must* be prohibited.

Cargo Handling

Employees who handle cargo are probably subject to more accidents and injuries than are other employees. This is because cargo handling usually requires physical effort on the part of the employee and the use of mechanized devices. Anyone involved in cargo handling should, therefore, be thoroughly trained in safe-operating techniques (Figure 3-3).

The following suggestions for handling materials can be used by employees as practical guidelines to handling cargo safely and efficiently:

- Do not pile or stack cargo too high. Avoid instability in cargo stacks.
- Pack all cargo firmly (either in the aircraft or on carts) to prevent its toppling.

- Use tarpaulins, cargo-restraining nets, side gates on carts, and other such items to prevent cargo from falling.

- Operate all mechanized units, such as cargoveyors and forklift trucks, in accordance with established instructions. Do not exceed the vehicle's rated load capacity. Carry loads centered and fully back against the fork carriage, and ask your supervisor if you have questions about the load. On an incline, always drive with the load upgrade. Always travel with the forks carried low, and do not carry loads that block your vision.

- Never attempt to lift, push, or pull more than one's personal physical capabilities allow. When lifting, use the squat lift (bend the knees, keep the back straight) if the load is below table height and can be lifted close to the body. If the load is large and/or heavy, get assistance to lift it. Use the stoop lift or assisted one-hand lift to lift small, light objects out of a container (see the Manual Handling section in Chapter 5 for detailed instructions).

- Avoid wearing jewelry (such as rings and identification bracelets). Such objects may catch on hooks, nails, buckles, locks, or straps and cause serious injury to fingers, hands, or arms.

- All cargo should be slid rather than lifted into small spaces. Lifting may cause fingers or hands to become jammed between objects.

- Avoid handling cargo by the metal or plastic strapping that is frequently used to bind heavy or awkward shipments.

- Set all cargo down easily (rather than dropping it) to avoid injuries to the feet and toes, as well as to prevent damage to aircraft flooring and to shipments.

- Wear appropriate gloves, shoes, and clothing.

- Exercise extreme care when entering the aircraft cargo areas from carts and tractors or when alighting from the aircraft onto vehicles. Entering and leaving aircraft is best done from stands.

- When handling live animal cargo, keep fingers and hands clear of the interior of cages or crates to avoid possible bites.

- When a poorly packaged shipment is observed, proceed with caution.

- All contents should be prevented from spilling out and possibly causing injuries.

- Neckties should be avoided, but if they are part of required uniform, make sure that ties are firmly clasped or tucked into their shirts to prevent possible catching in conveyor rollers or pinch points. A clip-on type of tie is desirable.

Weather

Unfavorable weather is as much to be reckoned with in conducting safe ramp operations as it is in conducting a safe flight. Rain, wind, and snow cause both employees and passengers to rush in conditions when footing and visibility are poor. Potential problems with ground equipment and aircraft are also compounded during inclement weather.

Foul-weather clothing serves to keep ramp workers comfortable and, hence, reduces the inclination toward undue haste. In addition, employees working under poor weather conditions must recognize the need to use extreme care both in their own physical movements and in the operation of portable and mobile service equipment on ramps.

Aircraft and support equipment require special care in bad weather. Some rules to follow are:

- Use protective devices, such as engine intake covers, cooler plugs, and pitot covers as weather conditions warrant.

- Keep footholds such as passenger boarding stairs, running boards on tractors and trucks, and ladders and work platforms clear of ice and snow.

- Keep handrails on boarding stairs clean and dry to encourage passengers to use them during rain, snow, or wind.

- Check the outermost portion of jet bridges frequently to ensure that the walking surface exposed to the weather between docking is clear of ice and snow or water.

- Keep vehicle lights and windshields clear of snow and grime to aid the driver's vision.

- Use foul-weather equipment on vehicles such as windshield wipers, defrosters, and frost shields. Such equipment should be properly maintained.

All possible steps should be taken to protect passengers from the elements. Covered passenger walkways are ideal. However, where these are not available, umbrellas or closed transportation from holding rooms to aircraft are helpful. During unfavorable weather, boarding and disembarking passengers should be closely supervised to prevent accidents.

Good maintenance of ramp surfaces is essential to employee and passenger safety, as well as to safe vehicle operation. Drainage systems should be maintained to carry away run-off from rainfall. Removal of snow and ice from ramps must be given a high priority. Material used to thaw ice and snow on walkways and ramps must be noncorrosive so as not to damage aircraft and equipment.

GROUND EQUIPMENT MOVEMENT AND PARKING

Ground service mobile equipment operates as a vital adjunct to flying activity. Efficient control of ground traffic is necessary both to avoid equipment damage and personal injury and to run a safe, on-time operation.

Organizing Vehicular Traffic

Regulations for airport vehicular traffic should cover the equipment operated on company premises and on airport roadways. For effective control, all groups concerned (airport management and airfield tenants) should coordinate efforts, agree on necessary rules and regulations, and accept responsibility for adherence and enforcement. These ends can best be achieved by establishing a local airport traffic committee consisting of airport management and tenant representatives.

These should be the prime activities of the airport traffic committee:

- Establish well-marked and controlled-traffic roadways, where possible.
- Post speed limits. Place signal lights and signs to indicate NO PARKING, SLOW, and STOP. Designate authorized parking areas and traffic lanes.
- Develop methods for enforcement of the established traffic rules.
- Periodically review the types and numbers of vehicles that use airport roadways and aircraft apron areas to determine whether there are needless traffic lanes.
- Review traffic rules and procedures periodically and modify them as conditions change.
- Review accident reports and modify rules, where possible, to eliminate future accidents of a similar nature.

After the operating requirements and driving rules recommended by the airport traffic committee have been completed and approved by airport administration and management of the various tenants, the committee should publish and distribute the documents to all tenants and vehicle operators.

Operating Requirements

Everyone who operates a motor vehicle on any airport service roadway or ramp area should carry a driver's permit at all times when on duty. Some airports and/or tenants may issue permits to their own employees. If so, the airport administrator should have the authority to revoke such permits.

An airport driver's permit should list the equipment that the holder is qualified to drive. To assist police officers, safety patrol officers, and others in authority, authorized drivers should be readily identified by a badge, uniform, armband, or other conspicuous means established by the airport traffic committee.

Tenants and their employees should be required to maintain vehicles in good working order. Especially important are the horn, headlights, rear lights, rearview mirrors, brakes, reflectors, steering mechanism, turn indicators, and windshield wipers.

All motor vehicles should display lights from one-half hour before sunset to one-half hour after sunrise, and at all other times when the airport obstruction lights are on or when there is not sufficient light to make persons and vehicles discernible at a distance of 150 m (500 ft).

Every vehicle authorized to operate on any public cargo ramp and apron area, public loading area, or public passenger ramp and apron area should display identifying symbols or numbers that can be clearly identified with field glasses or binoculars from an observation deck, such as the control tower (Figure 3-4). Enforcement of this rule should limit field traffic to regular tenant vehicles and to other authorized vehicles, such as supplier trucks and government agency vehicles.

Any motor vehicle authorized to operate in an aircraft landing area during daylight hours should be made conspicuous and identified by a paint scheme, checkered flag, or other such means. Vehicles operating in this area during hours of darkness should have an overhead, rotating, red light. In addition, motor vehicles operating in the aircraft landing area should have a two-way radio if aircraft movements are controlled by radio (or they should be accompanied by a vehicle so equipped).

Driving Rules

No vehicle should be operated carelessly or negligently or at a speed exceeding the limit. The operator must not be under the influence of intoxicating liquor or narcotics.

Vehicle operators in public areas should comply with rules of the road as established by the airport or airline. Traffic lights, signs, or mechanical or electrical traffic-control signals must be obeyed, unless an authorized representative of the administrator directs otherwise (Figure 3-5).

Lane requirements and safe following distances should be observed by vehicle operators. The rule for following distances is at least a two-second interval between two-axle vehicles. Longer intervals are required (four seconds or more) for larger, multiple-axle vehicles. More distance yet should be allowed under adverse driving conditions and for vehicles with loads.

Operators of ground vehicles must understand that aircraft *always* have the right-of-way. Ground vehicles should pass well to the rear of taxiing aircraft. When maneuvering around aircraft parked in the public cargo ramp and apron areas, ground vehicles should not move faster than a normal

Courtesy United Airlines, photo by Mike Sroka.

Figure 3-4. All vehicles authorized to operate on the airfield should be conspicuously marked so that they can be identified from the control tower with field glasses.

walk. They should be operated even more slowly on wet pavement, in congested quarters, and under other adverse conditions.

When an aircraft is parked on a public passenger ramp and apron area, the space between the aircraft and railings, fences, or passenger loading gates should not be used as a vehicle thoroughfare.

Vehicle operators must know and obey control tower signal lights. Tower signal lights and their meanings are:

- Steady RED light: *Stop.*
- Flashing RED light: *The vehicle is in a dangerous location and should be removed.*
- Steady GREEN light: *Clear to proceed.*
- Flashing WHITE light: *Return to origination point.*
- Alternating RED and GREEN lights: *Exercise extreme caution.*

When the airport includes a localizer building used in conjunction with the instrument landing system, vehicle operators should be familiar with its location. Flashing red lights are installed at both ends of such buildings. When the control tower turns these lights on, all vehicles should stop behind the yellow lines on the ramp on both sides of the instrument runway. Vehicles should not proceed until cleared by the tower or other authorized traffic control personnel.

Vehicles should enter restricted operational areas only with the specific permission of the administration. In addition, before entering or leaving restricted areas, such as runways, taxiways, and fuel storage areas, the operator of a vehicle may be required to get permission from the control tower or other authority each time.

In general, tank trucks should be forward of the aircraft wing when overwing fueling is in process and far enough away from the aircraft to avoid damage in case of emergency. Trucks should be positioned to permit rapid removal in the event of an emergency and should not be blocked by other equipment. (Fueling is discussed in detail later in this chapter.)

All emergency vehicles should be given the right-of-way during the emergency. All other vehicles not needed for the emergency may proceed only after the operators have determined that they are not entering the emergency area or the path of emergency equipment.

Operators should not park a vehicle, or leave it unattended, in these *public areas:* landing ramp and apron, passenger ramp and apron, cargo ramp and apron, or aircraft parking and storage. Exceptions can be designated only by administration.

Vehicles for hire should not load or unload passengers at any airport locations other than those designated.

Parking

Parking areas for ground support equipment should be located in ready proximity to the aircraft parking areas on the terminal ramp, as well as to the servicing positions around the parked aircraft. These points should be considered for safety in the arrangement of parking and service locations:

- Location of fuel overflow vents on aircraft in relation to the service vehicle position

- Possibility of exhaust vapors from service units entering aircraft cabins
- Avoiding water spillage (such as from lavatory and water-service units) in employee or passenger walkways
- Precluding aircraft settling onto adjacent equipment as fuel, cargo, and passengers board.
- Keeping exit ways clear for moving fueling vehicles in the event of fire
- Keeping a clear pathway from aircraft and passenger stands in case of emergencies
- Positioning stands, food carts, ladders, or cabin service vehicles and conveyors so they remain stable in high winds
- Clear access for cargo tractor trains and other vehicles
- Clear access to fire extinguishing equipment
- Working room for aircraft service personnel
- Free and clear access to the aircraft for emergency vehicles.

SERVICING AIRCRAFT

Aircraft servicing operations include fueling, providing passenger water and lavatory service, and deicing. Fueling is one of the most potentially hazardous servicing operations.

Millions of gallons of aircraft fuel are handled each year in servicing aircraft. Most of this fuel is handled safely because the potential fire hazard is recognized and the necessary precautions are taken. An understanding of fuel characteristics is important as a basis for establishing procedures to prevent fires, injuries to employees and the public, damage to aircraft and ground support equipment, and possible in-flight engine trouble.

This publication and others dealing with fuels (such as those of the National Fire Protection Association, petroleum companies, government agencies, and insurance companies and associations) define concepts necessary for a knowledgeable approach to safe fuel handling. Some basic information is given below.

Three essential requirements must be satisfied before a liquid fuel can be burned.

1. The fuel must be converted to a vapor.
2. The fuel vapor must be mixed in the correct

Courtesy Air Canada.

Figure 3-5. Airport ramps can become congested with ground service vehicles. Driving rules established for the airport should be strictly observed by operators.

proportion with air (fuel-air ratio).
3. A source of ignition must be present.

Properties of Fuels

Volatility. The tendency of a liquid to vaporize or change into a vapor is called volatility.

Flash Point. The minimum temperature at which a fuel gives off vapor in sufficient concentration to form an ignitable mixture with air near the surface of the liquid is the flash point. Ordinarily, the higher the vapor pressure (the pressure exerted by a volatile liquid, under any of the equilibrium conditions that may exist between the vapors and the liquid) of a fuel, the lower its flash point.

Flammable Limits. Gases and vapors of flammable liquids have a minimum concentration of vapor or gas in air below which propagation of flame does not occur on contact with a source of ignition. This is known as the lower flammable limit (LFL). There is also a maximum proportion of vapor or gas in air above which propagation of flame does not occur. This is known as the upper flammable limit (UFL).

For example, a gasoline vapor-air mixture with less than approximately 1.0% of gasoline vapor is too lean, and propagation of flame will not occur on contact with a source of ignition. Similarly, if there is more than approximately 8% of gasoline vapor, the mixture will be too rich to ignite. Other gases, such as hydrogen, acetylene, and ethylene, have a much wider range of flammable limits.

Flammable limits are determined at pressures of one atmosphere. Thus the range will increase with an increase of temperature or pressure, the UFL being more influenced than the LFL.

Flammable Range. The difference between the lower and upper flammable limits, expressed in terms of percentage of vapor or gas in air by volume, is the flammable range. It is sometimes referred to as the "explosive range."

For example, the limits of the flammable range of gasoline vapors are generally taken as 1.4 to 7.6%, a relatively narrow range. A mixture of 1.4% gasoline vapor (and 98.6% air) is flammable, as are all the intermediate mixtures up to and including 7.6% gasoline vapor (and 92.4% air). The range is the difference between the limits, or 6.2%.

Liquid Turbulence. Agitation during tank filling increases the fuel evaporation rate and vapor release. Because the flammability range is reached at a lower temperature than if no turbulence were present, the ignition hazard is increased.

Fuel Misting. Fuel misting, or atomizing, changes the ignition hazard of the fuel. Any fuel is more readily ignitable if it is atomized or broken up into extremely minute particles. It is this characteristic, for example, that provides the ease with which home oil burners can be ignited. Although the temperature may be low, the fact that liquid takes on the form of a very fine spray increases its ignition capability. Therefore, a pinhole developing in a hose during fueling operations could create a fuel mist, which can be an extreme fire hazard.

Ignition Sources

Static Electricity. Because static spark discharge is a constant threat to safe fueling, proper bonding and grounding are essential. When two dissimilar materials make physical contact and are then separated, a charge of static electricity is nearly always produced. Static electricity is generated when pumping any fuel through a system, such as a hose or pipe. The amount of static electricity generated increases linearly with the rate of flow. High fuel flow rates are normal today, with several thousand gallons of fuel often transferred in a relatively short period of time.

Static electricity can be generated by pumping fuel through a service hose, by allowing it to fall through the air from a filler spout into a tank, or by draining it from a tank or line into a container.

A charge may accumulate on an aircraft during flight or on the ground. Rain, snow, ice crystals, or dust blowing across the aircraft can create a heavy charge of static electricity. A passing cloud may also stimulate a charge. A servicing vehicle, like any other rubber-tired vehicle, may become charged too. Static can also be collected by induction from an electrically charged atmosphere.

Like water, static flows to points of lower potential. If the metallic structures on an airplane are bonded (or connected) electrically, the flow will continue until the potentials are equal. (Note the grounding wires in Figure 3-6a.)

Static electricity flows along the easiest path, just as lightning follows a highly conductive lightning rod and cable into the ground. If no easy path is provided, a charge builds up. When a charge is great enough, an electric spark jumps the shortest or most vulnerable gap. Often, this spark has sufficient energy to ignite flammable vapors.

CAUTION: Stray electric currents originating from improperly made connections between the ground power unit and the aircraft, or from electrical shorts in electric power sources, may also provide a source of ignition.

Smoking. Matches, cigarette lighters, and other smoking materials should not be carried by any employees engaged in fueling operations. The no-smoking rule should be rigidly enforced. Because fuel vapors may settle and travel long distances along the ground, they can create a hazard even a distance away from the fuel source. If passengers remain aboard during fueling operations, there should be a qualified attendant in the cabin to enforce the no-smoking rule and to direct evacuation if it should become necessary.

Excessive fuel odors, or any of the other hazardous conditions noted above, should cause fueling to cease until the condition is corrected. Passenger loading steps or loading bridges should remain in position during fueling, and an unobstructed exit way should be maintained for those on board to use in the event of emergencies.

Open Flames. Open flames are frequently employed in field maintenance work and as signal lights. Fueling should not be done while the following are within 15 m (50 ft) of an aircraft:

- Flareports and similar open-flame lights
- Welding or cutting torches, or blowtorches
- Exposed flame heaters (including portable gasoline or kerosene heaters).

There should be no fueling while the aircraft engines or aircraft combustion heaters are running. This includes wing and tail deicing heaters.

Sparks. Electrical circuits may arc when connections are made; arcing can also occur from faulty equipment. The following precautions are recommended to prevent electric sparks:

- Aircraft batteries should not be installed or removed during fueling operations.
- Battery chargers should not be connected, disconnected, or operated during fuel servicing.
- Aircraft ground-power units should be located as far away from fueling points as practical; they should neither be connected nor disconnected during fueling.
- Care should be taken in using electrically powered tools or other such equipment in or near aircraft during fueling. Battery-powered tools appropriate for use in this environment should be considered as alternatives.
- Aircraft electric switches that control units in the wing or tank areas and that are not necessary to the fueling operation should not be operated during fueling except in emergencies.
- Aircraft radios and radars should be off.
- Fueling should not be conducted within 30 m (100 ft) of energized airborne radar or within 90 m (300 ft) of energized radar installations.
- Photo flashbulbs should not be used in the immediate vicinity.
- Flashlights used near fueling points should be listed by Underwriters Laboratories for use in such locations.

Ramp Vehicles. Improperly maintained vehicles present a fire hazard during fueling operations. Such vehicle problems as electrical system shorts, arcs across terminals, sparks from exhausts, and backfires can ignite flammable vapors and should be corrected when first noticed in the vehicles.

No vehicles other than those performing aircraft servicing functions should be allowed within 15 m (50 ft) of the aircraft during fueling.

Footwear. Those working near the aircraft should be discouraged from wearing shoes or boots with metal nails, hobnails, metal cleats, or plates on the sole or heel. Such footwear creates sparks when it makes contact with other metal or concrete and damages wing surfaces and floor coverings.

Neighboring Turbine Aircraft. Fueling should not be carried on within 45 m (150 ft) directly downstream from the tailpipe of an operating turbojet engine, nor within 22.5 m (75 ft) directly downstream from an operating turboprop.

Fueling Operations

Positioning of Fuel Servicing Vehicles. A clear path should be maintained to permit rapid removal of fueling vehicles from the aircraft in an emergency.

Flow Rates. When the aircraft is being fueled, the maximum rate of gallons per minute as outlined in the aircraft operations manual should not be exceeded. Nozzle pressure should not exceed 345 kPa (50 psi).

Overwing Fueling from Tank Vehicles. This operation requires precautions against static electricity:

- A grounding cable should be connected from the service vehicle to a satisfactory ground.
- A grounding cable should be connected from the ground to an approved point on the aircraft.
- A bonding cable should be connected from the service vehicle to the aircraft.
- A bonding cable should be connected from the fuel nozzle to the aircraft before the tank cover is opened. This bond must be maintained until the fueling operation is completed and the fuel tank cover has been closed.
- Disconnections should be done in the reverse of the order stated above.

When mobile dispensing carts are provided with hydrant fueling systems, they should be grounded and bonded just as mobile fuel trucks.

Overwing Fueling from Hydrants, Pits, or Cabinets. This operation requires the following grounding:

- A bonding cable should be connected from the grounded dispenser to the aircraft. (A conductive fuel hose is not satisfactory bonding.)
- A bonding cable should be connected from the fuel nozzle to the aircraft before the tank cover is opened.
- When disconnecting, reverse the order.

Overwing Fueling from Drums or Cans. This procedure requires proper bonding and grounding connections, as do other methods. Drums should be placed near grounding posts to faciliate this. Connections should be in the following sequence. Before tank covers are opened, connect:

- Drum to ground
- Ground to aircraft
- Drum to aircraft
- Nozzle to aircraft
- When disconnecting, reverse the order.

When fueling is done from cans directly into the aircraft (an uncommon procedure that should be used only in an emergency), a funnel and a chamois may be the only way to filter the fuel before it enters the tanks. Because this procedure is likely to increase the charge of static electricity and the possibility of sparks, use the following precautions. Connect:

- Ground to aircraft
- Can to funnel
- Funnel to aircraft before tank cover is opened.

Under no circumstances should a plastic bucket or nonconductive containers be used for fueling.

Underwing Fueling. This procedure reduces the chance of ignition of flammable vapors by an electrostatic spark. The integral wing fitting and mating hose connections are completely closed and, therefore, automatically bonded. The fuel does not flow until the attachment is completed, and a "splash filling" is avoided. However, grounding and bonding of the aircraft and equipment as previously outlined (except for the nozzle-to-aircraft bond) are still necessary to protect against static electricity and stray currents (Figures 3-6a and b).

Unusual Terrain. When refueling is on ice, sand, desert terrain, or wherever else it is difficult to secure a satisfactory grounding, a compromise procedure is necessary. Since draining the static charge becomes impossible without an adequate ground, the potentials *must* be equalized to prevent a dangerous sparking discharge. Strict bonding practices must, therefore, be followed.

Lightning Storms. Extreme caution should be observed during electrical storms, including suspending fueling operations during severe disturbances.

Indoor Fueling. Fueling and defueling can be done indoors if guidelines provided by the NFPA are followed. (See References.)

Fuel Spills. Prevention of spills entails considerable care on the part of every employee involved in the fueling operation. Fueling equipment must be meticulously maintained. There must be tight observance of each detail of the fueling procedures.

In the event of a fuel spill, emergency shutdown procedures should be activated at once. All fuel spills, regardless of size, must be regarded as a potential source of fire. Specific action to be taken will depend on the size and location of the spill. Spills are discussed in more detail in Chapter 12, Planning for Emergencies.

Passenger Water and Lavatory Services

Water servicing regulations and water service equipment handling procedures should conform with sanitary requirements of the appropriate health authority. Careful attention should be given to water spillage which can be hazardous. Water freezing could create hazardous conditions on ramps and within the servicing areas of an aircraft. Precautions must be taken to make sure aircraft are heated properly and that water freezing is prevented. Electric water heaters require attention; they can burn out or suffer other damage.

In many instances, lifting devices, platforms, or access stands are used by workers to reach the water service areas of aircraft. Workers on such devices should use extreme care to prevent falls. They should wear safety harnesses and lanyards where conditions warrant them.

Operators of water service vehicles and other mobile water service equipment should be careful to prevent injury to themselves or damage to either the equipment or the aircraft. For example, rough handling of latching devices on water service access panels should be avoided to prevent damage to the aircraft.

For the most part, lavatory servicing requires the same precaution and care that is necessary for water servicing. In addition, attention should be given to the relationship between the locations of lavatory service panels and cabin air intakes. Sometimes, odors resulting from servicing can be drawn into the aircraft cabin through these intakes. If this occurs, intake fans should be shut off, as a temporary expedient. Engineering modification should be sought as a permanent solution.

Local health regulations pertaining to waste disposal must be closely followed to prevent contamination or spread of disease. For the same reason, lavatory service equipment should be kept in sanitary condition and good repair.

Deicing Operations

The presence of water, ice, and snow on control and aerofoil surfaces can have a very serious effect on aircraft operation. The aircraft's rapid rate of climb to, and descent from, high altitudes increases the possibility of icing conditions, in any season.

When freezing or near-freezing temperatures are likely to be encountered, an aircraft should not be dispatched with water or wet snow on its flying surfaces, control surfaces, hinges, or any other part likely to be adversely affected by such an accumulation. When it is known that a hazardous condition could result from accumulation of moisture, it is *extremely* important to keep the aircraft moisture-free.

Ice and snow that have accumulated on aircraft and that cannot be swept off by a broom, a rope, or muslin strips should be removed by an approved deicing fluid. Deicing fluid can be applied with mops, cloths, hand pumps, or power sprayers.

Figure 3-6a. This figure shows underwing fueling from a hydrant.

Figure 3-6b. This figure shows underwing fueling from a tank truck.

Courtesy United Airlines, photos by Mike Sroka.

Those applying the fluid should wear appropriate personal protective equipment.

It is important that the fluid be applied as uniformly as possible. No fluid should be permitted to enter any intakes, vents, or openings in the engines.

On aircraft that must be refueled over the wing, deicing should not be started until the fueling is completed. Deicing fluid on upperwing surfaces would present hazardous footing for employees engaged in fueling.

Deicing fluid should not come into contact with the exhaust stacks or other hot engine components. Although the fluid has a relatively high flash point, it can still be ignited.

Deicing fluid should not be used to remove ice or snow from props or prop-spinners. In many cases, deicing is accomplished electrically from the cockpit. (A cloth dampened with deicer fluid may be used; however, manufacturer's procedures should be checked.)

Special attention should be given to aileron and elevator sealing strips, hinges, airseal diaphragms, and flap telescoping rods. These areas may become congested with snow or slush following ice removal.

In some instances, a long aluminum tube with one end covered with a rubber hose can be used to remove ice by rubbing it across various surfaces. Under no circumstances should the aircraft be hit or pounded with these tubes in an attempt to break up ice concentrations.

All mechanized deicing equipment should be operated with extreme caution because of the close proximity to the aircraft. Aerial baskets, baskets attached to a boom used to raise workers to a work area, should be treated with extreme caution and operated precisely according to authorized methods. These units can be hazardous if there is not complete coordination between the person in the basket and the one at the driving controls (Figure 3-7).

Aircraft may also be deiced by placing them in heated hangars. When this is done, it should be ascertained that the aircraft is dry before moving it outside; otherwise, any moisture remaining after the melting process might refreeze. However, the aircraft may be moved outside without complete drying if a coat of deicing fluid is applied prior to removal from the hangar.

COMMUNICATIONS IN RAMP AREAS

One of the most important safety procedures in parking or moving aircraft on ramps involves proper signaling procedures. An aircraft, because of its weight and size, is a difficult object to stop, start, and maneuver in a restricted area.

Standard hand signals, with colored paddles during daylight and light wands in darkness, should be used by every operator (Figure 3-8).

Supervisory personnel must ensure that only qualified and competent employees are allowed to signal an aircraft. Signals should be given to the captain of the aircraft by only one person at any time.

Most operators require that passengers remain seated until the aircraft has come to a full stop—a difficult rule to control. Therefore, an aircraft should be signaled into the parking area in as smooth a manner as possible to preclude sudden stops and starts or extremely sharp turns. The signaler is essentially the eyes and ears of the flight crew while the aircraft is taxiing into or out of a parking area. The captain of an aircraft relies on the signaler to guide the plane safely, smoothly, and efficiently.

While an airplane is standing after it has been parked but before it is to begin taxiing, interphone or two-way radio communication has advantages over hand signals or the voice.

Interphones or Headset Systems. Various types of ground-to-aircraft interphones or headset systems are available. All who are assigned to use such equipment should fully understand its function and their responsibility. Interphones or headset systems should be well maintained to ensure correct operation at all times. Intermittent communications with breaks can easily be misunderstood, and, as a result, potentially dangerous conditions can be created. Voice communications procedures should be strictly followed. Unorthodox commands or acknowledgments must not be tolerated.

Courtesy Federal Express.

Figure 3-7. Workers in aerial baskets deice an aircraft at night.

Two-way Radios (Mobile or Walkie-talkie). Mobile radio or walkie-talkie systems provide an efficient method of ground-to-cockpit communications, provided that personnel are fully aware of the operating procedures and that the equipment is properly maintained. Such systems should be monitored at all times to maintain complete communication. Correct voice communications procedures should be closely followed, and horseplay or unauthorized conversation should not be tolerated.

PROTECTION AGAINST JET BLAST AND NOISE

Jet blast on terminal ramps is a hazard to employees, passengers, and equipment. Adequate ramp surfaces and ramp procedures can help reduce the possibility of jet blast damage.

Reducing Jet Blasts

To reduce jet blasts, concrete ramps in good condition probably make the most satisfactory surface. Airline and airport management should work together to ensure the proper maintenance of ramp surfaces. Concrete ramps that have begun to deteriorate by sinking, cracking, and crumbling generally require that an aircraft produce additional thrust to compensate for their bad condition.

A macadam surface may be less satisfactory than a concrete one since it has a tendency to "dish out" under the main aircraft gear in the hot sun; as a result, the aircraft needs to produce additional thrust for breakaway.

Poor weather conditions, regardless of the type of ramp, can cause increased jet blast. Ice and snow on the ramp surface will require greater thrust from the aircraft engine to begin the initial pullout. Airport authorities and tenant operators, therefore, should maintain ramps as free of ice and snow as possible.

Ramp equipment should be stowed so that it is unaffected by blast. This is essential to avoid personal injury and property damage. Blast fencing can help reduce injury and potential damage.

Aircraft should be parked to prevent any blasts from being directed at galleries or balconies where large gatherings of the public can be expected. Monitoring pilot techniques and surrounding conditions can help reduce blasts and their possible damaging results.

Hearing Protection

Sound enters the human ear in the form of pressure waves and travels through a maze of delicate channels, membranes, fluids, and bone structures. Fine, hairlike projections in the ear sense the pressure waves and, through the auditory nerve, transmit the sensation of sound to the brain. Some loss of hearing ability can normally be expected with age. However, personnel may experience an addi-

Figure 3-8. The chart shows basic hand signals used for communications in ramp areas.

HAND SIGNALS

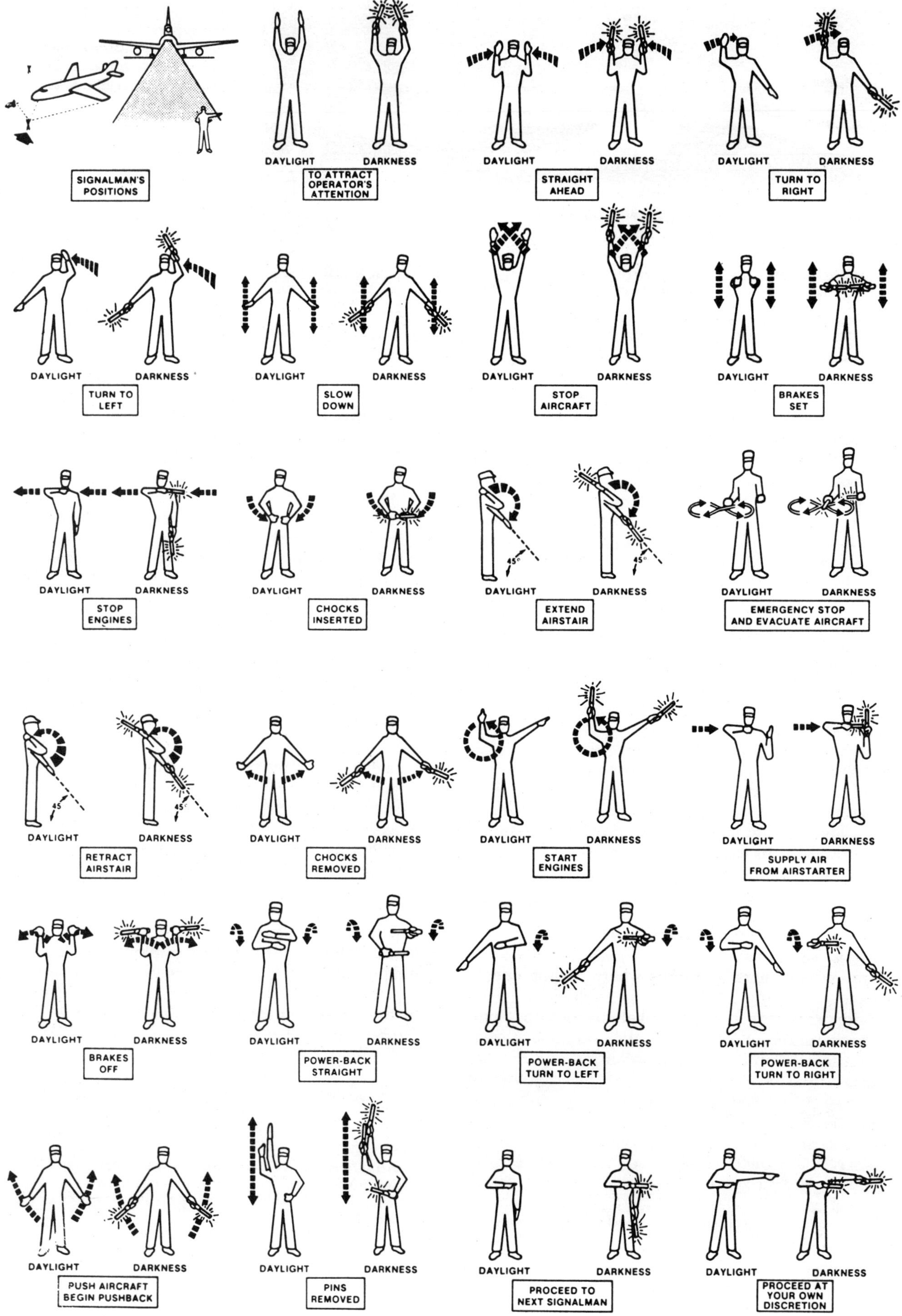

ACF467A(7-85)

Figure 3-9. A jet engine noise suppressor reduces jet roar and the hazard from jet blast during service tests. Service personnel still, however, must wear adequate hearing protection.

tional loss of hearing if they regularly subject themselves to noise from turboprops, jet engines, aircraft auxiliary power units, or other flight line noises without adequate hearing protection. Such a loss may not be immediately apparent; it may take several years for the loss to be recognized. Periodic audiometric tests will disclose progressive hearing losses. Such tests should be made every year on line employees and others exposed to high-noise-level areas.

It is essential that all ramp workers be aware of the noise hazard and that they be required to wear appropriate protective equipment. Wearing appropriate hearing protection equipment near turboprop or jet operations, either main engine or auxiliary power units, will help minimize hearing loss as a result of noise. Hearing protective equipment attenuates or reduces noise pressure levels at the ear. It does not eliminate noise. Using a jet engine noise suppressor also reduces jet noise and jet blast hazard (Figure 3-9). For more detailed information on the noise hazard, see Chapter 9, Personal Protective Equipment and Guarding.

FIRE PROTECTION

Fire extinguishers on ramps where fueling operations are conducted provide an immediate means of fire protection in an area likely to contain a high concentration of personnel and valuable equipment (see Chapter 7, Fire Prevention and Protection). Prominent and strategic positioning of portable fire extinguishers is essential so that they may be of maximum value in an emergency. The placement of portable extinguishers should comply with NFPA 10. (See References.) In order to ensure continued adequate protection, extinguishers should be used and maintained in accordance with NFPA 10. They should also be located in such a manner that easy access is possible in an emergency. Extinguishers should be placed upwind of the work areas at no greater distance than personnel could reasonably be expected to carry them. The size of the fire extinguisher must be compatible with the size of the aircraft in the vicinity.

Hose line stations of stationary extinguishing systems should be easily accessible. They should be placed so that the hose can be conveniently maneuvered to cope with emergencies most likely to occur. Hoses should also be protected from weather.

Fuel trucks operated away from airports should be equipped with extinguishers capable of handling fires in their engine, brake, and exhaust systems. When operating at the airport, trucks are adequately covered by the ramp distribution of fire extinguishers, as required under NFPA 10.

Flight line personnel should be familiar with the common types of aircraft fires, and the procedures to be followed by a cockpit crew and ground personnel if such fires occur. In addition, employees should know the locations of extinguishers, the classifications or types of fires on which each type of extinguisher is effective, the methods of handling extinguishers, and the danger areas to avoid when fighting fires.

A daily recorded "eyeball" inspection program for extinguishers should be followed to make sure they are available and ready to work if the need arises. Follow-up training of employees in the use and limitations of extinguishers should also be conducted periodically. For more detailed information on fire protection programs, see Chapter 7, Fire Prevention and Protection.

REFERENCES

American National Standards Institute, 1430 Broadway, New York, NY 10018.

Deicing/Anti-icing Fluid, Runways, and Taxiways, ANSI/SAE AMS 1426A.

National Fire Protection Association, Batterymarch Park, Quincy, MA 02269.

Aircraft Fuel Servicing, NFPA 407, 1985.

Aircraft Fueling and Ramp Drainage, NFPA 415, 1983.

Aircraft Maintenance, NFPA 410, 1980.

Portable Fire Extinguishers, NFPA 10, 1984.

MOORE
MOORE
CAUTION

UNITED
9735
UNITED
ORD
A.O.A.
UNITED

CHAPTER 4

Mobile Ground Service Equipment

Ground service equipment in position.

Top: courtesy Piedmont Airlines; bottom: courtesy United Airlines, photos by Mike Sroka.

Ground service equipment (GSE) includes both motorized and nonmotorized units that are needed to service aircraft safely and efficiently. This chapter lists design and procedural considerations in procuring, operating, and maintaining mobile ground equipment used in airports (Figure 4-1).

In the selection of proper ground service equipment, the function that the equipment is to perform must be evaluated. In evaluating the function, consider these factors:

- Types of aircraft to be serviced
- Possible use other than aircraft servicing
- Use of the equipment at other airports or at some off-airport location
- Minor changes or modifications that would allow for use in other ways than originally intended. These considerations may reduce or eliminate the need for additional pieces of ground service equipment. All changes or modifications may be done only with the manufacturer's approval.

EQUIPMENT DESIGN CONSIDERATIONS

All equipment should conform to appropriate standards, such as those of the American National Standards Institute (ANSI), the International Organization for Standardization (IOS), and the International Electrotechnical Commission (IEC). (See References at the end of this chapter.)

Controls

Controls and controlling circuits should be designed in a manner that failure within a control or its circuitry will not introduce an unsafe operating condition.

Controls should be grouped and located so that

Courtesy Federal Express.

Figure 4-1. Well-maintained ground service equipment promotes efficient, safe ground operations.

the operator can easily reach them with his or her operational hand.

The design and location of such controls should be in a manner that does not permit clothing to catch on them.

Controls should be sized and spaced to provide easy operation with a gloved hand.

Controls should be identified with permanently affixed and nonfading placards. The lettering or symbols on the placards should be easy to read from the operator's position and should contrast sharply with the background. Signs should indicate the function or motion of the control.

Controls and instruments exposed to the weather should be weatherproof. They should be protected from snow and ice accumulation.

Operations control and instrument panels, exclusive of driving controls, should be illuminated to a minimum of 5 foot candles (5 decalux), and not produce a glare to the operator.

Ground service equipment with automatic transmission shall have the transmission shift sequence conforming to Federal Motor Vehicle Safety Standard (FMVSS) No. 102. (See References. Other standards may apply outside the United States.)

Transmission shift selection should be located on either the right side of the steering column or to the right side of the operator. It should be sized to be handled with a gloved hand with a minimum of 7.5 cm (3 in.) unobstructed clearance.

All other operational controls should move in the direction of travel for the function that they control. They should be of the deadman type, unless the control is set to achieve a function to permit the users to accomplish another task. In these cases, such set controls should be detented or similarly locked into the operating positions to prevent inadvertent deactivation or reversing. Such controls should be readily available to the operator(s). Emergency-only operating controls need not meet this requirement.

ON-OFF switches should be on when in the up position, or if mounted horizontally, they should be on when they are away from the operator.

Foot-operated driving controls should be in the following sequence, left to right from the operator's position, as applicable: parking brake, light dimmer switch, clutch, foot brake, and accelerator.

Clutch, foot brake, accelerator, and functional foot controls should be a minimum size of 5 × 7.5 cm (2 × 3 in.) and provided with a slip-resistant material.

Foot controls should be spaced to provide easy operation with a booted foot.

Brakes

Based on the vehicle brake design, two systems should be provided for applying brakes: (1) The primary system (service brakes) should be pedal-operated to apply brakes simultaneously on all braked wheels. (2) The secondary system should be hand- or foot-operated to apply a braking action sufficient to hold the vehicle on the maximum grade that the vehicle can negotiate with rated capacity load, with the transmission in neutral and the engine idling on a dry, clean concrete surface.

The brake should be effective in restraining vehicle movement to either a forward or a reverse direction. Mechanical adjustment other than minute adjustments should not be available to the operator for the service brake.

Vehicle brake drive systems using unconventional energy (such as hydrostatic, electric, etc.) can employ that energy for both the primary and secondary brake systems.

Table 4-A gives maximum permissible stopping distances for single-unit vehicles, excluding reaction-time distance, from a minimum initial speed of 32 km/h (20 mph) on level, dry pavement using a maximum service brake pedal of 445 N (100 lb).

Table 4-A. Maximum Permissible Stopping Distances

Single-unit Gross Vehicular Weight	Stopping Distance (at 15 mph and max. load)
2,270 kg (5,000 lb) or less	7.6 m (25 ft)
2,270 to 4,540 kg (5,000 to 10,000 lb)	9.2 m (30 ft)
Over 4,540 kg (10,000 lb)	12.2 m (40 ft)

Vehicles towing unbraked trailers should be designed to have a towing restriction on them to ensure stopping the towed load in a distance not to exceed 30 m (100 ft) with a maximum load at 24 km/h (15 mph).

Manually moved units should have parking brakes (or other means) capable of holding a maximum capacity load on a 15% grade. The brakes should also be capable of holding an empty or capacity load when subjected to wind or blast load up to 145 km/h (90 mph). Wheel chocks or similar braking devices that accomplish this are acceptable.

Power-assisted brakes should be provided with a gross vehicular weight (GVW) of 14,600 kg (30,000 lb) or over unless the vehicle is braked by the drive system described earlier. Such brake systems, however, should meet the criteria for stopping distances. (Other standards for brakes may apply outside the United States.)

Stability

All ground service equipment should be stable when exposed to wind and/or jet blast loads of 129 km/h (80 mph) and should not tip when exposed to wind and/or jet blast of at least 145 km/h (90 mph). Units not designed for such winds, such as rollup boarding stairs, should be removed from the ramp or secured when high winds are predicted.

Lift units exposed to jet blast, wind, and irregular surfaces should be equipped with stabilizing devices, if necessary, that would preclude their overturning when exposed to wind or blast up to 145 km/h (90 mph). The point at which the stabilizing devices will be needed to ensure that the equipment remains stable during elevation must be determined. A safety device should be provided to ensure that the lift units do not exceed the predetermined elevation unless stabilizing devices are deployed and/or engaged.

Retraction of the stabilizing device should not be possible under normal or emergency conditions, until the unit has been lowered to within the stability previously discussed.

Stabilizer-activating devices should be located so as not to expose the operator to a personal injury.

Emergency stabilizer-raising controls should be provided and should be located so as not to expose the operator to injury.

Stabilizer ground contact pads should have the outside edges radiused a minimum of 6 mm (¼ in.) and should be smooth.

Stability devices that extend beyond the vehicle profile should be painted yellow or illuminated.

Calculations, test data, or actual tests should be available to show stability with and without stabilizing devices.

Fuel System

Fuel lines on GSE vehicles should be constructed of seamless annealed copper or steel tubing. Flexible fuel lines should only be used in locations where it is necessary to absorb vibration and prevent fatigue and failure.

Fuel lines should be secured with a minimum of 5 cm (2 in.) clearance to the exhaust and electrical systems.

Fuel tanks should be located and installed so that any overflow during filling or any leakage from the tank, lines, or fittings will not impinge on the engine, exhaust, electrical system, or other ignition sources or enter the operator's compartment.

Fuel tanks should be located for maximum protection from collision damage.

The filler and tanks should be designed to accept a minimum fill rate of 0.6 liter/sec (10 gpm) without splash back.

A clearly visible permanent marking that indicates the type of fuel to be used should be installed adjacent to the filler.

Fuel tank fillers should be located outside the vehicle, vent directly to free atmosphere, and be accessible from ground level.

All fuel tanks should be equipped with self-closing caps and an attached vent.

Operator's Compartment

If a vehicle has an enclosed cab, the cab should be well ventilated for the operator's comfort. Heat and/or cooling for the cab should be considered; this decision is to be based on local climatic conditions.

Vehicle operators should have clear and unimpaired visibility when running the unit. There should be maximum visibility based upon the functional requirements of the unit. Safety or tempered glass should be used.

Any vehicle equipped with a windshield should

be provided with a powered windshield wiper that wipes an area not less than 60% of the glazed area. On enclosed-cab vehicles, the windshield should be provided with a defogger and/or defroster.

Windshield washers should be installed on enclosed vehicles whenever a unit is used in any environmental area where the unit is subjected to wheel splash and spray from other units.

On open-cab vehicles with passenger seats, a hip guard a minimum of 7.5 cm (3 in.) high above the seat surface should be provided on the outside edge of the outside seats.

On open-cab vehicles where the operator's compartment is used as a work station, slip-resistant materials should be applied.

Seats should be provided with a backrest of no less than 33 cm (13 in.) high.

In enclosed-cab vehicles, a clearance of not less than 90 cm (35 in.) should be provided between the top of the seat cushion and the cab roof.

Foot supports (such as a floor rest) should be provided for all seat positions.

Door handles, latches, and hinges should be rugged, positive, and easily maintainable, and should conform to the requirements of Federal Motor Vehicle Safety Standards (FMVSS). (See References. Other standards might apply outside the United States.)

Horns should be located so that operators can reach them conveniently.

Rearview mirrors should be installed as required.

The maximum sound level generated by the equipment when operated at rated capacity or load should not exceed 85 dBA (A-weighted network) when measured at the operator's position and at a distance of 4.5 m (15 ft) from the equipment at a minimum of 8 positions at 45 degree (0.79 radian) radials. (This is an OSHA standard. Other standards might apply outside the United States.) If it is not feasible or reasonable to achieve the above requirement because of economic and/or engineering technology, the manufacturer should document the design limitations, giving all the economic and/or engineering considerations. This documentation should include profile readings taken at 0.6, 1.5, 3.0, and 4.5 m (2, 5, 10, and 15 ft) distances.

Hoisting/Lifting

A minimum design factor of 4 to 1 (to the yield of the material) should be provided on all structural members. Nonstructural members should be designed with a minimum design factor of 2 to 1 (to the material yield point) if possible. (See ANSI standards in References.) Deviations from these minimums should be approved by parties assuming the responsibilities. (Other standards may apply outside the United States.)

The maximum capacity of all hoisting equipment (including chains, cables, etc.) should be displayed in a readily visible location.

Fail-safe devices to prevent any free falling of materials should be provided.

Maintenance safety locks should be provided, and their use required.

A safe means of lowering or disconnecting materials should be provided in case of a malfunction.

Working Surfaces

Work platforms and walkways should have a slip-resistant surface.

Work platforms and walkways should have adequate handrail and/or guardrail protection and toeboards.

Stairs, ramps, and the rungs, cleats, or treads on ladders should be of slip-resistant material.

Ladders and stairs should be designed to support a minimum working load of 90 kg (200 lb).

Landings and working surfaces should be designed to support 113 kg (250 lb) per person on the landing or working surface at the same time.

Maneuverability

Wheels on all equipment should be of a type and size that will not cause undue wear to the surfaces over which they will normally operate. For nonmotorized equipment, the wheel type and size should minimize the push/pull efforts of the employees handling the equipment.

Driving wheels should have sufficient clearance—approximately 5.7 cm (2¼ in.) minimum—under normal load to permit the installation of tire chains.

All wheels should be equipped with fenders or other suitable devices to protect personnel and materials on the vehicles from spray or splashes.

A power-steering system should be considered for all vehicles with a GVW of 4,540 kg (10,000 lb) or over.

Exhaust Systems

Internal combustion engines (excluding gas turbine engines) should be fitted with either a baffle-type muffler or muffler fitted with a Society of Automotive Engineers (SAE) approved spark arrestor. (See References.)

The exhaust system, beyond the manifold, should be supported at least 7.5 cm (3 in.) clear of combustible materials, excluding flexible mountings, and at least 5 cm (2 in.) clear of fuel and electrical system parts and should not be subject to drippage of fuel, oil, or grease.

The surfaces and the discharge of exhaust systems should be located so that they will not expose employees to injury or materials to damage in normal operation.

General

Equipment having an effect on public health (such

as food, drinking water, and lavatory service equipment) should be certified by U.S. Public Health Services (USPHS) and/or other regulatory bodies in the country where the equipment will be operated.

Vehicles carrying materials that could subject the operator and/or occupants to injury should be equipped with attach points for load restraint.

All lamps, reflectors, and/or reflective tapes should be recessed or otherwise protected against damage by impact. They should meet the Federal Motor Vehicle Safety Standards (FMVSS), as well as the requirements of the local airport. If backup lights are provided, they should be automatically controlled by the shift selector when it is placed in reverse gear.

Unlicensed units with a length in excess of 2.4 m (8 ft) shall be equipped with clearance lights, reflectors, or reflective tape on both sides of the vehicle, visible at any angle not less than 80 degrees (1.4 radians) and a distance of 23 m (75 ft) illuminated by standard headlights.

A towed unit (singular or in train) that exceeds 2.4 m (8 ft) in total length shall be provided with either clearance lights, reflectors, or reflective tape on both sides and the rear. These lights, reflectors, or tape shall be visible at any angle not less than 80 degrees or a distance of 23 m (75 ft) when the source of illumination is up to 80 degrees, from normal to the clearance lights, reflectors, or reflective tape, and the observer is within 5 degrees (0.09 radians) of the source of illumination at a minimum of 23 m (75 ft).

Any unattached parts such as hitch pins, safety pins, props, etc., should be secured to the unit. This does not include oil caps, water-fill caps, or similar caps normally provided on the propulsion unit.

The tongues or tow-bars of units should be designed to minimize exposure to pinch points during coupling.

Fire extinguishers of 2A:10B:C rating (minimum) should be installed and readily accessible on all flammable liquid-dispensing units.

Cushioning devices should be installed on all equipment intended to be used in direct contact with, or in close proximity to, aircraft to minimize aircraft damage. Such cushioning devices should be tubular or D-section bumpers of suitable length, outside diameter, and wall thickness. Aircraft engineering and/or the aircraft manufacturer should approve the cushioning device to ensure that the cushioning materials adequately protect aircraft. Temperature range should also be considered in selecting the cushioning material.

Self-propelled electric vehicles intended for use in aircraft hangars should comply with the standards in NFPA 505, *Powered Industrial Trucks,* as well as other related standards such as the ANSI A92 series. (See References.)

Equipment for use in hangars or around aircraft servicing (such as an engine change unit) should comply with those provisions of NFPA that deal specifically with aircraft hangars and servicing. (See References.)

EQUIPMENT MAINTENANCE AND OPERATION

Some basic procedures to be followed in maintaining and operating ground service vehicles are given in this section.

Maintenance

The required number of operating hours and/or time period for scheduled maintenance and overhaul of all units and their components should be obtained from the vendor.

Equipment components and systems requiring routine and frequent inspections and maintenance should be readily accessible.

Whenever possible, major assemblies and components should be easily disconnected and removed from the equipment. The vendor should specify any assemblies and/or components requiring special procedures and/or tools required to do routine and nonroutine maintenance and overhaul.

All doors and panels should be provided with securing devices to retain them in the open or closed position. These devices should be capable of withstanding jet blast or ambient winds. They should be installed so that the doors, when open, do not create a personal injury hazard.

All parts subject to high operating temperatures and all sprockets, gears, belts, and other moving parts should be suitably guarded if operating and/or maintenance personnel might accidentally contact them. For more detailed information on procedures for shop areas where GSE is maintained, see Chapter 5, Hangar and Shop Operations.

All units and parts requiring service and/or lubrication should be easily accessible. Pressure lubricating fittings should be used wherever possible.

All ground equipment should be checked periodically, and the interval between checks should depend on the amount of usage the vehicle receives. All items needing correction should be noted, and supervisors or other appropriate authorities should be informed so that they can schedule the repairs.

Checklists should be made to aid maintenance inspections. For nonmotorized equipment, a checklist should include:

- Ease of operation of the equipment
- Condition of tires and wheels
- Cracks in panels and framework
- Broken welds or missing fasteners

- Condition of hitches
- Condition of hoses, bumpers, fittings, and step treads.

Checklists for motorized equipment should include all the items for nonmotorized vehicles listed above, as well as the following:

- Condition of grounds and power cables
- Condition of guards and guardrails
- Operation of lights, horns, mirrors, and alarm, if so equipped
- Operation of foot and hand brakes
- Pedal travel on brakes and clutch
- Engine, instrument, and windshield wiper tests
- Operational damage.

Figure 4-2 shows three sample checklists.

Fluid levels and lubrication schedules on ground equipment should be maintained as specified by the manufacturer. Any other specific checks or service called for by the equipment manufacturer's manual should also be added to the checklist.

Operation

Both motorized and nonmotorized ground service equipment should be parked in designated areas at the terminals between flights. The parking brakes on the equipment should be set, and the gear selector placed in NEUTRAL or PARK position, unless otherwise specified by company policy.

When servicing the aircraft, equipment should be placed in preassigned positions at the aircraft. These positions should be previously specified and illustrated on printed positioning guides (Figure 4-3). A positioning guide should be provided for each type of aircraft the equipment is to service.

When equipment must be either towed or pushed (towing is desirable), it should only be accomplished by qualified personnel.

Procedures for boarding of last-minute cargoes and passengers should be established by company and/or local policy. These procedures should be established as an exception and not as a routine part of operations. Flight crews should be advised when last-minute boarding is to take place; the operation should be under the full direction of only one person.

Aircraft and pedestrians should *always* have the right-of-way. Ground equipment should never move across the path of boarding or disembarking passengers or taxiing aircraft.

Operation of equipment under any part of the aircraft should be clearly defined for type of aircraft and GSE (Figure 4-4).

No equipment should be permitted to contact an aircraft unless the unit is specifically required to do so to perform its function. If the unit is required to contact the aircraft, auto-leveling devices should be considered.

As soon as a vehicle is positioned at the aircraft, the gear selector should be placed in the NEUTRAL or PARK position, the parking brake set, the wheel(s) chocked, and the engine turned off (if not required for the function of the unit).

Ground equipment should always be maintained in good repair. Units in need of repair should be reported immediately by the user to his or her supervisor. The unit must be sent to the appropriate shop for repair as soon as possible.

An OUT-OF-SERVICE tag, to be attached by the supervisor or a designee of the supervisor, is suggested for all units in need of repair. The tags should list the following information:

- Type and number of the unit
- Time removed from service
- Reason for removal from service
- Signature of the person removing the unit from service.

The OUT-OF-SERVICE tag should remain on the vehicle until it is returned to service by maintenance personnel. The tag should be affixed in a location where an operator will notice it, to prevent inadvertent use of a unit in need of repair.

Normally, only units licensed for highway usage need be equipped with safety belts. However, local management should evaluate specific requirements and needs, considering the amount of usage of a unit. If in management's opinion, safety belts would protect the operator and/or passenger(s), they should be installed. If installed, they should be in conformance with FMVSS requirements.

In units that come equipped from a vehicle manufacturer with safety belts, it can normally be assumed that the belts are correctly installed. Reinstallation of belts should not be done without authority of the ground equipment, maintenance, engineering, and/or safety groups.

Vehicles operated away from the airport must have a valid highway license plate(s) and/or special permits. Such units should carry an accident report form and a copy of the insurance certificate.

PERSONNEL CONSIDERATIONS

This section is about the duties of those who operate ground service equipment. It covers the issues of their qualifications and the training they should receive.

Figure 4-2. The forms on the next six pages are safety inspection checklists for motorized automotive equipment, cargo and baggage carts, and cargo and baggage dollies. Permission is given to photocopy these checklists. **(Text continues on page 52.)**

AUTOMOTIVE EQUIPMENT SAFETY CHECK LIST
CONTRÔLE DE SÉCURITÉ DES VÉHICULES MOTORISÉS

UNIT SERIAL CODE *NUMÉRO DE SÉRIE*	DATE	TIME *HEURE*

NOTE: In checking each item, follow the instructions carefully on the reverse side of this sheet. Check all items where applicable.
REMARQUE: *Pour la vérification de chaque élément, suivre attentivement les instructions portées au verso. Vérifier tous les éléments, au besoin.*

PRIORITY 1 (P.1): Tag unit and route to Ground Equipment Maintenance immediately.
PRIORITÉ 1 (P.1) *Étiqueter le véhicule et l'envoyer immédiatement à l'Atelier d'entretien du matériel de piste.*

PRIORITY 2 (P.2): Tag unit and route to Ground Equipment Maintenance **within** 24 hours.
PRIORITÉ 2 (P.2): *Étiqueter le véhicule et l'envoyer dans les 24* ***heures*** *à l'Atelier d'entretien du matériel de piste.*

ATTENTION: Attach the **white** copies of unserviceable tags to this sheet. As required.
IMPORTANT: *Le cas échéant, joindre au présent imprimé l'exemplaire* ***blanc*** *des étiquettes de réforme.*

NO. *N°*	ITEM *ÉLÉMENT*	SVBLE. *EN BON ÉTAT*	WITHDRAWAL *RETRAIT* P.1	WITHDRAWAL *RETRAIT* P.2	REMARKS *OBSERVATIONS*
1	DOORS *PORTIÈRES*				
2	FUMES *VAPEURS*				
3	HEATER/DEFROSTER *CLIMATISEUR/DÉGIVREUR*				
4	WINDOWS *FENÊTRES*				
5	WIPERS *ESSUIE-GLACE*				
6	MIRRORS *RÉTROVISEURS*				
7	HORN *KLAXON*				
8	WARNING HORN/IND. LIGHTS *AVERTISSEUR SONORE/VOYANTS*				
9	PEDALS *PÉDALES*				
10	HANDBRAKES *FREINS À MAIN*				
11	SPEEDOMETER *COMPTEUR DE VITESSE*				
12	FOOTBRAKES *FREINS AU PIED*				
13	TIRES *PNEUS*				
14	LIGHTS -DIRECTIONAL FLASH *FEUX -INDICATEURS DE DIRECTION/CLIGNOTANTS*				
	-HEADLIGHTS *PHARES*				
	-BRAKE/BACK-UP *FEUX DE FREINAGE/DE RECUL*				
	-FLOOD *PROJECTEURS*				
	-BEACON *FEUX À ÉCLATS*				
15	GEARSHIFT SAFETY SWITCHES *INTERRUPTEURS DE SÛRETÉ CHANGEMENT DE VITESSE*				
16	ANTI-SKID SURFACES *SURFACES ANTIDÉRAPANTES*				
17	ACCESS LADDERS *ÉCHELLES*				
18	GUARD/GUIDE RAILS *RIDELLES*				
19	PALLET STOPS *CALE-PALETTES*				
20	TAIL GATE *PORTE À RABATTEMENT ARRIÈRE*				
21	PINS AND HOLDERS *GOUPILLES ET PORTE-GOUPILLES*				
22	TOW HITCH *ATTELAGE DE REMORQUE*				
23	FIRE EXTINGUISHERS *EXTINCTEURS*				
24	FIRST AID KIT/BLANKET *TROUSSE DE PREMIERS SOINS/COUVERTURE*				
25	INTERCOMM. SYSTEM *SYSTÈME D'INTERCOMMUNICATION*				
26	HOSE CONNECTIONS *RACCORDS DE TUYAU SOUPLE*				

ACF905(10-76)

SIGNATURE ______________________

INSTRUCTIONS — SAFETY CHECK LIST

1. **DOORS** - Check the operation of all doors. They must open and close freely. **PRIORITY 1:** missing handles. **PRIORITY 2:** damaged handles.
2. **FUMES** - Report immediately any obvious vehicle exhaust fumes in cab. **PRIORITY 1 ONLY.**
3. **HEATER/DEFROSTER** - This must be fully operational during winter operations (i.e. from the time vehicle has been winterized until the spring changeover). Check that the defroster hoses are not damaged or disconnected **PRIORITY 1 ONLY.**
4. **WINDOWS** - First, clean all dirty windows. Inspect **all** windows - front, side and rear - for cracks or scratches. **PRIORITY 1:** impaired visibility. **PRIORITY 2:** visibility not impaired.
5. **WINDSHIELD WIPERS** - Must be fully operational. **PRIORITY 1:** unserviceable motor, missing blades or broken arms. **PRIORITY 2:** worn blades.
6. **MIRRORS** - First, clean all dirty mirrors. Check that the mirrors are secure and the glass is not broken. **PRIORITY 2 ONLY.**
7. **HORN** - For vehicles so equipped, sound of horn must be loud and clear. A broken horn requires immediate repair. **PRIORITY ONLY**
8. **WARNING HORN/INDICATOR LIGHTS** - On vehicles so equipped, check that the warning horn is functional and that indicator lights are operational. **PRIORITY 1 ONLY.**
9. **PEDALS** - Ensure that brake and clutch pedals have rubber pads or anti-skid material that is intact and not excessively worn. **PRIORITY 2 ONLY.**
10. **HANDBRAKES** - With engine running at idle RPM: **a) standard transmission:** set handbrake, release clutch slowly, engine should cut-off as clutch engages drive shaft. **b) automatic transmission:** set handbrake and select DRIVE; unit must remain stationary. **PRIORITY 1 ONLY** for both transmissions.
11. **SPEEDOMETER** - On vehicles so equipped, check that the indicator needle registers when vehicle is in motion (5-10 mph). **PRIORITY 2 ONLY.**
12. **FOOTBRAKES** - With vehicle in motion, check operation of footbrake. Pedal should not go more than half the distance to the floorboard. Depressed pedal should feel firm and not spongy. **PRIORITY 1 ONLY.**
13. **TIRES** - Check that tires are adequately inflated. **PRIORITY 1 ONLY.**
14. **LIGHTS** - **All** lights listed must be fully operational. **PRIORITY 1:** all lights, as well as beacon lense. **PRIORITY 2:** all lenses, except beacon lense.
15. **GEARSHIFT SAFETY SWITCHES** - Check operation of gearshift safety switch to ensure that engine cuts off at idle RPM or governed RPM, depending on the vehicle. **PRIORITY 1 ONLY.**
16. **ANTI-SKID SURFACES** - All anti-skid surfaces must be intact. **PRIORITY 1:** missing or "torn-off". **PRIORITY 2:** excessively worn surfaces.
17. **ACCESS LADDERS** - Ensure that ladders are properly secured. **PRIORITY 1:** a ladder that is in immediate danger of falling off. **PRIORITY 2:** loosened ladders.
18. **GUARD/GUIDE RAILS** - Inspect locking devices and hinges on guard rails and ensure that all rails are securely in place. **PRIORITY 1:** rail is missing or in immediate danger of falling off. **PRIORITY 2:** loosened rails.
19. **PALLET STOPS** - Ensure that all stops can be raised and lowered freely. **PRIORITY 1:** if stops do not operate. **PRIORITY 2:** if stops are sticky or slow to operate.
20. **TAIL GATE** - Damaged or missing lock pins, hinges and chains must be immediately repaired. **PRIORITY 1:** only if both pins are missing. **PRIORITY 2:** in any other case.
21. **PINS AND HOLDERS** - Pins in food service trucks (except 747 trucks) must be secured with chains and stowed in the holders provided. Ensure that all holding racks and bungee cords are functional. **PRIORITY 1:** missing or inoperable pins or bungee cords that will impair unit operation. **PRIORITY 2:** any other conditions.
22. **TOW HITCH** - Ensure that the return spring on the hitching mechanism is functional. On equipment with pin-type hitches, pins must be securely attached to the vehicle. **PRIORITY 1:** if spring is inoperable. **PRIORITY 2:** if spring operation is sticky, or pins are not properly secured.
23. **FIRE EXTINGUISHERS** - On vehicles so equipped, check for damaged handles, pins, levers, mounting brackets and broken seals. In the event of any of these, replace fire extinguishers immediately. Also, verify that any gauges on the unit register "charge". **PRIORITY 1 ONLY.**
24. **FIRST AID KIT/BLANKET** - Supervisors must ensure that their vehicles carry a sealed aircraft-type first-aid kit (part number 25-70002-1) and a sealed blanket. These items are to be picked-up from the A.S.M.'s office. **PRIORITY 1 ONLY.**
25. **INTERCOMM. SYSTEM** - Check operation of intercommunication system. **PRIORITY 2 ONLY.**
26. **HOSE CONNECTIONS** - Inspect connecting mechanism to ensure positive locking. **PRIORITY 1.**

INSTRUCTIONS

1. ***PORTIÈRES*** - *Vérifier le fonctionnement de toutes les portières. Elles doivent ouvrir et fermer aisément.* ***PRIORITÉ 1:*** *poignées manquantes.* ***PRIORITÉ 2:*** *poignées abîmées.*
2. ***VAPEURS*** - *Signaler immédiatement toute fuite de gaz d'échappement dans la cabine.* ***PRIORITÉ 1 SEULEMENT.***
3. ***CLIMATISEUR/DÉGIVREUR*** - *Doit fonctionner parfaitement au cours de l'hivers (c'est-à-dire pendant toute la période d'hivernisation du véhicule) S'assurer que les tuyaux de dégivrage ne sont ni endommagés ni débranchés.* ***PRIORITÉ 1 SEULEMENT.***
4. ***FENÊTRES*** - *Commencer par nettoyer les fenêtres sales. Inspecter toutes les fenêtres avant, côtés et arrière - pour déceler toute fêlure ou rayure.* ***PRIORITÉ 1:*** *visibilité contrariée.* ***PRIORITÉ 2:*** *visibilité non contrariée.*
5. ***ESSUIE-GLACE*** - *Doit fonctionner parfaitement.* ***PRIORITÉ 1:*** *moteur défectueux, balais manquants ou bras cassés.* ***PRIORITÉ 2:*** *balais usés.*
6. ***RÉTROVISEURS*** - *Commencer par nettoyer les rétroviseurs sales. S'assurer qu'ils sont tous bien fixés et que le verre n'est pas cassé.* ***PRIORITÉ 2 SEULEMENT.***
7. ***KLAXON*** - *Le timbre du klaxon, dont sont munis certains véhicules, doit être fort et clair. Faire réparer immédiatement tout klaxon défaillant.* ***PRIORITÉ 1 SEULEMENT.***
8. ***AVERTISSEUR SONORE/VOYANTS*** - *S'assurer, sur les véhicules qui en sont équipés, du bon fonctionnement de l'avertisseur sonore et des voyants.* ***PRIORITÉ 1 SEULEMENT.***
9. ***PÉDALES*** - *S'assurer que les pédales de frein et de débrayage ont des patins de caoutchouc ou un matériel antidérapant entiers et pas trop usés.* ***PRIORITÉ 2 SEULEMENT.***
10. ***FREINS À MAIN*** - *Moteur au ralenti: a)* ***transmission manuelle:*** *mettre le frein à main, relâcher lentement la pédale de débrayage, le moteur devrait caler au moment de l'embrayage; b)* ***transmission automatique:*** *mettre le frein à main et passer à DRIVE, le véhicule doit rester immobile.* ***PRIORITÉ 1 SEULEMENT*** *pour les deux transmissions.*
11. ***COMPTEUR DE VITESSE*** - *S'assurer que l'aiguille du compteur enregistre bien la vitesse du moteur en marche, sur les véhicules qui en sont munis (5-10 mi/h).* ***PRIORITÉ 2 SEULEMENT.***
12. ***FREINS AU PIED*** - *Véhicules en marche, vérifier le fonctionnement des freins au pied. La course de la pédale doit s'arrêter à mi-chemin du plancher. La pédale enfoncée doit présenter une résistance ferme et non élastique.* ***PRIORITÉ 1 SEULEMENT.***
13. ***PNEUS*** - *S'assurer que leur pression de gonflage est adéquate.* ***PRIORITÉ 1 SEULEMENT.***
14. ***FEUX - Tous*** *les feux mentionnés doivent fonctionner parfaitement.* ***PRIORITÉ 1:*** *tous les feux, y compris les feux à éclats.* ***PRIORITÉ 2:*** *tous les feux, sauf les feux à éclats.*
15. ***INTERRUPTEUR DE SÛRETÉ - CHANGEMENT DE VITESSE*** - *Vérifier le fonctionnement de l'interrupteur de sûreté afin que le moteur cale au ralenti ou au régime contrôlé, selon le véhicule.* ***PRIORITÉ 1 SEULEMENT.***
16. ***SURFACES ANTIDÉRAPANTES*** - *Elles doivent toutes être intactes.* ***PRIORITÉ 1:*** *défaut ou déchirure.* ***PRIORITÉ 2:*** *usure extrême.*
17. ***ÉCHELLES D'ACCÈS*** - *S'assurer qu'elles sont bien fixées.* ***PRIORITÉ 1:*** *échelle risquant de tomber.* ***PRIORITÉ 2:*** *échelle desserrée.*
18. ***RIDELLES*** - *Vérifier les dispositifs de sûreté et les charnières et s'assurer que toutes les ridelles sont bien en place.* ***PRIORITÉ 1:*** *ridelle manquante ou risquant de tomber.* ***PRIORITÉ 2:*** *ridelles desserrée.*
19. ***CALE-PALETTES*** - *S'assurer que tous les cale-palettes peuvent aisément être levés ou abaissés.* ***PRIORITÉ 1:*** *cales qui ne fonctionnent pas.* ***PRIORITÉ 2:*** *cales lentes ou difficiles à faires fonctionner.*
20. ***PORTE À RABATTEMENT ARRIÈRE*** - *Les goupilles de sûreté, charnières et chaînes abîmées ou manquantes doivent être immédiatement réparées.* ***PRIORITÉ 1:*** *seulement si les deux goupilles manquent.* ***PRIORITÉ 2:*** *dans tout autre cas.*
21. ***GOUPILLES/PORTES-GOUPILLES*** - *Les goupilles pour les camions du commissariat (sauf pour les camions de 747) doivent être attachées à l'aide de chaînes et rangées dans les porte-goupilles. S'assurer que les barres de maintien et les amortisseurs en caoutchouc fonctionnent bien* ***PRIORITÉ 1:*** *goupilles et amortisseurs manquants ou inutilisables, pouvant entraver le fonctionnement du véhicule.* ***PRIORITÉ 2:*** *toutes autres conditions.*
22. ***ATTELAGE DE REMORQUE*** - *S'assurer que le ressort de rappel de l'attelage fonctionne bien. Véhicules munis d'un attelage à goupilles: celles-ci doivent être bien attachées au véhicule.* ***PRIORITÉ 1:*** *si le ressort est inutilisable.* ***PRIORITÉ 2:*** *si le fonctionnement du ressort est difficile ou si les goupilles ne sont pas bien fixées.*
23. ***EXTINCTEURS*** - *Le cas échéant, déterminer si les poignées, goupilles, leviers, supports de monture ou les plombs sont abîmés. Si c'est le cas, remplacer immédiatement les extincteurs. S'assurer également que tout manomètre indique une pleine charge.* ***PRIORITÉ 1 SEULEMENT.***
24. ***TROUSSE DE PREMIERS SOINS/COUVERTURE*** - *Les Responsables doivent s'assurer que leurs véhicules possèdent une trousse scellée de premiers soins du modèles pour avions (numéro de catalogue 25-70002-1) et une couverture sous emballage scellé. S'approvisionner au bureau de Chef des services Avions.* ***PRIORITÉ 1 SEULEMENT.***
25. ***SYSTÈME D'INTERCOMMUNICATION*** - *Vérifier le fonctionnement du système d'intercommunication.* ***PRIORITÉ 2 SEULEMENT.***
26. ***RACCORDS DE TUYAU SOUPLE*** - *Vérifier le mécanisme de raccordement et s'assurer du verrouillage.* ***PRIORITÉ 1.***

CARGO/BAGGAGE CART SAFETY CHECK LIST
CONTRÔLE DE SÉCURITÉ DES CHARIOTS À FRET ET BAGAGES

NOTE IN CHECKING EACH ITEM, FOLLOW THE INSTRUCTIONS CAREFULLY ON THE REVERSE SIDE OF THIS SHEET. A UNIT HAVING A SAFETY DISCREPANCY IN ANY OF THE ITEMS BELOW, MUST BE TAGGED **IMMEDIATELY** AND TURNED OVER TO R.E.M.S.

REMARQUE *SUIVRE ATTENTIVEMENT LES INSTRUCTIONS AU VERSO POUR LA VÉRIFICATION DE CHAQUE ÉLÉMENT. TOUT CHARIOT DONT UN DES ÉLÉMENTS CI-DESSOUS EST DÉFECTUEUX DOIT ÊTRE ÉTIQUETÉ ET ENVOYÉ* ***IMMÉDIATEMENT*** *À L'ATELIER D'ENTRETIEN DU MATÉRIEL DE PISTE.*

ATTENTION ATTACH THE **WHITE** COPIES OF UNSERVICEABLE TAGS TO THIS SHEET.

IMPORTANT *LE CAS ÉCHÉANT, JOINDRE AU PRÉSENT IMPRIMÉ L'EXEMPLAIRE* ***BLANC*** *DES ÉTIQUETTES DE RÉFORME.*

CARGO *FRET* ☐

BAGGAGE *BAGAGES* ☐ DAY *POSTE DE JOUR* ☐ AFTERNOON *POSTE DU SOIR* ☐ NIGHT *POSTE DE NUIT* ☐

RAMP *AIRE DE TRAFIC* ☐

UNIT SERIAL CODE *N° DE SÉRIE*	SVCBL. *EN BON ÉTAT*	BRAKES *FREINS*	TOW HANDLES *TIMON*	PANELS *PANNEAUX*	LOCKING PINS HOLDER *GOUPILLES DE VERROUILLAGE ET PORTE-GOUPILLES*	TOW HITCH *ATTELAGE DE REMORQUE*	TIRES *PNEUS*	REMARKS *OBSERVATIONS*

ACF905C(12-76)

DATE *DATE*

SIGNATURE *SIGNATURE*

INSTRUCTIONS - SAFETY CHECK LIST

1. **BRAKES—** Brakes should grip evenly on both wheels. Check by putting cart in motion and applying brakes. Tow handle should **not** turn fully to one side.
2. **TOW HANDLE —** Ensure that at least one spring and one stop are operative and that the handle itself is not twisted or bent.
3. **PANELS —** Ensure that panels are not torn and hinges are not broken.
4. **LOCKING PINS/HOLDERS —** All pins must fit through the brackets when panels are in the vertical position.
5. **TOW HITCH —** Ensure that the hitch is secure and the spring is functional.
6. **TIRES —** Check for flat or badly deflated tires.

INSTRUCTIONS - CONTRÔLE DE SÉCURITÉ

1. ***FREINS —*** *Le blocage des deux roues doit se faire également. Véhicule en marche, appliquer les freins. Le timon ne doit pas pivoter.*
2. ***TIMON -*** *S'assurer qu'au moins un ressort et un taquet fonctionnent et que le timon lui-même n'est pas tordu.*
3. ***PANNEAUX -*** *S'assurer que les panneaux ne sont pas tordus et que les charnières ne sont pas brisées.*
4. ***GOUPILLES DE VERROUILLAGE ET PORTE-GOUPILLES -*** *Toutes les goupilles doivent entrer dans les supports quand les panneaux sont en position verticale.*
5. ***ATTELAGE DE REMORQUE -*** *S'assurer que l'attelage est bien fixé et que le ressort fonctionne.*
6. ***PNEUS -*** *Vérifier la pression des pneus.*

CARGO/BAGGAGE DOLLY SAFETY CHECK LIST
CONTRÔLE DE SÉCURITÉ DES REMORQUES À FRET ET BAGAGES

NOTE: In checking each item, follow the instructions carefully on the reverse side of this sheet. Check all items where applicable
REMARQUE: *Pour la vérification de chaque élément, suivre attentivement les instructions portées au verso. Vérifier tous les éléments, au besoin.*

PRIORITY 1 (P.1): Tag unit and route to Ground Equipment Maintenance immediately.
PRIORITÉ 1 (P.1): *Étiqueter le véhicule et l'envoyer immédiatement à l'Atelier d'entretien du matériel de piste.*

PRIORITY 2 (P.2): Tag unit and route to Ground Equipment Maintenance **within** 24 hours.
PRIORITÉ 2 (P.2): *Étiqueter le véhicule et l'envoyer dans les **24 heures** à l'Atelier d'entretien du matériel de piste.*

ATTENTION: Attach the white copies of unserviceable tags to this sheet, as required.
IMPORTANT: *Le cas échéant, joindre au présent imprimé l'exemplaire blanc des étiquettes de réforme.*

CARGO *FRET* ☐	RAMP *AIRE DE TRAFIC* ☐	BAGGAGE *BAGAGES* ☐
DAY *POSTE DE JOUR* ☐	AFTERNOON *POSTE DU SOIR* ☐	MIDNIGHT *POSTE DE NUIT* ☐
SINGLE CNTR.DOLLY *CHÂSSIS ROULANT POUR UN CONTENEUR* ☐	DOUBLE CNTR.DOLLY *CHÂSSIS ROULANT POUR DEUX CONTENEURS* ☐	PALLET/CNTR.DOLLY *CHÂSSIS ROULANT - PORTE PALETTES* ☐

	1	2	3	4	5	6	7-8	9-10	
UNIT SERIAL CODE *Nº DE SÉRIE*	WHEEL ALIGNMENT *PARALLÉLISME DES ROUES*	TIRES *PNEUS*	TOW HANDLE *TIMON*	TOW HITCH *ATTELAGE DE REMORQUE*	LOCKING PINS & HOLDERS *GOUPILLES DE VERROUILLAGE ET PORTE—GOUPILLES*	TOW HANDLE LOCK *VERROU DU TIMON*	CASTERS AND ROLLERS *ROULEMENTS À BILLES ET À ROULEAUX*	BED-ROTATE CNTR. LOCK HANDLES *MANETTES DE VERROUILLAGE DE LA PLATE-FORME PIVOTANTE ET DU CONTENEUR*	SERVICEABLE *EN BON ÉTAT*

ACF905D(10-76)

Date ____________________ Signature ____________________

INSTRUCTIONS

1. **WHEEL ALIGNMENT** - With tow handle lined up in the forward direction, all four wheels must be in alignment. **PRIORITY 1**
2. **TIRES** - Check for flat or badly deflated tires. **PRIORITY 1.**
3. **TOW HANDLE** - Ensure handle is not twisted or bent. **PRIORITY 2.**
4. **TOW HITCH** - Pin must operate freely and spring must be intact. **PRIORITY 1.**
5. **PINS AND HOLDERS** - Pins on pallet dollies must be secured by a chain and placed in the holders provided. **PRIORITY 1:** more than one pin missing. **PRIORITY 2:** one pin missing or chains not secured.
6. **TOW HANDLE LOCK** - Check that the locking mechanism holds the handle firmly in place **PRIORITY 1.**
7. **CASTERS** - Must be intact and rotate freely. **PRIORITY 2.**
8. **ROLLERS** - All rollers must be in place and rotate freely. **PRIORITY 1:** missing or bent rollers. **PRIORITY 2:** stiff rollers.
9. **BED-ROTATE HANDLES** - When activated, must release locking mechanism and spring back when handle released. Table must rotate freely. **PRIORITY 1:** both handles not functioning. **PRIORITY 2:** one handle not functioning or table not operationg freely.
10. **CONTAINER LOCK HANDLES** - When activated, must depress locks and locks must spring back when handle is released. Operation of locks must not be sticky. **PRIORITY 1.**

INSTRUCTIONS

1. ***PARALLÉLISME DES ROUES*** *- Lorsque le timon est dans l'axe longitudinal, les quatre roues doivent être parallèles à cet axe.* ***PRIORITÉ 1.***
2. ***PNEUS*** *- Vérifier l'état et la pression des pneus.* ***PRIORITÉ 1.***
3. ***TIMON*** *- S'assurer qu'il n'est pas tordu.* ***PRIORITÉ 2.***
4. ***ATTELAGE DE REMORQUE*** *- La goupille doit jouer librement et le ressort doit être intact.* ***PRIORITÉ 1.***
5. ***GOUPILLES ET PORTE-GOUPILLES*** *- Les goupilles sur les châssis porte-palettes doivent être fixées à l'aide de chaînes et rangées dans les porte-goupilles.* ***PRIORITÉ 1:*** *plus d'une goupille manquante.* ***PRIORITÉ 2:*** *une goupille manquante, ou chaînes non fixées.*
6. ***VERROU DU TIMON*** *- S'assurer que le mécanisme de verrouillage maintient fermement le timon en place.* ***PRIORITÉ 1.***
7. ***ROULEMENTS À BILLES*** *- Les billes doivent être en place et rouler librement.* ***PRIORITÉ 2.***
8. ***ROULEMENTS À ROULEAUX*** *- Les rouleaux doivent être en place et rouler librement.* ***PRIORITÉ 1:*** *rouleaux manquants ou faussés.* ***PRIORITÉ 2:*** *rouleaux grippés.*
9. ***MANETTES DE LA PLATE-FORME PIVOTANTE*** *- Lorsqu'elles sont actionnées, les verrous doivent s'abaisser et revenir à leur position normale quand elles sont relâchées. La plate-forme doit pivoter librement.* ***PRIORITÉ 1:*** *aucune des deux manettes ne fonctionne.* ***PRIORITÉ 2:*** *une manette ne fonctionne pas, ou la plate-forme ne pivote pas librement.*
10. ***MANETTES DU CONTAINER*** *- Lorsqu'elles sont actionnées, les verrous doivent s'abaisser, et revenir à leur position normale quand elle sont relâchées. Il ne doit pas y avoir grippage.* ***PRIORITÉ 1.***

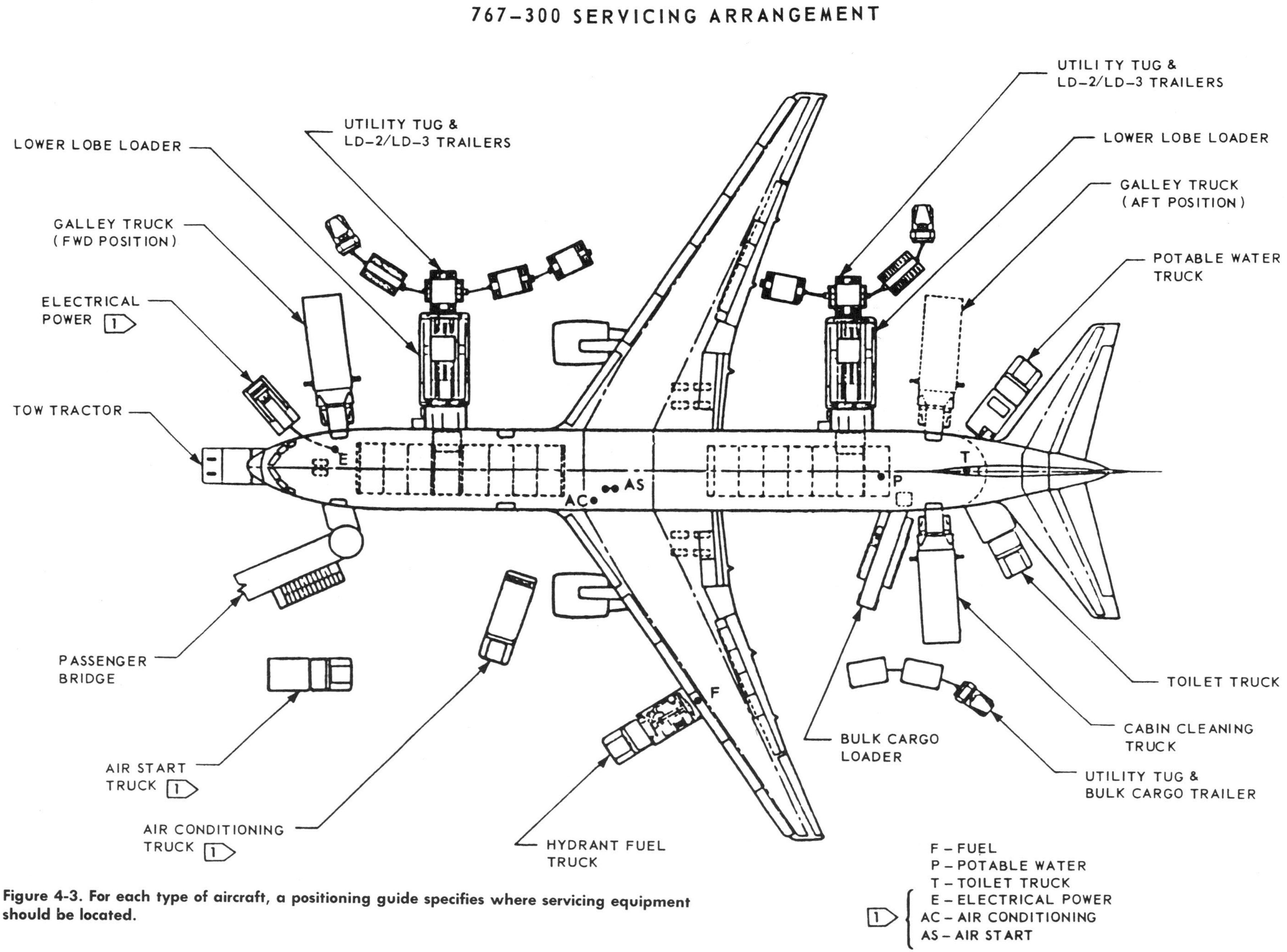

Figure 4-3. For each type of aircraft, a positioning guide specifies where servicing equipment should be located.

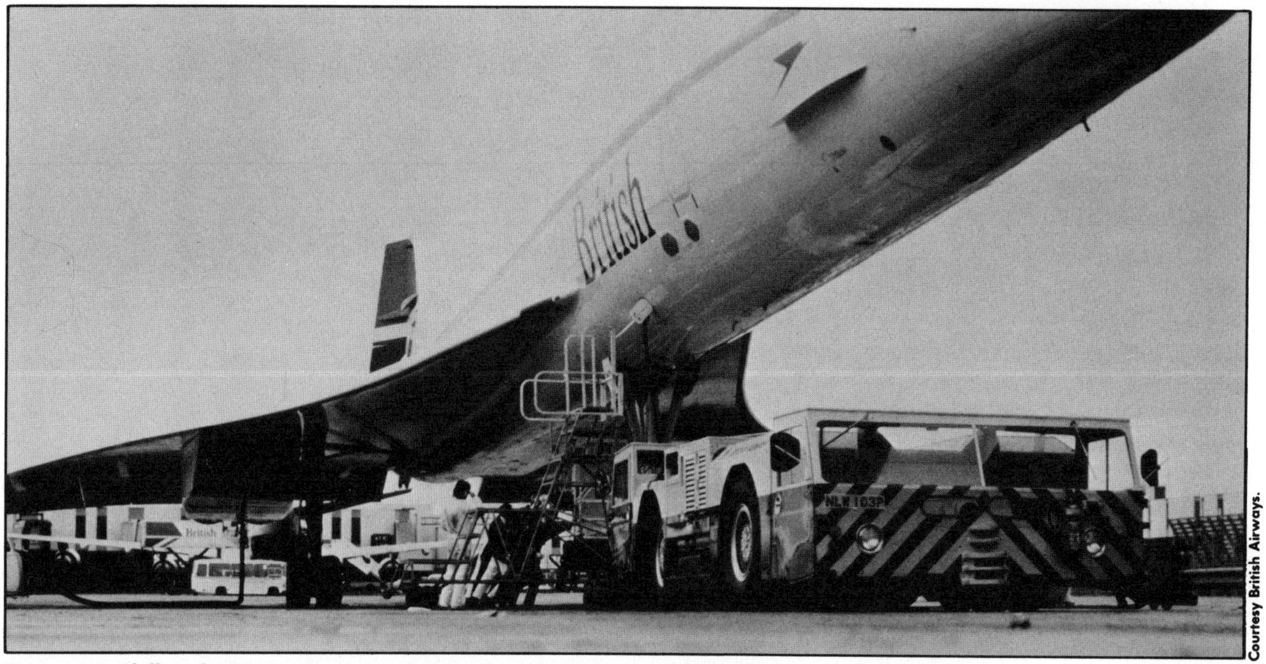

Courtesy British Airways.

Figure 4-4. Skill and experience are needed to service specialty aircraft properly.

Personnel Qualifications

Only certified personnel should be permitted to operate equipment. They should be trained to operate and handle the equipment for optimum functioning of the unit. Trained operators should be tested by a qualified instructor and certified as authorized unit operators. Periodic renewal of a unit operator's certification should be considered.

Strict supervision should be maintained to make sure only certified operators handle equipment.

Operators should possess a valid driver's license in the state, area, province, or country in which they operate. In addition, special permits may be required by local airport authorities.

To establish an operator's qualifications, the following procedures are often used:

- Vision is checked. Visual acuity should be suitable in each eye. Standards may be agreed to by both the company and the airport authority.
- Color vision should be checked by charts or other methods approved by the company medical department and/or insurance company.
- Depth perception should be checked by an accepted method approved by the company medical department and/or insurance company.
- Hearing should be checked in accordance with requirements approved by the company medical department and/or insurance company.
- Physical fitness is tested. The level of fitness required should be based on the employee's job duties. Included in examinations should be the person's physical capability to operate any piece of equipment associated with the job. If restrictions on the employee are established, based upon the physical examination, supervisory and/or management personnel should ensure that the person is not exposed to undue hazards.

Personnel Responsibilities

When an operator's vision is restricted in critical areas (such as when positioning certain equipment at an aircraft and removing it from the aircraft), it should be a unit operator's responsibility to use a guide during positioning and/or removal.

Company requirements should specify that when units are equipped with safety belts, the vehicle operator is responsible for seeing that occupants use the safety belts. (A notice or decal posted on the dashboard or similar convenient location will be helpful in enforcing company policy regarding safety belt usage.)

No vehicle (motorized or nonmotorized) should carry riders unless such a practice is authorized by company procedures and/or the responsible supervisor. Even then, riders should not be permitted on any unit unless an approved seat and/or approved seating/standing area with handrails or restraints is provided.

Unit operators should be responsible for the safe operation of the unit which they handle. Before using any vehicle, operators should make sure that:

- The area is clear of other equipment, personnel, and anything else that would interfere with safe operation.
- Cable, cords, hoses, and other accessories are properly stowed.
- Doors are closed and secured.

- Horns, lights, windshield wipers, and washers operate properly.
- The unit has adequate fuel, oil, water, and other required operating fluids. (The above can vary by location based upon company and station policy regarding assignment of responsible groups to maintain and check these items.)

Operators should report units in need of repair to their supervisors. The supervisor is responsible for putting an OUT-OF-SERVICE tag on the unit. The OUT-OF-SERVICE tag should remain on the unit until it is returned from maintenance.

Operators of GSE should observe maximum speed limits. In areas away from the terminal or hangars, the speed limits are usually established by local authorities. When a GSE is approaching or leaving an aircraft or is inside a hangar, terminal, or building, the prescribed speed limit is usually a maximum of 8 km/h (5 mph), which is equivalent to a walking pace. Inside aircraft parking areas or immediately outside hangars, a maximum of 16 km/h (10 mph) is usually prescribed. Speed should be reduced when heavy traffic, bad weather, or other adverse conditions exist.

Vehicles approaching an aircraft should be stopped while they are still a safe distance from the aircraft to make sure their brakes are serviceable.

a. Vehicles equipped with manual transmission should approach the aircraft in the lowest gear ratio.

b. Vehicles equipped with automatic transmission should approach the aircraft in the lowest gear range.

Ramp equipment should not approach an aircraft that has its engines running, unless it has been specifically cleared into the area by the ground personnel directing the operation.

Training Programs

A training program should be established to make sure that all unit operators are taught safe procedures and practices to handle the vehicle(s) they will be required to operate. Where possible, simulations using mock-ups of aircraft doors and loading docks should be provided as part of the training.

It is recommended that the appropriate training manual and procedures for each piece of equipment be used.

During training, special emphasis should be placed on:

- Preuse equipment check
- Defensive driving (driving to save lives, money, and time in spite of conditions around you and the actions of others)
- Working with guide personnel
- Operating in emergencies.

Vehicle operators should be tested for the following:

- Parking
- Backing
- Turning
- Positioning
- Use of hand and/or turn signals
- Stopping and starting
- Observing clearances
- Nervousness
- Lack of confidence or overconfidence.

Signaling

For the safe movement of ground service equipment, operators, as well as those who guide them, should be trained in the use of hand signals. Verbal signals should be avoided because they can be misunderstood.

The use of approved guide signals is recommended. In the event the operator does not understand the signal, loses sight of the guide, or communication is hampered in any way, the operator should immediately stop until the discrepancy is remedied. Conversely, when the guide feels the operator is not following given signals, he or she should signal the operator to stop.

Refer to Figure 4-5 for hand signals.

The IDENTIFICATION signal is used to attract the operator's attention. The guide extends both arms above the head in full view of the operator. The operator must indicate to the guide that he or she has seen the signal.

The ADVANCE signal is given as long as it is safe for the vehicle to move. The guide moves both arms forward and back in unison from the elbow while the arms are held above the waist with palms facing inward. The rapidity of arm movement will indicate the desired speed of advance.

To signal SLOW DOWN, the guide holds both arms down with palms toward the ground moving the hands up and down several times.

The signal for STOP, given with the guide positioned in front of or at the rear of a vehicle, is to cross arms repeatedly above the head. The rapidity of the arm movement should be related to the urgency of the stop—that is, the quicker the arm movement, the quicker the stop.

When signaling TURN from the front or rear of a vehicle, the guide:

Figure 4-5. Ground equipment operators follow the signals of a guide. The chart shows the recommended signals. Verbal signals should be avoided.

a. Stands in the most advantageous position

b. Extends one arm in the direction the turn is to be made

c. Moves the other arm in a back and forth motion above the head.

Operating a lift truck around aircraft is hazardous because the raised portion of the truck is particularly likely to make a damaging contact. When directing this operation, the guide signals RAISE by extending the arm forward, above the waist, with *palms up,* and moving both arms up and down in unison. The STOP signal stops the lift. The guide signals LOWER by extending both arms with the palms down and then moving them up and down. Again, the STOP signal is the same.

In positioning a train of carts/dollies to a loading/unloading position, the driver does not have the proper perspective to align the loading/unloading equipment. The guide under these conditions will station himself or herself in a position in full view of the driver and will indicate to ADVANCE THE TRAIN by holding the arm on the driver's side forward and upright from the elbow, with the side of the hand facing forward. The guide extends the other arm forward above the waist and waves it back and forth parallel to the ground.

To signal STOP TRAIN of carts/dollies, the guide drops the upright arm in a sharp, chopping motion.

CATERING OPERATIONS

An important element of airline service is providing food and beverages to passengers aboard flights. Catering service requires materials handling and the operation of mechanized equipment while the aircraft is on the airport ramp.

Food Service Handling

Several potential hazards for personnel involved in food service handling should be noted.

- Jamming fingers while opening or closing galley doors
- Tripping or falling over galley units set in narrow galleys or aisles
- Bumping head on open galley compartment doors
- Jamming fingers while inserting or removing ovens, food units, and tray carriers
- Burning hands and fingers when handling ovens
- Getting scratches and cuts from jagged metal edges while handling metal galley units that need repair
- Spraining of the back as a result of improper lifting procedures while handling galley units
- Falling out of galley doorways after hi-lift food trucks or other means of access have been removed
- Falling off hi-lift trucks or other means of access
- Lowering bodies of hi-lift trucks without warning (This can injure personnel and damage equipment.)
- Galley units falling or being blown out of aircraft doorways or food trucks
- Falling after attempting to board hi-lift trucks or other such vehicles by unauthorized methods
- Getting scratched as a result of handling broken glass or cutlery in the galley.

Operational Guidelines

Food service vehicles comprise a considerable part of the ground equipment that converges on an aircraft during the loading/unloading operation. While food service vehicles usually have special features not found on the typical ramp service vehicle, they should be operated according to the general instructions outlined earlier in this chapter.

Because many of these vehicles are operated by nonairline employees working on a contract basis, it is most important that such operators be required to comply with the same procedures as the airline's own employees. The following safety guidelines outline the procedures needed to safely operate and maintain these vehicles.

Throughout this section, the terms *helper* and *guide* are used interchangeably. For those companies that provide both a driver and a helper on a truck, the helper will be the "guide." If only a driver is provided, then when a guide is required to help position a vehicle against an aircraft safely, a member of the ground service crew must serve as the guide.

Qualifications

All drivers and helper/guides should meet the qualifications outlined earlier in this chapter. They should also be trained in the special procedures of each airline for which they provide service.

Supervisors should make periodic observations of a driver's operating habits and performance. Violation of operating procedures should be discussed with the driver *on the spot*, to make sure he or she is aware of these errors. Violations will be reported to the driver's supervisor at the earliest opportunity.

Drivers are required to check equipment prior to use. Checks should include, but not be limited to, brakes, lights, windshield wipers, and horn. (See the checklists in the section on Maintenance earlier in this chapter and on pages 74-76 in Chapter 5.)

If any of these items are found inoperative, the problem should be reported to the supervisor. The equipment should be recorded for maintenance or tagged OUT OF SERVICE, depending on the seriousness of the problem.

General Airport Driving Rules

The following airport rules should be observed at all times:

- Because of the danger of jet blast, the operator should avoid driving vehicles behind aircraft that have engines running. Look to see if the "anticollision" lights on the aircraft are on. This means that engines are running or are about to be started.
- Aircraft *always* have the right of way.
- A guide should be used when moving trucks and when raising truck bodies or extending platforms when a truck is positioned at the aircraft.
- The guide should stand where he or she can observe the most likely point of contact with aircraft, other GSE, or people (Figures 4-6 and 4-7).
- Drivers must always follow the rule that when they lose sight of the guide, either in the mirror or directly, they must immediately stop.
- The truck must be positioned at an aircraft in such a manner that no part of the aircraft will contact the truck if the aircraft settles.
- While waiting for the arrival of aircraft, trucks should stop only in "authorized" areas and out of the path of passenger loading bridges or other ground equipment. When a vehicle is parked on the ramp, unattended, the truck body must be fully lowered, parking brake set, and engine off.
- Vehicle bodies should not be raised during periods of high wind. In most cases, a velocity of 64 km/h (40 mph) can be critical. Company procedures should be based on the truck manufacturer's specifications.
- Controls for raising bodies must be of the constant-pressure type and should never be blocked or bypassed.

Loading

The requirements listed in this section and the ones that follow must be met to make sure that aircraft are catered safely and properly. The following rules should be observed in loading catering trucks:

- All drivers and helpers should be familiar with galley requirements, to make sure that correct equipment and supplies are put on the trucks.
- Equipment must be handled carefully to avoid personal injury, food spoilage, or equipment damage.
- All equipment aboard trucks must be securely stowed to prevent shifting in transit.
- Rear doors of trucks must be closed and latched at all times except when personnel are actually

Figure 4-6. A service truck is guided through a ramp area. Notice the distance between the truck and the airplane wingtip.

entering or leaving the truck body. This is to ensure the safety of personnel and to prevent anything from blowing out of or falling from trucks.

Positioning Trucks at Aircraft

Catering vehicles should approach aircraft so that operations will be completed properly, minimizing personal injury and potential property damage.

The operator should then come to a second stop approximately 2.5 m (8 ft) from the aircraft. At this point, the helper will dismount and guide the truck to the final position at the aircraft. Standard hand signals should be used in positioning the truck.

The truck should be positioned so that the bumper will be a short distance from the aircraft skin when the truck is raised to the proper working level. This distance ensures that the truck will not come into contact with the aircraft regardless of the movement of the aircraft.

Truck brakes should be set, and the transmission/gear train placed in the correct mode to elevate the truck body. At the same time, the helper should be placing the chock(s) fore and aft of a front wheel of the truck (Figure 4-8).

NOTE: The use of one or two chocks is the option of the company operating the truck. When only one chock is provided, it will be placed in *front* of the wheel.

NOTE: The use of one or two chocks is the option of the company operating the truck. When only one chock is provided, it will be placed in *front* of the wheel.

If at any time during the raising of the truck body, the guide believes the platform is coming too close to the aircraft, he or she should give the STOP signal. The truck body should be lowered and the truck repositioned to provide sufficient clearance.

Raising Truck Bodies

The helper should assist the driver during the raising operation by closely watching the clearance between the truck and aircraft.

The truck body should be raised only high enough to suit the type of aircraft being catered. Where the airline uses a bridge to roll equipment directly into the aircraft, the platform must be at doorsill height.

Truck bodies must not be raised if an outward-opening door of the aircraft is open; a failure in the controls could cause the body to continue to rise too high and damage the door.

Whenever possible, trucks should be positioned so that platforms are not under the aircraft door, to preclude any damage if the aircraft settles during loading.

Prior to servicing, the truck platform guardrails (where provided) must be installed to prevent personnel from falling off.

Figure 4-9 shows how stabilizers extend as the body of the vehicle moves upward to service the aircraft.

Servicing an Aircraft

Before opening the galley door, catering personnel should knock on it twice to alert anyone inside that it is being opened. Doors should then be opened carefully and moved to the latched position, to prevent jet blast or wind from damaging them.

If, while the door is being opened, it becomes evident that the evacuation slide is still connected, the door should be closed and the airline crew should be instructed to disconnect the slide. An inflating slide can injure personnel on the truck or in the aircraft.

The clearance between aircraft and truck should be checked periodically to make sure no part of the aircraft comes in contact with the truck.

Nothing that can be blown off should be left on the truck platforms. Any equipment that must be staged on the platform should be properly secured.

Aircraft galley equipment will be handled carefully to ensure correct operation in flight. Any

Courtesy United Airlines, photo by Mike Sroka.

Figure 4-7. When the vehicle is about 2.5 m (8 ft) from the aircraft, the guide should stand near the plane to direct the vehicle into its final position.

Figure 4-8. A helper pushes the front-wheel chock into place before the body of the vehicle is raised to service the aircraft.

unserviceable items should be brought to the attention of the appropriate airline representative.

When catering is completed, catering personnel should check that all galley doors and compartments are properly closed and locked. They should tidy up the galley area and be sure nothing is left behind that could be a problem to the flight attendants.

Leaving the Aircraft

Procedures for a truck to leave the aircraft are basically the reverse of positioning the catering truck. The following additional items are required:

- The aircraft door should be closed slowly and carefully; the door should be correctly positioned and latched properly.
- Both the driver and helper should survey the ramp around the truck to make sure the area below is clear of personnel and equipment.
- The driver should lower the body only after he or she has closed the front door, the helper has closed the rear door, and the area is clear. Before leaving the truck body, the driver should make sure the rear door is closed.
- When the driver is seated and has started the engine, the helper will remove the chock from *behind* the front wheel (where applicable), and will leave the *front* chock in place.
- The helper or guide will take a position at the rear of the truck—about 3 m (10 ft) behind the truck—where he or she is in full view of the driver in the mirror and where he or she can accurately observe the most critical point of clearance between the truck and the aircraft (Figure 4-10).
- After the driver has backed the truck approximately 2.5–3 m (8–10 ft), the guide should give the STOP signal, pick up the chocks, and stow them on the truck. The guide should then return to the rear of the truck and direct the driver away from the aircraft.
- Backing the truck away from the aircraft can be more critical than positioning it. The driver must drive slowly, while observing clearance from the aircraft, and being alert for signals from the guide. If the driver loses sight of the guide, he or she must *stop* immediately and not proceed farther until visual contact is reestablished.
- When the truck is clear of the aircraft and surrounding equipment, the guide returns to the cab of the truck and the workers proceed to their next assignment.

Courtesy United Airlines, photo by Mike Sroka.

Figure 4-9. As the body of the service truck is raised, the stabilizers extend automatically.

Courtesy United Airlines, photo by Mike Sroka.

Figure 4-10. A guide directs a food service truck driver away from the aircraft after servicing operations are finished.

Special Procedures and Precautions

Certain aircraft, because of special configurations or means of operation, require additional procedures or precautions in the catering operation. This is particularly true of wide-bodied aircraft because of their height. Such precautions are necessary to protect personnel and to prevent damage to the aircraft.

Procedures must be developed for servicing each type of aircraft, if the aircraft operator does not already have such procedures.

Some of the hazard points that must be addressed and highlighted in the procedures are:

- Unusually low wing areas of BAC 111 and DC-9 aircraft
- Trailing edges of the left wing of Boeing 727 "stretch" aircraft, because of the location of the rear galley door
- Cabin doors of the 747, 757, 767, DC-10, and L-1011. All these doors are power-operated (by compressed gas) in the emergency mode. Catering personnel must never operate these doors from inside the aircraft, as a powered opening and slide deployment can result if the door mechanism is not in the "disarmed" mode.
- With aircraft that are catered by loading complete food units, the catering truck must be positioned to have its platform level with the aircraft doorsill. If a bridge plate is used, it should have a means of being secured so that it does not move when the food containers are transferred from the truck to the aircraft (or vice versa).
- High-lift trucks used to service wide-bodied aircraft should have an interlock installed that prevents the body from being raised higher than regular jet aircraft height unless the stabilizers are extended (Figure 4-9).

REFERENCES

American National Standards Institute, 1430 Broadway, New York, NY 10018.

Airline Ground Support Vehicle-Mounted Vertical Lift Devices, Safety Standards for, ANSI A92.7-1981.

Boom-Supported Elevated Work Platforms, ANSI A92.5-1980.

Elevating Work Platforms, Manually Propelled, ANSI A92.3-1980.

Vehicle Mounted Elevating and Rotating Aerial Devices, ANSI A92.2-1979.

Work Platforms, Self-Propelled Elevating, ANSI A92.6-1979.

International Electrotechnical Commission, 3 rue de Varembe, CH-1211 Geneva 20, Switzerland.

International Organization for Standardization, 1 rue de Varembe, CH-1211 Geneva 20, Switzerland.

National Safety Council, 444 N. Michigan Ave., Chicago, IL 60611.

Accident Prevention Manual for Industrial Operations, 9th ed., 1988.

National Fire Protection Association, Batterymarch Park, Quincy, MA 02269.

Aircraft Hangars, NFPA 409, 1985.

Aircraft Maintenance, NFPA 410, 1980.

Powered Industrial Trucks, Including Type Designations, Areas of Use, and Maintenance and Operations, NFPA 505, 1982.

Society of Automotive Engineers, AGE 2C (Subcommittee), 400 Commonwealth Dr., Warrendale, PA 15096.

U.S. Department of Transportation, 400 Seventh St. SW, Washington, D.C. 20590.

Federal Motor Vehicle Safety Standards (FMVSS) in Code of Federal Regulations, Title 49, Part 571.

UNITED
MAX TOWING
10 MPH
GOV CHARGE
AT 78
REMOVE TOWBAR
FROM AIRCRAFT

CHAPTER 5

Hangar and Shop Operations

Aircraft maintenance in hangars and shops brings together representatives of nearly every aircraft trade and skill, along with many other categories of support personnel. This concentration of personnel, the limits of space in which they work, the variety of activities they perform, and the size and weight of the aircraft and equipment involved create a significant safety challenge. To assure safe operations, safety programs must be established and the safest practices and procedures must be strictly followed.

This chapter will cover requirements to safely meet this challenge. It is divided into three sections: hangar operations, shop operations, and materials handling in these areas.

HANGAR OPERATIONS

Environmental control in hangars requires intensive industrial engineering and maintenance programs. Continual attention must be directed to the main power systems of the hangar itself. Housekeeping must be of a high quality, and floors and equipment must be maintained in excellent condition. Further, personal work habits must be in accord with safe practices. Finally, workers should wear the kind of clothing appropriate for the operation being performed. Controlling these factors can help reduce the potential for accidents around aircraft.

General Rules for Hangar Facilities

Housekeeping. In hangars, housekeeping is a continuous operation. The very nature of the work produces oil spills, used parts, dust, grime, and debris on work surfaces. A sound housekeeping program should result in cost savings by reducing accidents. Here are some basic housekeeping rules for hangars:

- Keep floors clean and free from oil, grease, fuel, and trash at all times.

- Keep aisles, walkways, and exits clear.
- Avoid concentrations of equipment, toolboxes, and other materials around aircraft undergoing overhaul, since these items can form obstacles.
- Mark areas of operation and protective devices.
- Guidelines for positioning aircraft should be clearly visible and kept intact.
- Dispose of oily rags, empty oil cans, and other combustible waste in metal containers with self-closing lids. Place the containers in convenient locations in the work area, and empty them on a regular schedule.

Electrical Equipment. Both fixed and portable electrical equipment in hangars and around aircraft should be of an approved type according to the *National Electrical Code* (National Fire Protection Association 70; see References).

All electrical equipment in hangars should be continuously inspected to detect defects that may have arisen as a result of use or misuse.

Compressed Air Systems. Compressed air lines in hangars should have only standard, approved fittings, without makeshift modifications. Hose lines should be approved for the pressures involved. Hoses should be securely connected in place to eliminate both tripping hazards to people and damage to hoses. The operator should check hoses before use to make sure they are securely connected to the proper pipe outlets. Air hoses should receive periodic inspections. Defective hoses should be replaced immediately. High- and low-pressure chucks for servicing systems should not be interchangeable: It should be impossible to interchange low-pressure systems with a high-pressure supply.

Aircraft Painting and Cleaning. Painting and cleaning operations usually involve the use of flammable and/or toxic substances. Every effort should be made to protect employees from exposure to hazardous materials. Employees should be provided with proper protective equipment and should use it. Other necessary controls should be used as suggested by the Material Safety Data Sheet (MSDS) available in the United States from the manufacturer, distributor, or supplier of the substance. In the United States, check also the requirements of OSHA Hazard Communication Standard mandated by the OSHAct. Other standards may exist outside the United States.

Whenever possible, the least flammable and least toxic materials should be used. Flammable solvents should not be used in the cabins of aircraft. The least flammable paints and solvents should be used on aircraft exteriors.

All hazardous materials should be properly identified by (1) name, (2) health hazards they pose, (3) safety hazards they pose, and (4) control measures for them. Employees exposed to these materials should be provided with training on these four points for each potentially hazardous material. (For more detailed information on dealing with these materials, see Chapter 8, Hazardous Materials and Processes.)

Aircraft Docking and Dedocking

Before an aircraft is placed within docks or removed from them, the hangar door alarms should be checked and the area should be clear of all obstructions.

The steps in positioning or docking an aircraft are:

- Warn workers of an approaching aircraft by posted signs or other means.
- Make sure that qualified operators are at the aircraft controls during the entire operation.
- Post observers at each wing tip and at the tail to warn the operator of the tug of unseen hazards.
- Make sure that all aircraft enter in the exact guidelines.
- Position aircraft and attach ground plugs before closing the hangar doors. (Wheels should also be chocked as required.)
- Draw dock structures into position before removing WARNING signs.
- Make sure that all movable structures are locked into position, guardrails in place, and utilities connected.

The steps in dedocking, or removing, an aircraft are:

- Remove all equipment and personnel from a dock.
- Disconnect grounds, power, air pressure, and other utilities.
- Remove movable structures around the aircraft.
- Open the hangar doors.
- Position a qualified operator in the aircraft and at the controls.
- Connect tugs, picket the aircraft at both wing tips, and place one person outside hangar doors to guide the tug operator to ensure that no other approaching traffic or personnel are in the path of the tug and the aircraft.
- Check that the aircraft is guided clear of all obstructions and position on ramp.
- Place chocks in position.
- Set aircraft brakes before disconnecting towbars.

- Make sure that if a towbar is returned with the tug, it is visible to other traffic; have it either lighted or otherwise conspicuously marked.
- Close the hangar doors.

Aircraft Fuel Systems

Aircraft fuel system service and maintenance personnel should strictly observe the provisions of applicable maintenance manuals. In maintaining aircraft fuel systems, consider the two basic hazards: fire and health.

Fire Hazards. Aviation gasoline (avgas), jet A, and JP fuels are classified as flammable or combustible liquids, depending upon grade. All precautions covering fire prevention practices should be observed in their handling. In addition, the area in which aircraft fuel systems are being maintained should be kept free of flammable materials, oxidizers, and acids. Fire hazards are thoroughly covered by the National Fire Protection Association (NFPA) standards and the U.S. Air Force *Manual 32-3.* (See References.)

Skin Contact with Fuels. Fuels may irritate the skin on contact and may cause dermatitis with repeated exposure. Here are some rules those handling fuels should follow:

- Remove liquid fuels from the skin immediately with soap and water.
- Remove any fuel-soaked clothing.
- If the eyes or face come into contact with fuel, flush the area immediately, preferably at an eye wash fountain. Seek medical treatment promptly.

Inhalation of Fuels. Fuels are toxic if inhaled or swallowed. Benzene, a component of avgas, is a known carcinogen, or cancer-causing agent. Fuels can cause narcosis, an effect on the central nervous system involving a stupor or unconsciousness. For example, more than 1,000 parts per million (ppm) of JP vapor will produce a "naptha jag," which is similar to alcohol intoxication. The maximum allowable concentration of JP-4 vapor in air is 200 ppm. For jet A fuel, the maximum allowable concentration of vapor in air is 300 ppm. (These threshold limit values for aliphatic petroleum hydrocarbons are set by The American Conference of Governmental Industrial Hygienists.)

Workers should wear special protective clothing such as face shields, full-coverage suits, gloves, boots, and air-supplied breathing apparatus either when a gross contamination hazard is present, such as may occur during a fuel spill, or when high concentrations (over 200 ppm) of vapor are detected.

Fuel Cell and Tank Repair. Maintenance of aircraft fuel cells and tanks requires thorough knowledge of hazards and procedures. Fire and inhalation hazards are usually present. Strict adherence to prescribed safety standards is mandatory. Repairs should be made only by qualified personnel and only in areas where spark or flame producing devices are excluded.

Defueling. Before tank work, defueling should be carried out under supervision at least 15 m (50 ft) from any building or other aircraft. Defueling may be conducted within the hangar if an installed hydrant defueling system is available and approved for use.

Here are rules and procedures to follow before defueling:

- Open the fuel cell filler cap.
- Open the vent line.
- Have a Class B:C fire extinguisher of sufficient capacity placed near the aircraft.
- Ground and bond both the aircraft being drained and the fuel truck. (For a detailed explanation of grounding and bonding, see the section Servicing Aircraft in Chapter 3, Ramp Operations at Passenger Terminals.)

For the defueling process:

- Do not perform any other work on the aircraft during defueling.
- Do not carry out fuel transfers during an electrical storm.

Venting. Here are the procedures for venting:

- Perform venting after defueling and before opening the tank access plates.
- Use an approved blower having nonsparking blades and an isolated, nonsparking blower motor that is U.L. listed for conditions.
- Employ forced air or positive pressure, rather than negative pressure while venting.
- Utilize a grounded hose for venting.
- Do not leave the hose hooked up after venting is completed.

Aircraft Jet A Fuel Tank Entry Safety Procedures

Fuel tank entry for removal of residual fuel or for maintenance of fuel tanks requires close adherence to procedures. The following procedures contain minimum requirements for protecting the health and safety of workers and for protecting equipment and facilities during certain aircraft fuel tank entry. Procedures apply *only to entering aircraft fuel tanks that have contained jet A/Kerosene fuel.*

Definition of Equipment and Terms. The list below contains the basic terms relating to fuel tank entry.

1. ***Acceptable combustible gas indicator (CGI).*** This is defined as a CGI that has been calibrated to measure jet A fuel vapors and is capable of accurately measuring 15% and 5% of the lower explosive limit (LEL) or capable of accurately measuring 15% of the LEL and 300 parts per million (ppm) of jet A fuel vapor.
   NOTE: Before purchase of a new CGI or use of a CGI already on hand, the capability of the selected CGI to accurately measure jet A/Kerosene vapors in the ranges between 5% of the LEL (300 ppm) and 15% (1400 ppm) of the LEL should be certified in writing by the CGI manufacturer. The CGI should be initially calibrated for jet A fuel vapors by the manufacturer. CGIs capable of these measurements probably will be "dual range" instruments.
   All CGIs used for fuel tank atmosphere tests should be recalibrated at least once a year. Recalibration should be done by the manufacturer or by qualified technicians using calibration procedures recommended by the CGI manufacturer.
2. ***Fire safe condition.*** This occurs when the fuel tank atmosphere contains 15% of the LEL or less of jet A fuel vapors.
3. ***Health safe condition.*** This occurs when the fuel tank atmosphere contains 5% or less of the LEL or 300 ppm or less of jet A fuel vapors.
4. ***Lower explosive limit (LEL) [sometimes called lower flammable limit (LFL)].*** This is the minimum concentration of a combustible gas or vapor in air that will ignite if an ignition source is present.
5. ***Parts per million (ppm).*** This indicates the parts of vapor or gas per million parts of air (a standard measurement used to determine health hazards).

Required Safety Precautions Prior to Fuel Tank Entry. The following safety procedures should be followed before fuel tank entry:

- Properly ground the aircraft to an approved and identified ground.
- Bond to the aircraft and ground all barrels, cans, funnels, suction guns, etc., used in draining tank sumps and/or removing residual fuel.
- Drain the residual fuel into suitable containers. Remove the containers from the repair area immediately, and take them to a proper fuel storage area.
- Pull and tag electrical circuit breakers for the fuel quantity system and the tank boost pumps and valves before opening the fuel tank.
- Shut down all motorized equipment or place it at least 15 m (50 ft) from the fuel tank opening until the tanks are determined to be in a FIRE SAFE CONDITION. After a FIRE SAFE CONDITION is obtained, it is permissible to use ground power equipment and other electrical, gasoline, or LP-powered equipment as required.
- Prohibit radar or high frequency radio transmissions within 90 m (300 ft) of an open fuel tank until a FIRE SAFE CONDITION is obtained.
- Prohibit open-flame or spark-producing equipment or devices within 15 m (50 ft) of any open fuel tank until a FIRE SAFE CONDITION is obtained.
- Locate at least one wheeled dry chemical (or equivalent) fire extinguisher having a rating of 80 B:C and a minimum capacity of 57 kg (125 lb) of agent within 15 m (50 ft) of any aircraft undergoing fuel tank maintenance.
- Permit fuel system maintenance only in areas that have free access for fire-fighting or other emergency equipment.
- FOR RESCUE USE ONLY: Provide at least two air-supplied respirators and an acceptable and adequate air supply for immediate availability at the aircraft any time that personnel are working inside a fuel tank.
  NOTE: Air-supplied respirators are not required for rescue purposes if a HEALTH SAFE CONDITION has been determined immediately prior to the rescue entry.

Fuel Tank Atmosphere Conditions. The concentration of fuel vapor determines whether, and under what conditions, fuel tank entry is possible.

- All jet A fuel vapors inside a fuel tank must be considered explosive and toxic until testing confirms otherwise. Workers exposed to excessive concentrations of jet A fuel vapors may experience headache, nausea, and dizziness. Extremely high concentrations of the vapors may act as an anesthetic, and, depending on concentration and length of exposure, can cause death.
- Fuel vapor concentration is measured in percentage of the lower explosive limit (LEL) or in parts of fuel vapor per million parts of air (ppm).
- The condition of the fuel tank atmosphere will determine the equipment necessary for tank entry (Table 5-A).

The following are required procedures for ventilating tanks and measuring fuel vapor:

- Initial tank entry
  a. Force-ventilate fuel tanks with venturi or equivalent air movers for at least 30 minutes before the first entry after tanks are opened. Test the tank for fuel vapor with an acceptable combustible gas indicator (CGI) before the first entry.
  b. Maintain forced ventilation at all times a fuel tank is occupied. The ventilation must be sufficient to reach all parts of the tank.

Table 5-A. Condition of Fuel Tank Atmosphere

Contamination Level	Tank Atmosphere	Tank Entry Permitted
Not fire safe	Greater than 15% LEL	No
Fire safe	15% LEL (1400 ppm) or less	Yes, with NIOSH-approved organic vapor cartridge or air-supplied respirator
Health safe	5% LEL (300 ppm) or less	Yes, without a respirator

Data source: Air Transport Committee, National Safety Council.

- Subsequent tank entry
  a. Each day that tank entry is performed, test the fuel tank atmosphere at least before the first entry to determine the personal protective equipment requirements as defined in Table 5-A.
- Records
  a. Maintain a record of all fuel tank atmosphere test results. Include in this record:
  —Identity of the employee performing tests
  —Identification of the CGI used
  —Date and time of the test
  —Aircraft and fuel tank numbers and test results
  b. Keep this record in the immediate supervisor's files for at least the duration of the job.

Personal Precautions. Workers engaged in fuel tank repairs are required to observe the following precautions:

- If toxic chemicals are used inside the tank, wear respiratory equipment approved for the specific chemicals.
- If clothing becomes saturated with fuel or solvent, remove clothing immediately, flush the affected area with water, and launder the clothing before reuse.
- Do not carry matches or cigarette lighters inside fuel tanks.
- Do not carry tools or other loose objects in pockets while inside fuel tanks.
- Do not wear clothing that is likely to produce static electricity, such as wool, silk, and synthetics. Cotton is acceptable.

The following are the procedures for use of standbys:

- Have a worker standing by outside the tank at all times when workers are completely inside a fuel tank that is not in a HEALTH SAFE CONDITION—that is, for either or both of the following:
  a. Fuel vapor concentration in the tank is above 5% LEL (above 300 ppm).
  b. Workers are required to wear respiratory protection because of toxic materials inside the tank.
- Workers assigned to standby duty are to maintain constant visual or verbal contact with the personnel inside the tank during the job so they can promptly call for help or assist those inside the tank if the need arises.

Tool and Equipment Requirements. The following are guidelines for tools used inside fuel tanks.

- Inside fuel tanks, use only droplights, flashlights, and other electrical equipment listed by Underwriters Laboratories Inc. for Class I, Group D, Division 1 atmospheres.
  NOTE: Only the probe of CGIs may be taken inside fuel tanks.
- Use only clean, lint-free cotton rags or cheesecloth for wiping up inside fuel tanks. *Do not* use rags of wool or synthetic materials.

Fuel Tank Rescue Requirements. Although fuel tank entry is safe when proper precautions are taken, all workers should be familiar with the following methods for dealing with potential emergencies.

Prolonged breathing of fuel vapor in excess of limits established as HEALTH SAFE can cause dizziness and unconsciousness. At the first sign of the slightest dizziness while inside a fuel tank, the affected person should:

- Signal the standby, if a standby is required.
- Get out of the tank as calmly and as quickly as possible.

If a person in the fuel tank is experiencing difficulty, but *is still conscious,* the standby or other employees should:

- Alert other employees to stand by in the event additional help is needed.
- Get a fresh-air supply to the person in the tank. It might be possible to push either an open air line or a rescue air-supplied respirator to the person in the tank (see Required Safety Precautions Prior to Fuel Tank Entry on page 66). *Do not use oxygen inside the fuel tank!*

NOTE: In a situation where there is only one standby, the standby should *not* enter the tank, but rather should seek help first. There must be at least one other person outside the fuel tank when any person enters it to make a rescue effort.

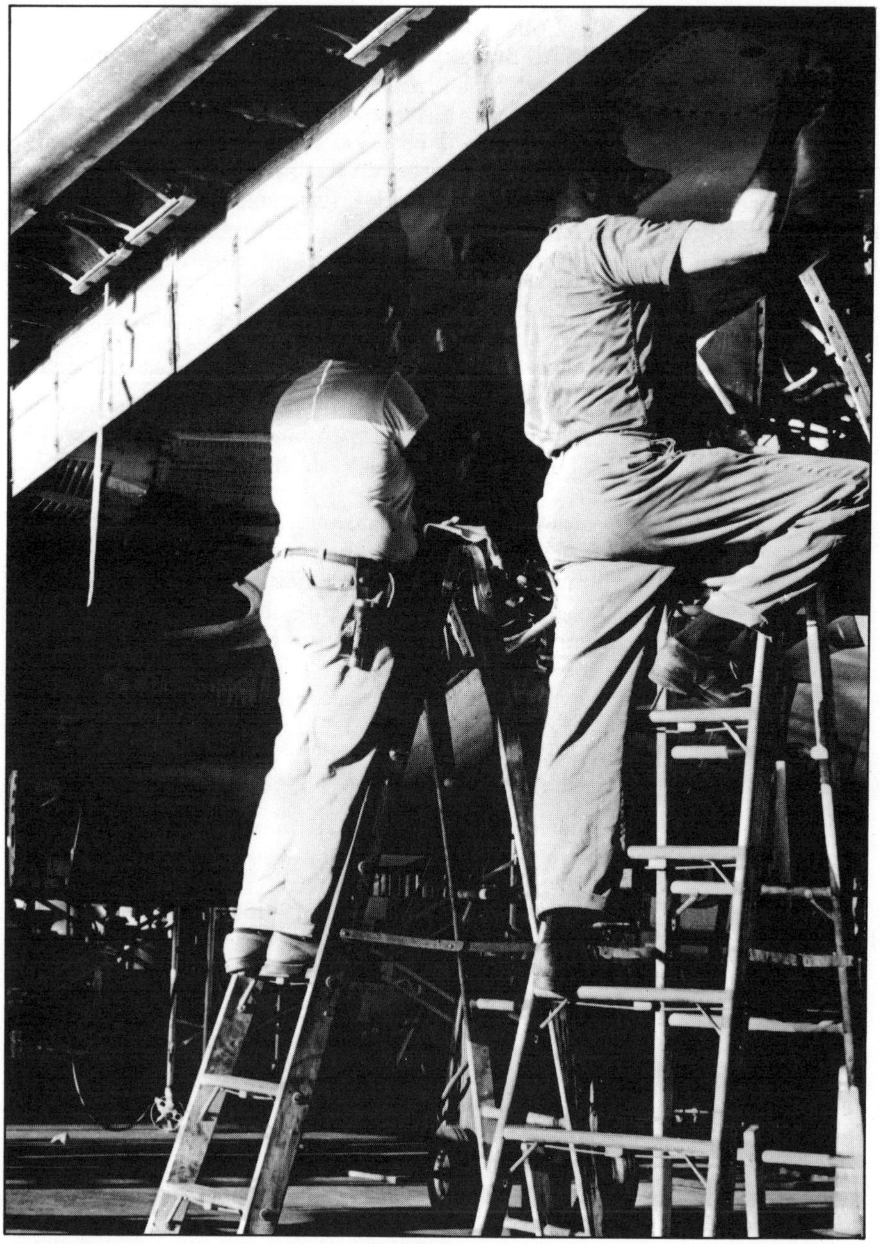

Figure 5-1. Because of the possibility of electrical shock and because of the presence of flammable vapors around aircraft, manual hand tools, pneumatic tools, and wooden ladders should be used for repair work on aircraft.

- When the victim revives, give calm matter-of-fact instructions to help him or her out of the tank. Avoid exciting the victim or having him or her perform any unnecessary exertion.
- Support the person getting out of the tank so that he or she does not incur injury as a result of dizziness or nausea.

If an unconscious person cannot be revived, the standby or other employees should:

- Remove the victim from the tank immediately.
- Send someone for emergency medical assistance.
- Start mouth-to-mouth resuscitation or cardiopulmonary resuscitation (CPR) (as appropriate) as soon as the unconscious person is removed from the tank. Limited space and/or contaminated air will normally prevent applying mouth-to-mouth resuscitation or CPR inside the tank.

Electrical Systems and Electronic Equipment

Short circuits, overloading, accidental grounding, poor electrical contacts, and misuse are all potential sources of accidents involving electrical power in a hangar. All electrical systems used in aircraft—primary power supplies, communications equipment, and electronic equipment—produce or use extremely high voltage. Severe electric shock or electrocution is an ever-present hazard to those repairing electrical equipment, whether it is low-voltage (600 v or less) or high-voltage (over 600 v). Standard safe practices must be followed for all work on electrical systems.

Use only wooden or plastic ladders when servicing electrical equipment or electrical systems (Figure 5-1).

Ground fault circuit interruption installations should be provided as established by local electrical codes and as considered necessary.

Personnel throughout the aviation industry, but particularly those in maintenance, are exposed to hazards created by improper use of electrically powered equipment. Serious injury, even death, can result from unsafe use of electrical power. Major damage to materials and property can also result from explosions and fires caused by improper use of electrical equipment.

Inspection. All electrical equipment facilities should be regularly inspected by qualified personnel. Explosion-proof and vapor-tight equipment should be regularly maintained to comply with *National Electrical Code* or other applicable standards.

Personnel. Only trained and qualified electricians should be permitted to install and maintain electrical facilities and supply lines. Personnel working on electrical circuits should avoid wearing loose clothing. Also, they should not wear jewelry or metal objects that can conduct electricity and thus cause shock, burns, or electrocution.

Grounding. Aircraft should be grounded to proper grounding plugs at all times when within hangars or undergoing maintenance. Grounding circuits should be periodically tested to make sure that resistance levels are below 25 ohm.

Ground wires should be located to minimize damage and wear. Large metal equipment complexes, such as aircraft docks, should be permanently bonded and grounded.

Controls. Electrical controls on circuits within hangars should be suitable to the location. They should be positioned to minimize the possibility that anyone will accidentally come into contact with them.

Repair. Only qualified personnel should repair the electrical circuitry in hangars. Electrical circuits to be repaired or installed should have the line switch locked "OPEN" and tagged to prevent the circuit from becoming accidentally energized. Only the person tagging and locking the switch should be permitted to remove the tag and lock. People trained in rescue procedures, mouth-to-mouth resuscitation, and cardiopulmonary resuscitation should be immediately available when repair work is being done.

Warning signs. There should be adequate warning signs in areas where hazardous electrical facilities exist, particularly around high voltage apparatus.

Wiring. All wiring within hangars should be installed by qualified electricians, and all conductors protected by conduit or armor. Temporary or makeshift wiring, other than extension lights, should be prohibited in hangars. Workers should assume that all conductors are "energized."

Overloading. Electrical circuit overloading is dangerous and should not be permitted at any time. All primary systems within hangars should be equipped with circuit breakers or other accepted means to prevent accidental overloading. Circuit breakers should be reset only after the circuit is tested and the overload has been eliminated.

Cords and Receptacles. Electrical cords on portable lamps should be heavily insulated (see *National Electrical Code* or other appropriate standard). Workers should make sure that the cords are long enough for the job and should avoid stretching and breaking them. Extension cords should not be used. All cords must be inspected regularly for signs of deterioration. Damaged or frayed electrical cords should be replaced immediately. Wall plugs must not be interchangeable with those of different voltages.

Low Voltage Systems. Low voltage systems (600 v or less) should receive the same respect given high voltage circuits. Severe shock and death can be caused by 100 v or less if a good contact is made. Regardless of voltages, follow safe practices.

High Voltage Systems. High voltage systems (above 600 v) expose all service people to hazards. The treachery of electrical voltage is that its presence cannot be detected by human senses until injury occurs. Therefore, everyone should treat all electronic and communication devices with caution.

Standard practices should require power to be turned off for work on electronic, communication, or energizing equipment. If an adjustment can only be carried out when the circuit is "hot," or energized, the servicing should be done by qualified personnel who are properly trained.

Repair workers should not use metal rules or uninsulated tools near electrical voltage circuits. Service personnel should not use hand tools (such as screwdrivers) to make energy tests on any piece of electronic equipment. Serious burns can result from this practice.

Circuits should be deenergized when work is in progress. Equipment should be grounded according to manufacturer's instructions and procedures. Grounding "hot" circuits should be done at the exact point of the intended repair or adjustment prior to making contact with that particular area of the energized equipment. (Grounding may be needed on both sides of the circuit or equipment). Grounding should be used on all circuits being worked on that could contain residual energy, such as capacitors, or circuits that could be energized. It should not be removed until repairs are completed. The system should not be energized until grounding is removed.

Equipment safety devices, such as interlock switches, disconnect relays, or automatic circuit breakers are designed to give protection to electrical circuits and equipment. Because these devices are subject to failure, repair workers should take other necessary precautions, such as manually disconnecting or locking out control switches when working on electrical equipment. Safety interlocks should not be deliberately decommissioned. Where appropriate, nonmetallic ladders and extension cords with ground fault circuit interrupters should be used.

When antenna repairs are undertaken, power should be grounded out at the transmitter, and a warning tag indicating work in progress applied.

Electronic equipment carrying high voltages (above 600 v) should not be unplugged with the power on.

High Voltage Switches. Electrically operated high voltage switch gears should not be manually closed on any energized electrical circuit.

Radar Systems. Neither weather radar nor any other type of radar emission should be allowed in hangars because radar in sufficient intensity may cause damage to human tissue, particularly to the eyes. Another reason to exclude radar operations from hangars is that radar beams might activate hangar warning systems by causing localized heating. Radar is also dangerous near fueling operations for the same reason.

Cathode-ray Tubes. Because of the high vacuum present in cathode-ray tubes (CRTs), anyone working on them should prevent bumping, scratching, or cracking them. A violent implosion may result if a CRT is damaged or handled too roughly.

Courtesy Air Canada.

Figure 5-2. Aircraft service docks should be strongly built of noncombustible materials. Workers at elevated heights should wear safety harnesses and lifelines.

In the event of an equipment fire in a chassis that has CRTs, use of carbon dioxide (CO_2) gas extinguishing agents should be avoided. As the gas expands, it becomes very cold. The contact of the cold gas with the warm glass of a CRT will result in a violent implosion. Halon extinguishing systems are preferred.

When maintaining or removing CRTs, workers should wear safety glasses. They should also wear rubber gloves as protection against implosion. Proper grounding procedures should be followed.

Engine Starters. Like other electrical apparatus, high energy ignition systems have the potential to kill. Therefore, only employees who are properly trained and technically qualified should work on high energy ignitions.

Control Systems In Aircraft

Serious damage can be done to aircraft (and personal injury may also result) if aircraft controls are operated without the use of correct procedures. Here are some basic procedures for operating controls:

- Mechanics should make certain that all personnel and equipment are clear of the moving surfaces on the aircraft before operating any controls in the cockpit.
- Place placards on the controls in the cockpit with warning signs when work is in progress on either surfaces or linkages. Only maintenance personnel actually involved in doing the work should remove the placards.

Walking and Working Surfaces

In the United States, OSHA regulation 1910.28 specifies that walkways, scaffolds, and stairways used to service wing and tail assemblies on aircraft should be constructed of materials sufficiently strong to provide a safety factor of at least 4. [A safety factor is the ratio of the ultimate (breaking) strength of a member or piece of material to the actual working stress or to the maximum permissible (safe load) stress when in use.] Walkways, scaffolds, and stairways should be of stable design and adequately secured to the floor or aircraft dock. Work platforms more than 1.2 m (4 ft) in height and 0.75 m (30 in.) above the floor or surrounding area must be equipped with guardrails and toeboards, in compliance with federal and state standards (Figure 5-2).

When the nature of the repair makes it necessary for the worker to step on the aircraft, the worker should use designated walkways. Under no circumstances should personnel step on control surfaces, air scoops, fairings, or other parts that are not designed for walking. All walkways, scaffolds, and platforms should be suitably guarded for the work to be undertaken. Personnel working on unguard-

Figure 5-3. The picture shows the control panel of a high-altitude test chamber. Vacuum pumps take the test chamber to a pressure altitude of 15,000 m (50,000 ft) in less than one minute. The chamber tests turbocompressors, the devices that provide cabin pressure for passenger comfort.

ed, elevated surfaces should wear lifelines and safety harnesses.

Horseplay in any form should be forbidden in and around all aircraft during maintenance operations. Horseplay is dangerous to both people and aircraft.

Aircraft Pressurization and Air-Conditioning Systems

Air Control Systems. These systems on an aircraft are usually composed of a turbocompressor assembly, heat extraction assembly, reheat assembly, and valves and ducts. Maintenance on them inside a hangar should be confined to functional checks of components (Figure 5-3). Pneumatic test equipment, which involves ducting to carry high-temperature compressed air to an aircraft, is widely used to test pressurization, air conditioning, and pneumatic installations on an aircraft. From a personal safety point of view, external lines carrying high-temperature compressed air to an aircraft should be well insulated and installed so as to be inaccessible to workers. Air ducts and nozzle attachments should be maintained in the best condition possible and should have locking devices built into an aircraft coupling. Standard fan guards with mesh small enough to prevent fingers from contacting fan blades must be provided.

Turbocompressor Run-in. Temperatures and pressures of intake air should not exceed published limits. Guards for compressors should be installed and kept tight during run-ins. No differential pressure should be permitted to build up in the cabin of an aircraft unless this is a requirement of the test and well posted.

Freon Compressors and Condensors. Compressor guards should be in place and tight during functional tests or run-ins.

Heaters. Where heaters are an integral part of the air conditioning system, their exhaust should go into the atmosphere during tests.

Spill Valve Test. The pressure surge necessary to trip the spill valve should not exceed maximum published pressure.

Anti-icing Functional Test. For such tests, the control surfaces may be heated to as much as 93 C (200 F). Personnel in the area should be warned of all hazardous hot surfaces.

Pneumatic Pressure. This is used inside hangars to actuate certain controls of the aircraft, such as the reverser mechanisms of certain turbojet engines. Aircraft cockpit controls and selectors are to be posted with warning placards when pneumatic pressure is being supplied to an aircraft. When controls are being tested pneumatically, no one should be in a position to be injured and all personnel in the area should be made aware of the test.

Landing Gear

Landing gear maintenance involves the use of aircraft jacks and hydraulic lift tables. To protect personnel from injury, landing gear and the elevating means must be carefully monitored, and prescribed procedures strictly followed.

Aircraft Jacks. These are the principles basic to jacking operations:

- All jacks should be properly rated for the job for which they are being used. They should be in good working order.
- Place jacks firmly on a flat surface. Correctly position jacks under the aircraft jackpoints, as identified by the manufacturer.
- Alert all personnel in the area of the jacking operation.
- Make sure that the area around the aircraft, on all sides, is clear, in case one or more jacks fail under the load or the aircraft moves off the jackpoints.
- After the aircraft is jacked to the desired height, make sure that the jacking controls are protected from accidental operation.

Hydraulic Lift Tables. Follow these procedures before the aircraft is positioned:

- Check the hydraulic lift tables to see that their controls, wiring surfaces, and fluid levels are in order.
- Also check that the table operates full travel.

Follow these procedures in positioning the aircraft:

- Alert all personnel that an aircraft is being positioned for jacking.
- Check that the jacks are properly placed and serviceable.
- Position the aircraft on the table in line with the jack assembly.
- Lower both tables simultaneously with the rear wheel assembly. The tables should stop just clear of the jackhead.
- Check the alignment and the lower tables until the weight is off the undercarriage.
- Then lower the aircraft onto the nose jack.

Undercarriage Work

This section covers basic procedures for work on the undercarriage of aircraft.

For removal of wheels or an assembly:

- Use a table to support the part being removed.
- When the component is disengaged from the wheel assembly or the aircraft, use the necessary equipment to roll it away.

For a swing test of undercarriage assemblies:

- Lower the table or raise the jacks until all the wheels are clear of the floor.
- Alert all personnel of the test.
- Check that no mechanics are working in the wheel-well area of the aircraft.
- Begin the test only when the area is clear and posted with appropriate signs.

After a swing test:

- Warn all workers before the aircraft is lowered.
- Lower the aircraft by degrees to make sure that the gear can take the full weight of the aircraft.

It is recommended that tires be inflated only when enclosed in a tire cage. They should be inflated in shops whenever practical. When it is necessary to inflate tires in hangars, use appropriate metering equipment for the job. Under no circumstances should personnel inflate tires or struts directly from a high-pressure cylinder.

Radiography

Radiography in the aircraft industry involves:

- Radioactive isotope iridium-192 (Ir-192)
- Portable x-ray units of 130 to 200 KVP
- Transport and storage facilities for radioactive materials.

All procedures concerning radiography must be in accordance with appropriate local, state, and federal regulations.

Iridium-192. This radioactive isotope should be stored in a lead-lined room, radiation-free to 165 KVP in any direction. The isotope itself must be encapsulated at all times, with only beams exposed when required. Weekly readings must be made of the lead-lined room, and readings must be taken of the capsule before every use.

X-ray Units. These units should be stored and locked in isolated confines when not in use. Daily readings should be taken of the shielding of the x-ray tube head to trace any radiation leakage through the tube walls.

Personnel Safety Precautions. Technical personnel

working in radiography should at all times wear two pocket dosimeters. These should be zeroed every morning and checked at the end of each shift. To determine cumulative dosages, exact dosimeter reading records should be maintained for each person. In addition, each worker should wear a film badge, and the results on the badges should be checked by an outside agency. Permissible dosage limits are available from government regulatory bodies.

Each employee working with radiation should receive a preplacement medical examination. A blood count should be taken of each employee every six months; a full annual medical checkup is also recommended.

When x-ray equipment is set up in a shop or hangar, all employees not associated with the operation should be cleared from the area. Using meters, the x-ray technicians and operators should establish a safe boundary limit and mark it off with standard warning signs. In addition, audible or flashing light warnings should be used to alert personnel of the operation being conducted.

The area must be constantly surveyed during operation of x-ray units. The location should be checked for scattered radiation patterns. Each time the location of use is changed, the new area must also be checked for scatter patterns.

SHOP OPERATIONS

Careful adherence to accepted safety standards and precautions will greatly reduce the hazards present in shop areas and operations.

The principles in this section should be taught to, and practiced by, shop personnel in their regularly assigned jobs. Supervisors, ground safety personnel, and others responsible for training and safety should familiarize themselves with these standards. They should assume the responsibility for instructing subordinates in the various provisions.

The medical department, which is responsible for evaluating workers' physical capability for the job requirements, should recommend appropriate action when examinations indicate that workers do not have physical qualifications for a particular job.

General Principles

Principles to be followed in the physical aspects of a safety program for shop operations are:

Analyze. Analyze the potential hazards of each job and provide safer methods, materials, procedures, facilities, or equipment.

Isolate. Operations which may be potentially hazardous to passersby or people not specially equipped should be isolated by a screen or done in a separate room, if possible. Painting, for example, must be done in a separate, well-ventilated room. Small welding jobs may only be screened off.

Guard. Provide a barrier guard that prevents the operator from putting hands or any part of the body in danger.

Layout. For safe, efficient production, be sure operations and facilities have proper lighting, ventilation, aisle, and work space.

Identify. Use colored lights, barriers, signs, audible signals, and other means to mark potentially hazardous areas or operations.

Principles of Machine Guarding

Improved machine design or installation of guarding removes much of the threat to safety for the operator of a machine. There are two general classifications of machine guarding: (1) power-transmission guarding (which includes all equipment from the prime mover to, but not including, the point-of-operation), and (2) point-of-operation guarding (where the actual work of the machine takes place).

In the interest of safety and economy, machinery should be purchased with appropriate guarding. Establish a procedure that the purchasing staff consult the safety department on current safety standards or specific needs for optimum protection of machinery before buying equipment.

Guards should be designed to give maximum protection to the operator yet not interfere with the normal operation of the equipment. For instance, in order to permit changing drive belts, making adjustments, or lubricating, machine guards may have to be designed with hinged or removable sections.

When machinery and power-transmission equipment do not have guards as part of their design, suitable enclosures or barricades should be installed to prevent injury resulting from persons contacting moving parts or hazardous substances.

Guarding is covered in more detail in Chapter 9, Personal Protective Equipment and Guarding.

Machine Shop Layout

For maximum safety, machines should be located to provide sufficient space for the operator to handle materials and perform routine job operations without interference from his or her own equipment or nearby operators. Machines should be firmly secured to the floors, bases, or stands.

If equipment contains heavy or high-speed moving parts that may disengage or disintegrate and strike nearby persons, it should be located behind shielding that will fully contain flying fragments.

Lighting at the point of operation and in the immediate areas should be adequate to eliminate excessive glare or shadows.

Materials-handling equipment should be installed to assist the operator in handling awkward or heavy parts.

Machine controls should be conveniently located for the operator. Power disconnects or stop switches should be located within easy reach of machine operators. Controls for drag lines, conveyor systems, and like equipment should be installed at intervals not exceeding 30 m (100 ft) to allow for immediate shutdown in an emergency.

At no time should stop switches be made inaccessible by covering them or blocking them off. Power controls or disconnects should be locked in the OFF position when repairs are necessary. Suitable identification signs should be posted at control switches.

Machines, or their appropriate parts, should be color-coded according to established standards to help distinguish them and to improve visibility, thereby reducing the accident potential.

Handling Hazardous Materials

All hazardous materials used in shops should be subject to appropriate, effective control measures.

The most effective means of controlling hazardous materials is to substitute a nonhazardous material for a harmful type. Where a substitution can be made, make certain that a different hazard is not created by the new material.

The procedures to follow for the control of hazardous materials include these:

- Inventory all chemicals and other materials with hazardous properties used in the workplace. Acquire the appropriate Material Safety Data Sheet (MSDS) for the materials. These sheets list the hazards of a substance, give precautions on safe handling, and recommend control measures. (For a sample MSDS, see Chapter 8, Hazardous Materials and Processes, Figure 8-1.)
- For those hazardous materials received without adequate labeling, properly identify and label them. Review governmental regulations on process or transfer container labeling requirements. Depending on U.S. government regulations, it may be necessary to report chemicals manufactured by your organization and sold to others.
- Inform workers who may be exposed to hazardous materials. Workers should know the hazardous substances to which they are exposed, their nature, the protective measures to take in handling them, and the safe practices required on the job. Maintain a record of such training.
- Establish a means to notify contractors in your facility of the hazards the contractors' employees may be exposed to while working on the facility.
- Establish a written program on hazardous materials to conform to legal requirements.
- Describe emergency procedures and the nature of the hazard in the program.

For a more detailed discussion of hazardous substances and programs for controlling them, see Chapter 8, Hazardous Materials and Processes.

Personal cleanliness is most essential in operations involving possible skin contaminants. Workers should be informed of the need for personal cleanliness. In order to encourage and facilitate personal cleanliness, suitable washrooms, showers, and locker rooms should be available.

Supervisors should make certain that all safety regulations and standards are strictly observed. They should give short safety talks at frequent periods to all employees under their jurisdiction.

Particular Hazards in Shops

Fire Hazards. Flame-producing equipment should be prohibited in the shop, except in areas such as those for welding. In areas where flame-producing equipment is used, safety controls should be established. Smoking should be forbidden except in designated areas.

Only explosion-proof electrical equipment and fixtures should be used in paint shops. All electric-power machinery should be effectively grounded. Other equipment should be arranged as prescribed by manufacturer's recommendation, military standard, or other directives.

Shops should be adequately ventilated to prevent accumulation of dangerous gases and vapors. Special exhaust systems should be provided in battery rooms, painting booths, and for confined welding jobs.

Carbon Monoxide. Carbon monoxide is one of the common gases to which personnel in shop operations are exposed. Flexible tubing attached to vehicle exhaust pipes should be used to carry carbon monoxide and other exhaust gases outside the shop. General exhaust ventilation should also be provided to prevent accumulations of this poisonous gas.

Floor Drains and Spills. Shop floor drains should not be connected to sanitary sewer lines. Whenever possible, shop operations should be laid out so that flammable liquids will not drain into floor drain systems. Such liquids should be drained into suitable containers. The containers should be held for disposal by a reputable treatment and disposal facility.

Emergency procedures for material spills as recommended by the manufacturer (refer to MSDS) should be followed in the event of a spill. If a hazardous spill occurs, drains should be adequately flushed with water or treated with a neutralizing/nonreactive agent specified for such a spill, then inspected by the authority having jurisdiction. If the spill enters a public sewer system, a local agency should be contacted.

Boxes of suitable absorbent materials should be provided in vehicle maintenance shops to be used on grease or oil spills. After absorbent material has been applied to a spill, the floor should be thoroughly cleaned.

Shop floors should be constructed to slope toward drains equipped with grease traps. These traps should be cleaned out at frequent intervals.

Welding Hazards. Welders should wear the necessary gloves, aprons, helmets, or shields when actually performing welding operations. They should also be careful to wear filter goggles of the shade appropriate for the type of welding equipment being used. Before welding or other heat-producing work is performed on a vehicle, gas tanks and other fuel containers should be removed from the vehicle. They should then be drained, purged, and filled with water or otherwise rendered safe by filling them with inert gas.

Battery Handling. Shop personnel handling batteries should be provided with rubber gloves, aprons, and suitable eye protection. When handling electrolyte, workers should wear chemical safety goggles and face shields, rubber gloves, and aprons. A water source suitable for the size of the operation should be provided for workers to wash off acid that may splash on their eyes or bodies. There should be a continuous flow eyewash station in the immediate vicinity.

Machine Shop Operations. Maintenance personnel using grinding wheels or cutting tools that produce flying chips or dust should wear impact safety goggles or face shields. Mechanics working under vehicles should wear safety goggles to prevent dirt from entering their eyes.

Shop machinery, such as lathes, abrasive wheels, and portable electric tools should be guarded according to federal, state, or provincial standards.

Pits. Guardrails should be placed around grease or repair pits. All pits should have steps and handrails to permit safe entrance and exit. Pits should be built with drains equipped with oil or grease traps. Pit drains should not be connected to sanitary sewers. In addition, there should be a local exhaust system to remove flammable vapors.

Repair and grease pits should be cleaned regularly with soap or cleaning solution and water or a caustic solution. Pit contamination is a potential health, fire, and accident hazard. In order to prevent accumulation of hazardous gases, an engine normally should not be operated while a vehicle stands over a repair pit unless exhaust gases are safety ducted to the outside, away from fresh air intakes.

Compressed Air. Compressed air is used in many shop operations, such as spray painting, tire inflation, and fuel line cleaning. When handled properly, compressed air is not hazardous. However, many mechanics are tempted to use air under high pressure to clean work benches, vehicle chassis, parts, or even their skin or clothing. This practice is extremely dangerous because the air pressure blows around metal parts, dirt, and debris.

If the air pressure is strong enough, flying particles can be forced through clothing, or into the flesh or eyes. Air itself can be forced into the bloodstream, with potentially fatal results. Mechanics should never engage in horseplay with compressed air.

Compressed air pressure should be reduced to minimal operational requirements and should never exceed 207 kPa (30 psi) for cleaning purposes. Chip guarding should be provided. Approved nozzles are to be used on air hoses.

Controlling Hazards. Whenever practical, processes creating health or safety hazards should be isolated as completely as possible. Physical isolation in circumstances where personnel must work nearby may mean the use of protective shields, barriers, and other similar devices. Noise-attenuating or noise-deflecting barriers may be advisable.

Certain operations may call for employees to wear personal protective equipment such as respirators, hoods and helmets, safety glasses, face shields, hearing protection, and gloves (Figure 5-4). Rules for the use of such equipment should be enforced.

Ground Equipment Maintenance

A procedure should be established to ensure that ground service vehicles are checked daily. Units that an operator finds to have defective components should be removed from service immediately, tagged with a description of the defect or defects, and routed to the shop for correction before being returned to service. For additional information on the maintenance of ground equipment, see Chapter 4, Mobile Ground Service Equipment

Inspection. Inspections of ground vehicles should cover these items:

- *Brakes.* Check floor brakes for smooth and effective operation. When the brakes pull a vehicle to one side or the other, there is a braking deficiency. Such deficiencies should be corrected immediately. If brakes allow vehicles traveling at 32 km/h (20 mph) to move more than 9 m (30 ft) after they have been fully applied, the brakes should be considered defective. (For more specific stopping distances, see the GVW figures in Table 4-1, in Chapter 4.) Hand brakes should be capable of holding vehicles on a reasonable grade when only two-thirds of the handle travel has been taken up. (Brake pedals and clutch pedals, when applicable, should have a skid-resistant surface.)

- *Lights.* Check all lights on a vehicle for burned-out lamps. Headlight beams should be adjusted to ensure that the area in front of a vehicle is properly and evenly illuminated, without glare to approaching drivers. Operate switches and trace any loose or broken connections to their source and repair. Check that the lenses and reflectors of vehicle lights are clean and securely fastened in place. Check directional signals and backup lights, if applicable.

- *Windows.* Check that the windows of all vehicles

Courtesy Air Canada.

Figure 5-4. Each successful project is a result of a combination of factors, including proper equipment and materials, skillful workers, good procedures, and correct protective gear.

are clean and free of obstructions. Cracked windshields and windows will distort and limit a driver's vision and endanger the safety of drivers and protection of property. They should be replaced as soon as possible.

- *Rear-view mirrors.* Every vehicle should have at least one rear-view mirror. Check that these mirrors are clean and properly adjusted. The mirror fastening should be secure enough to prevent dislocation by vibration while vehicle is moving.
- *Horns.* Test vehicle horns for satisfactory operations and sufficiently loud warning signal.
- *Windshield wipers.* Check windshield wipers for satisfactory operation. Check that blades and arms are in place and securely connected. Blades must contact the glass properly to provide a driver with a clear field of vision.
- *Seats.* If removable seats are installed, the clamps should hold them securely.
- *Fire extinguishers.* Check that extinguishers are mounted in an accessible place; they should be readily removable and protected from damage. They should be inspected, serviced if necessary, and ready for use at all times.
- *Towing connections.* Towing connections should be maintained in good condition. Check the locking mechanisms for security. Operators should connect the brake lines and safety chains before moving the tow vehicle-trailer.
- *Wheels.* Before operating vehicles, drivers should check the wheel mountings, rims, and axle flange nuts to be certain they are secure. Tires should be gauged and inflated to specified pressures at the frequency recommended by the manufacturer.
- *Other items.* Passenger stands, ladders, work stands, steps, and handrails should be checked for good repair and security. Skid-resistant material should be replaced if worn or missing.

See also the checklists for maintenance of ground service equipment in Chapter 4, Ground Service Equipment, Figure 4-2.

Fueling of Vehicles. Vehicles should not be fueled indoors as a routine practice. Indoor fueling may sometimes be performed under controlled conditions—and then only when approved by the fire marshal or other authority having jurisdiction.

Vehicles taking on fuel, and those not in use and unattended, should have their engine stopped and the parking brake applied. No vehicle should be operated unless entirely free of fuel leaks. During fueling, the nozzle of the hose should constantly contact the intake pipe of the vehicle's fuel tank to provide an effective bond and prevent the discharge of static sparks.

Maintenance Operations. Motor vehicle maintenance activities such as painting, welding, and battery work should each be carried on in a separate part of the shop where the operations of one kind will not be hazardous to another. Adequate general illumination should be provided for all operations, and, where necessary, include supplemental lighting.

Vehicle Lift Safety

All vehicle lifts should be equipped with a safety device to prevent accidental lowering. The device can be a simple mechanism such as a safety leg, which locks in a vertical position as the lift is raised; or it can be a restricted orifice device, which permits controlled lowering in the event of a hydraulic failure. As an added safety feature, air-oil-operated hydraulic lifts should be equipped with a lock that prevents raising by air if the oil supply is low. A safety device meeting this requirement is called a "low-oil lock." This is a removable device that prevents compressed air from entering the lift cylinder assembly; the arrangement prevents the plungers from being raised above the oil supply in the air-oil reservoir.

Roll-on lifts should be equipped with stop chocks to prevent the vehicle from moving while the lift is hoisting, lowering, or in the elevated position. Preferably, stop chocks will automatically spring into position when the vehicle enters the lift.

Drivers should not be permitted to remain inside vehicles that are on moving or elevated lifts, unless a specific operation requires it. If on an elevated lift inside a vehicle, the driver must keep the doors closed to reduce the fall potential.

All automotive lifts should be marked with the name of the manufacturer, lift capacity, and date of installation. These markings should be stamped or etched on a metal plate permanently attached to the lift in a position where it can be checked.

All vehicle lifts should be equipped with "deadman" controls, which automatically turn to NEUTRAL or OFF when released by an operator. Controls should be conveniently located near the lift.

Chassis and axle supports should be designed to transfer the load to the lift rails. No makeshift devices should be used for chassis and axle supports.

Other Maintenance Precautions

Shop employees should use mechanical devices, such as dollies or hoists, to help them mount or remove large, heavy tires.

The rated load of jacks should be legibly and permanently marked on them in a prominent location by casting, stamping, or another suitable means. Operators should make sure that the jacks have a rating sufficient to lift and sustain the load. Jacks should also be inspected and tested in compliance with ANSI guidelines. (See References.) After a vehicle has been raised by a jack, it should be securely blocked to prevent falling. At no time should mechanics place any part of their body directly under the wheels of a jacked or blocked vehicle.

Mechanics should keep their clothing free of grease and oil. Clothing contaminated with flammable substances should not be worn or stored in clothing lockers. Workers should not wear neckties, loose clothing, wristwatches, rings, or other jewelry when working near or with equipment.

All hand and portable power tools should be used and maintained according to the highest standards. Tool kits should be inspected periodically and defective tools replaced immediately. For detailed information on tool inspection and maintenance, see the National Safety Council's *Accident Prevention Manual for Industrial Operations, Engineering and Technology* volume, Ninth Edition. (See References.)

Power cables and cords on portable electrical equipment should be made of heavy, armored rubber, or similar material, to prevent damage from oil, grease, and chafing. The cables should be constructed to provide automatic grounding of the equipment through integral conductors. Mechanics using portable electrical tools and lights should not string cables across shop floors. Serious injuries can be caused by tripping over power cords and cables.

Shop Traffic

Shop entrances and exits should be clearly marked and lighted to prevent accidents. Appropriate traffic signs should be posted at entrances and exits. Drivers entering or leaving shops should sound their vehicle's horn to warn personnel of oncoming traffic. In the interest of safety, a maximum limit of 8 km/h (5 mph) should be enforced in and around shops.

Driveways and the areas around shop entrances should be kept clear of ice and snow and treated with sand, ashes, calcium chloride, rock salt, or other similar materials if these areas become slippery. Shop floors and inside entrances should be cleared of ice and snow brought in on the wheels of vehicles.

Paint Shop

Painting operations present three potential hazards to health and safety: fire, toxicity, and mechanical hazards.

Fire. Paints and thinners must be kept away from

sources of ignition. They should be stored in approved flammable liquids storage cabinets. Housekeeping standards should be meticulously maintained. Masking materials, paper, and soiled rags used in painting should be deposited in self-closing metal containers. Combustible materials stored in hangars and shops should be kept to a minimum. Paint booths must be posted with NO SMOKING signs. All paint containers and drums must be properly grounded to ensure against static electricity buildup.

Toxicity. Painting is to be done in approved paint booths with mechanical ventilation. Employees who paint outside of booths should wear properly fitting, approved paint respirators at all times and should change filters regularly. All employees required to wear respirators should be trained in their proper fit, testing for fit, use, cleaning requirements, and limitations. Protective clothing made of material other than rayon, nylon, silk, wool, and certain plastics should be worn by workers who paint. For optimum protection against static electricity buildup from protective clothing, wear cotton.

Mechanical Hazards. Spray painting equipment should be kept clean and in good repair. Pressure hoses should be inspected for wear and replaced as necessary. Care should be taken in placing pressure hoses so that people will not trip over them and lines will not be cut by passing vehicles. Work stands should be of the correct height and size so that painters can work with reasonable ease and comfort. High-pressure paint nozzles should not be pointed at any operator. The recommendations contained in NFPA 33 (see References) should be closely followed for these operations.

Battery Charging

Potential hazards in battery shops are corrosive or toxic chemicals and explosive gases. Battery shop workers should be thoroughly trained in their jobs and familiar with safe operating procedures. Nickel-cadmium and silver-zinc batteries should be serviced in an area isolated from lead-acid batteries. Sufficient explosion-proof ventilation should be provided to prevent acid fumes from entering the nickel-cadmium or silver-zinc battery shop. When both acid and potassium hydroxide electrolyte batteries are handled in the same shop, the equipment for the two kinds of batteries should be kept separate and carefully labeled. Implements that have been used to service nickel-cadmium alkaline, silver-zinc, or nickel-iron alkaline batteries should be used on those types only.

Tools or metal parts should not be laid on a battery or stored in such a position that they may fall on a battery. Workers should not wear rings, wristwatches, or other jewelry. They should use nonsparking lifting devices and explosion-proof (nonsparking) hand trucks to handle heavy batteries. When manual lifting is necessary, workers should obtain sufficient help to prevent injury.

Lead-acid battery charging equipment should be located in well-ventilated, fire-resistant rooms. Excessive charging of lead-acid batteries should not be permitted, since this produces excessive quantities of hydrogen gas, creating a highly explosive gas mixture in the shop's atmosphere. A lead-acid battery should be allowed to cool down in accord with specifications after removing it from the charger. Work should not be done immediately on a battery that either has run down under heavy load or has just been charged. In both cases, the battery may be gassing rapidly and may explode if heat is applied. See details in the National Safety Council Data Sheet 635, *Lead-Acid Storage Batteries.* (See References.)

Silver-zinc batteries do not generate any harmful gases during normal charging or discharging, so there is no need for exhaust fans and nonsparking equipment.

To prevent burns when handling electrolyte, shop workers should wear protective chemical safety goggles and face shields, rubber gloves, and aprons. When mixing electrolyte, they should always pour the acid or potassium hydroxide into the water slowly. The water should never be poured into the chemical because rapid heat generation may cause explosive steam expansion. A tilter should be used to pour acid from a carboy. When acid is siphoned, workers should use a rubber suction ball—*never* their mouths—to start the action. Deluge showers and continuous flow eye wash fountains must be provided in all battery shop operations.

In order to keep concentrations of hydrogen gas below the ignition point, battery shops using electrical equipment must be mechanically ventilated. Because large charging rooms may charge 50 or more 24-volt batteries and create ignitable hydrogen gas concentrations, mechanical ventilation is necessary. (See CFR 1910.178g.305(J) (7) for U.S. requirements.)

Smoking and open flames should be strictly forbidden in battery shops. Care should be taken to remove unnecessary sources of ignition, including electrical-spark-producing devices, from the immediate area of battery vents when hydrogen concentrations are possible. (Explosive limits in air for hydrogen are 4–75% by volume.) Electrical facilities and spark-producing equipment used in battery shops should conform to the explosion-proof provisions of the *National Electrical Code.* (See References.)

Batteries should be handled with extreme care to avoid spark-producing short circuits. Workers should use terminal straps to handle batteries at all times. These straps should be kept free of grease or other foreign substances.

Floors in the battery shop should be kept clean and dry to prevent injuries from slipping and falling. Floors and battery racks should be made of acidproof materials like finished oak. Floors should be covered with acid-resistant paint. If metallic battery racks are used, they must be grounded to prevent sparking. (See CFR 1910.178(g).)

Courtesy Piedmont Airlines.

Figure 5-5. A worker prepares to inflate a tire, using a remote chuck.

Tire Service

Shop personnel should use mechanical devices, such as dollies, to help them mount or remove large, heavy tires.

Guard cages should be used when inflating tires, particularly those mounted on wheels with lock rings. When such wheels are mounted on vehicles, several lengths of chain, fitted with positive catches, should be passed through the wheel openings and around the tire rim before inflating. A rim lock ring that releases from a wheel during tire inflation or mounting can be propelled from the tire at a lethal velocity. (Figure 5-5.)

MATERIALS HANDLING

Workers should receive thorough instruction in safe lifting and carrying procedures, as well as in the use of personal protective equipment for handling materials. Adequate supervision is necessary to ensure that safe practices are being observed at all times by those who handle material. Wearing rings, jewelry, loose clothing, and improper footwear during handling operations is extremely hazardous and should not be permitted.

Proper planning in materials handling is also an important safety element. Materials should be handled in logical sequence, and unnecessary handling procedures should be avoided.

The principles in this section apply in all areas—including shops and hangars. For more specific information on cargo handling, see Chapter 6, Air Cargo Operations.

Manual Handling

These factors must be considered in establishing safe lifting limits for workers: physical differences, periods of sustained lifting, height of lifting, distance and frequency that the load is carried, and the size and shape of a load. (For more specific information, see, in References, NIOSH *Work Practices for Manual Lifting* and National Safety Council Lifting Calculator.) Workers should be required to take a medical examination to determine the suitability of assigning them to manual handling duties.

General pointers that can be given to those who handle materials include:

- Inspect materials for slivers, jagged or sharp edges, burrs, rough or slippery surfaces.
- Grasp the object with a firm grip.
- Keep fingers away from pinch and shear points, especially when setting down materials.
- When handling long objects, keep hands away from the ends to prevent them from being pinched.
- Wipe off greasy, wet, slippery, or dirty objects before trying to handle them.
- Keep hands free of oil and grease.

In most cases, gloves, hand leathers, or other hand protectors should be used to prevent hand injuries. Extra caution must be used when working near moving or revolving machinery.

Use of Body Weight. Employing the correct positioning of the feet and the flexion and extension of the knees, the weight of the body can be effectively used to push and pull objects and to initiate a forward movement, such as placing an object on a shelf or walking.

When lifting an object from the ground, the thrust from the back foot, combined with the extension of the knee joints, will move the body forward and upward, and for a brief period it will be off balance. However, this position is immediately countered by bringing the back leg forward, as in walking, and by this time the lift is completed. This forward movement of the body results in a smooth transition from lifting to carrying. Do not "jerk-lift" a load as this multiplies the stress to the lower back.

Here are some techniques for specific situations.

- If the object is too bulky or too heavy to be handled by one person, help should be sought.
- Before lifting the load to be carried, the worker should consider the distance to be traveled and the length of time that the grip will have to be maintained. The worker should select a place to set the load down and rest in order to allow for the loss of gripping power during a long-distance carry. Pausing to rest is especially important when negotiating stairs and ramps.
- *To place an object on a bench or table,* the worker should first set it on the edge and push it far enough onto the support to be sure it will not fall. The object should be released gradually as it is set down. It should be moved in place by pushing with the hands and body from in front of the object. This method prevents pinched fingers.
- It is especially important that an object, placed on a bench or other support, be securely positioned so that it will not fall, tip over, or roll off. Supports should be correctly placed and strong enough to carry the load. Heavy objects should be stored at approximately waist height.
- *To raise an object above shoulder height,* the worker should lift it first to waist height, then rest the edge of the object on a ledge, stand, or hip, and shift hand position, so the object can be boosted after the knees are bent. The knees should be straightened out as the object is lifted or shifted to the shoulders. As in the case of lifts originating at ground level, the upper extreme of muscle stress begins at shoulder height. Good job design should be applied to eliminate or minimize above shoulder lifting.
- *To change direction,* the worker should lift the object to the carrying position and turn the entire body, including the feet. Avoid twisting the body. In repetitive work, the person and the material should both be positioned so that twisting the body when moving the material is unnecessary.
- To deposit an object manually in a tight space, it is safest to slide it into place with the hands in the clear.

Instructions for three major lifting techniques are given below.

Squat Lifting Techniques. Here are six steps to good squat lifting techniques:

- Keep feet parted—one alongside, one behind the object.
- Keep back straight, nearly vertical.
- Tuck elbows and arms in, and hold load close to body.
- Grasp the object with the whole hand.
- Tuck your chin in.
- Keep body weight directly over feet.

Assisted One-hand Lift. In this method, the worker rests one hand on top of the container, bends over to grasp an object in the container, and then pushes down with the nonlifting hand resting on top of the container to force the upper body back to a vertical position. This method features using the large arm and shoulder muscles to perform the lift instead of the vulnerable muscles of the lower back. By using the nonlifting hand to raise the upper body, stress is distributed across the shoulders and arm muscles and reduced in the lower back.

For a good assisted one-hand lift, follow these steps:

- Place the nonlifting hand on the container top, bend over container, and assume lift position.
- While bending over, kick the foot on the same side as the nonlifting hand rearward to provide forward body balance (optional).
- Reach and grasp object to be lifted.
- Push down with the nonlifting hand on the container top, raising the upper body to a vertical position. (Be sure to let the nonlifting hand, not the back, do the work!)

As with any lifting technique, there are limitations to its use. The application of the assisted one-hand lift assumes that the object to be lifted can be grasped by one hand, that it is not too long that it becomes awkward to handle and that the weight is not excessive. Studies show that a load weight of 6.8–9.1 kg (15–20 lb) would not be excessive for most workers to lift with one hand.

The assisted one-hand lift technique also may be used to lift objects off the floor or pallet flats by placing the nonlifting hand on a spot above the knee and pushing down on it after grabbing an object with the other hand.

Team Lifting and Carrying. When two or more people carry one object, they should adjust the load so that it rides level and so that each person carries an equal part of the load. Test lifts should be made before proceeding.

When two people carry long objects, they should carry them on the same shoulder or walk in step. Shoulder pads will prevent cutting of the shoulders and reduce fatigue.

When a gang of workers carries a heavy object, the supervisor should make sure that proper tools are used. Work direction should be provided; frequently, a whistle or direct command can signal "lift," "walk," and "set down." The key to safe gang carrying is to make every movement in unison.

Mechanical Handling: Basic Principles

Mechanical materials handling equipment should be used whenever loads are too heavy or bulky to be lifted and carried safely by hand. Forklifts, conveyors, hand trucks, chutes, rollers and cranes, when properly used, simplify materials handling and greatly reduce hazards.

Although mechanical handling equipment is intended to reduce hazards involved in manual handling, unsafe use of hoists and trucks presents increased danger. Only fully trained or adequately supervised operators should use such equipment. They should be put through selection and training programs similar to those required for motor vehicle operators. Each operator should be given complete instructions in the proper use of equipment, and the training should include safe standards of operation, inspection, preventive maintenance, and materials-handling practices.

Where mechanical handling equipment is used, the aisles should have sufficient clearances for the equipment. There should be adequate clearances at loading docks, through doorways, and where turns must be made. Aisles should be at least two feet wider than the widest vehicle in use, and they should be clearly marked by guidelines painted on the floor. Obstructions, such as columns and posts, should be painted, preferably with diagonal stripes of black and yellow. Wooden guards, preferably painted with black and yellow stripes, should be used at the corners of stacked materials to prevent accidental dislodging and to protect the stacks.

Where handling equipment run by internal combustion engines is used in closed areas, there should be adequate ventilation to prevent accumulations of dangerous carbon monoxide gas. If natural ventilation is not sufficient, or forced ventilation cannot be provided, the engines should be equipped with enclosed exhaust piping direct to the outside away from outside air intakes. The piping system should be checked for leaks. As an alternative, electric-powered machines might be used.

Hand trucks should be pushed rather than pulled whenever practical. Truck handles that expose workers' hands to possible injury should be equipped with knuckle guards. When trucks are not actually in use, the handles should be effectively locked in a vertical position. Positive-action braking mechanisms should be provided on all hand trucks.

Loading Handling Equipment

On all handling equipment, the center of gravity of the load should be kept low by placing the heavier objects on the bottom and the lighter objects on the top. Side stakes, straps, or lashing materials should be used on high loads where there is a danger of toppling. Maximum load limits should be posted on all equipment, including cranes and hoists. Overloading should not be permitted under any circumstances. Equipment should be safely unloaded from the top down.

Often the size and shape of a particular load requires the use of special attachments on existing equipment. The development of forklift truck attachments to handle special loads has increased the versatility of the forklift truck. Special attachments such as rams, detachable cranes, and fork extensions are available. In most cases, their use modifies the rated capacity and imposes weight limitations. Any modifications must be considered when such attachments are used to handle excessively large or bulky loads. Only attachments approved by the forklift manufacturer should be used. Overhead guards should be provided on all high-lift forklifts and other equipment where operators are in danger from falling objects. Overhead guards should be maintained free of any material that may obstruct an operator's vision.

Safe operating speeds should be set for each type of special-purpose handling vehicle. No vehicle should exceed 8 km/h (5 mph) inside warehouses or other buildings, regardless of its safe operating speed. On long hauls out of doors, speeds may be increased (within local speed limits) to the vehicle's safe maximum. Operators should use common sense to determine how fast they should safely travel with particular loads. The operator is responsible for the safe operation of the vehicle and transport of the load.

Loaded vehicles should not be put into motion until the load is properly stacked and secured. Drivers should be particularly careful when approaching doorways, aisle crossings, and other intersections; they should be observant at all times. Ramps, doorways, and other physical features of warehouses and loading docks present a hazard to vehicle operators. Where possible, the conditions should be altered to reduce the hazard, or handling procedures should be revised.

When it is necessary to park vehicles inside warehouses, leave them only in an approved area, which has been authorized by the supervisor having jurisdiction. When a vehicle is parked, its brakes should be set, the ignition turned off, and the keys pulled. Unless the vehicle is equipped with an adequate passenger seat, and specific authorization is given, no person other than the driver should be allowed to ride on any materials-handling vehicle.

Fueling Forklift Trucks

Materials-handling vehicles should not be fueled indoors unless NFPA guidelines are followed in their entirety. (See References, NFPA 30.) Such vehicles should not be fueled in areas where flammable vapors may accumulate or where hazardous materials are stored. Fuel should be transferred only at designated safe locations, and the ignition turned off during fueling. At least two Class 20:B:C fire extinguishers should be kept ready during all fueling operations in case of a fuel spill or fire.

Precautions should be taken to prevent a fuel spill. If a small spill does occur, it should be neutralized, completely removed, or allowed to evaporate before a vehicle's engine is started.

Whenever large amounts of fuel are spilled, the fire department should be notified immediately to remove the hazard. While waiting for the fire department, materials-handling people should stand by the spill with suitable fire fighting equipment. Where fuel-filling pipes are located close to the engine manifold or another source of ignition, the vehicle should be shut down and the engine allowed to cool before it is fueled. Much materials-handling equipment has been set on fire by spilling fuel on hot engines or exhausts.

Equipment waiting to be refueled should remain at least 7.5 m (25 ft) from the servicing area while other vehicles are being fueled. (Floors should be marked.) No vehicle should be fueled inside a building unless the NFPA guidelines are followed in entirety. During servicing, the operator should turn off the engine.

Rules for Operating Materials-Handling Vehicles

The following section lists general standards of safe operation for materials-handling vehicles. All operators should be required to observe these standards.

- Drivers should not operate equipment unless it has been specifically dispatched. The only exception is during extreme emergencies or when the equipment must be quickly moved to prevent its being damaged or becoming a source of damage or injury.
- Before using any piece of equipment, the driver should be properly trained in its use and should be listed as qualified to operate the vehicle.
- Before operating it, the driver should check the operability of the machine, using a checklist.
- Materials-handling vehicles should not be shifted from forward to reverse without coming to a complete stop.
- Riding clutches excessively abuses vehicles. Loads should be carried in the gear that allows the vehicle to move smoothly without excessive use of the clutch. Generally, the heavier the load to be moved, the lower the gear to be used.
- Operators should drive at speeds that permit complete control at all times. Posted speed limits should be strictly observed. Drivers should be particularly careful when operating on slippery surfaces.
- Drivers should make certain that their vehicle has sufficient clearance through doorways, at loading docks, in aisles, or where turns are made. Before passing through a doorway, operators should check for adequate clearance on all sides and at the top of a load. They should make certain that overhead doors are raised to maximum height before entering or leaving.
- When entering or leaving a building, or at intersections where the view is restricted, vehicle drivers should stop, sound the horn or bell, and proceed with caution.
- Drivers should be prohibited from carrying loose materials on any handling equipment.

- Operators should not be permitted to eat, drink, or smoke while driving, nor engage in any unnecessary conversations.

- Drivers are responsible for safe delivery of loads. Unsafe loads should not be hauled. If a driver believes any load cannot be moved safely, the driver should immediately inform the supervisor, and then follow instructions.

- Materials-handling vehicles should be parked in spaces approved by the appropriate authority. No vehicle should be parked in front of fire alarm boxes, fire extinguishers, safety equipment, or in aisles or other areas where it would become a safety hazard or interfere with emergency equipment. When parking equipment with gas tanks mounted higher than the carburetors, fuel should be turned off at the tanks, particularly when vehicles are parked inside warehouses. Preference should be given to the use of battery-operated forklift trucks inside buildings whenever practical.

Forklift Trucks. Forklift truck operators should travel with forks close to, but not touching, the floor. With the forks close to the floor, the vehicle is less likely to hit and damage materials if it turns sharply. When traveling with a load, drivers should keep the forks close to the floor to prevent their field of vision from being obstructed by the material being transported. On an incline, the load should be kept on the uphill side.

Forklift trucks should be parked only in specified areas off the aisles. Forks must be lowered flat on the floor, the operating levers left in neutral, the ignition turned off, keys removed, and the hand brake set. This procedure should be followed at all times.

Drivers should always face or look in the direction in which they are moving. When moving a load too high to see over, operators should travel in reverse to give themselves a clear field of vision.

Gasoline-powered forklift trucks must never be left unattended with the motor running. This wastes fuel and creates excessive carbon monoxide concentrations if in confined areas.

Operators should not operate their trucks with wet or greasy hands. Serious accidents can result if a driver's hands slip on the steering wheel and control of the vehicle is lost.

Operators should not permit any person or persons to ride on the forks or other parts of their vehicles. Forklift trucks are not built to carry passengers.

However, in cases where permission has been granted to use a forklift truck to lift a worker to the top of stacked materials, an approved platform and cage or safety pallet should first be securely attached to the lift. The person being raised should take a safe position where he or she is in no danger of falling or catching hands or clothing on the truck as the cage moves upward. A proper safety harness and lanyard should be used. Persons should not be transported from one place to another in a safety pallet.

Forklift operators should use general highway driving rules indoors as well as outdoors, keeping to the correct lane, stopping at blind intersections, and using horn and arm signals. Horns should be used for necessary warning only. Horns should not be blown to attract the attention of other workers.

At least three truck lengths should be maintained between moving vehicles to reduce the potential of collision or toppling a load if the front truck should stop suddenly. Operators should keep their legs within the vehicle when it is moving. Serious injuries have been caused when drivers' legs have been pinched between the truck and obstacles in narrow operating areas.

Forklift truck drivers should not carry empty pallets stacked higher than eye level. This can cause an unsteady load and a possible source of injury or property damage. Forklift trucks should be conspicuously marked with their rated lifting capacity.

Tractors. Tractors are used for a variety of materials-handling operations, particularly where extremely heavy loads are to be moved considerable distances. The following precautions should be observed in tractor operations:

- Passengers should not be allowed to ride on tractors unless adequate seats have been installed.

- No more than four trailers, loaded or empty, should be pulled by any tractor. In order to avoid jackknifing, trailer trains should be arranged with the heaviest trailer load next to the towing vehicle, the next heaviest second in line, and so on.

- Tractor operators should make certain that couplings are secure before moving a trailer or train.

- Tractors with trailers in tow should never exceed 8 km/h (5 mph).

Cranes and Hoists

Lifting devices include a large group of cranes, derricks, hoists, elevators, and jacks. Slings, ropes, chains, and cables are used with lifting machines or as separate lifting aids (Figure 5-6). The hazards of lifting devices include swinging or falling loads, exposed moving parts, structural failures, and snapping cables and ropes.

All cranes and hoists should be installed, maintained, and inspected in accordance with applicable governmental requirements. Many lifting device failures can be prevented if proper inspection and maintenance procedures are followed. Operators on each shift should inspect lifting devices and lifting aids for operational condition and defects.

Figure 5-5. When working with overhead lifting devices, operators should be trained to use them safely.

When such equipment is not assigned to one operator, designated individuals should be responsible for making a daily inspection. Conditions that make equipment unsafe for operation should be reported immediately, and repairs arranged.

- Before any crane or derrick is moved, the route of travel should be checked to be certain that adequate clearance exists along the entire route. Operators should be particularly alert for overhead powerlines. During actual movement, the hook should be secured against swinging and the boom be lowered to within approximately 3 m (10 ft) off the ground. A red warning flag or light should be placed at the exposed end of the boom. Warning flags should be squares of red material measuring 0.3 m (12 in.). Heavy materials should not be carried at the end of the boom while equipment is being moved from one location to another.
- All cranes and derricks should be kept at least 0.6 m (2 ft) away from walls, overhead trestles, columns, and other structures.
- Safe load limits and boom angle indicators should be installed in plain sight on all cranes and derricks, for both maximum and minimum positions. These position load limits should not be exceeded.
- Cranes and derricks should be equipped with braking devices capable of stopping a weight of at least one and one half times the rated maximum load. "Deadman" type braking devices are preferred.
- Ladders, steps, handholds, and similar devices should be provided for safe access to cabs. Platforms with railings and toeboards should be installed for workers' protection.
- All exposed machinery and dangerous moving parts should be guarded against contact by personnel.
- Under no circumstances should personnel be permitted to ride loads being moved.
- At least two full turns of cable should remain on drums at all times.
- Booms, buckets, or other loads should not be swung over the heads of workers below.

- Booms should be placed directly over loads when lifting. If needed, snatch blocks should be used to move loads into position under the boom.

- When outriggers are to be used, they should be extended fully. For rubber-tired mobile cranes, the outriggers must be extended fully, elevating the tires completely off grade to reduce possible turnover. The crane should be leveled as for other operations.

- The swing radius of the crane should be guarded to prevent employees from being injured by the crane counterweight or by pinch-points.

- Tag lines should be used on free swinging loads to help guide them and to prevent their striking nearby objects.

- Booms not in use should be lowered to the ground, or onto resting platforms, to remove tension from cables and drums.

- Except as specified by maintenance requirements, no maintenance work should be performed on cranes or derricks while they are operating.

- No part of a lifting device (particularly the boom) or its load should be permitted to come within 3 m (10 ft) of live electrical powerlines rated 50,000 volts (50 kv) or less. Greater clearance is required for powerlines over 50 kv.

  NOTE: For powerlines rated over 50 kv, clearance between crane and/or load and lines must be a minimum of 3 m (10 ft) plus 1 cm (0.4 in.) for each 1 kv over 50 kv. Where this is impractical because of the location of the operation, electric current should be shut off. A permanent sign should be placed in the cab of the equipment in full view of the operator, reading: DANGER DO NOT OPERATE THIS EQUIPMENT WITHIN 3 M (10 FT) OF ELECTRICAL POWERLINES OF 50 KV OR LESS.

- If the boom of a rubber-tired crane should contact a hot wire, the entire piece of equipment will become charged and, being insulated from ground, the circuit breaker may not operate. When this happens, operators should not step to the ground as their bodies may complete a circuit. If it is absolutely necessary to leave the equipment, operators should jump clear.

- Cranes should be equipped with positive stops to prevent running off the ends of jibs, rails, or bridges.

- Only authorized, fully trained personnel should be permitted to operate cranes and derricks.

- No one must be allowed to perform repairs on crane booms unless authorized by manufacturer's service representatives or certified by the company as a crane boom repair specialist.

In general, all lifting or overhead carrying devices should be fitted with adequate equipment to protect operators from falling objects, swing loads, and cable failures. An efficient, audible warning device should be provided when hoisting operations or moving equipment might endanger people working in the area.

Appropriate head protection should be worn by crane crew personnel when such protection is needed to protect workers from falling objects or impact hazards. Safety-toe shoes should be worn by all workers involved in crane, hoist, or derrick operations.

Monorail hoists should not be used to move an object by a side pull, unless properly designed for that purpose. Monorail hoists operated in swivels should be equipped with one or more safety catches that will support the load should a suspension pin fail. Both the track and its supports should be inspected frequently for signs of weakening and wear. Rail stops should be provided at the ends of a monorail track. Such rail stops should extend at least as high as the radius of the wheels.

At switches, turntables, and transfer tables, automatic bumpers should drop into position to prevent the trolley from running off the open ends of the fixed and movable track if they are not properly lined up with each other. Conversely, the track should be interlocked with the bumpers so that the track cannot move until the rail stops are in position. Maximum load capacity should be plainly marked on each side of a monorail and should be clearly legible from the ground or floor.

REFERENCES

American National Standards Institute, 1430 Broadway, New York, NY 10018.

Identification of Piping Systems, Scheme for the, ANSI A13.1-1981 (R1985).

Jacks, ANSI/ASME B30.1-1986.

Department of the Air Force, The Pentagon, Washington, D.C. 20330.

AF Manual, 32-3.

National Fire Protection Association, Batterymarch Park, Quincy, MA 02269.

Aircraft Hangars, NFPA 409, 1985.

Aircraft Maintenance, NFPA 410, 1980.

Flammable and Combustible Liquids Code, NFPA 30.

National Electrical Code, NFPA 70.

Spray Application Using Flammable and Combustible Materials, NFPA 33.

National Safety Council, 444 N. Michigan Ave., Chicago, IL 60611.

Accident Prevention Manual for Industrial Operations, 9th ed., 1988.

Industrial Data Sheets

Lead-Acid Storage Batteries, 635.

Mounting Heavy-Duty Tires and Rims, 411.

Portable Ladders, 665.

Lifting Calculator.

Underwriters Laboratories Inc., 333 Pfingsten Road, Northbrook, IL 60002.

U.S. Department of Health and Human Resources, National Institute for Occupational Safety and Health (NIOSH), Cincinnati, OH 45226.

Work Practices Guide for Manual Lifting, NIOSH Technical Report 81-122.

FEDERAL

SAA 0211 FE
AAK 9102 FE
SAA 0171 FE
SAA 0916 FE
SAA 1527 FE
SAA 0650 FE
45 FE
AAE 9526 FE

CHAPTER 6

Air Cargo Operations

Top: The air cargo docking area should be well organized and illuminated so that every operation proceeds efficiently.

Lower left: Cargo cart loading crews should stow freight evenly with heavy pieces on the bottom to ensure stability.

Lower right: This cargo aircraft is in dock, positioned for loading.

Courtesy Federal Express.

Safety and health laws directly and indirectly control international air cargo operations. Because the airfreight terminal is a 24-hour-a-day complex with hundreds of employees, mechanized processing and loading systems, and services to suit every shipper and industry, accident prevention is essential in running a smooth, profitable operation. (See Figure 6-1.) If passengers and cargo are on the same plane, special safety procedures must be observed. The key to greater safety is training: a well-trained work force is the most valuable asset.

It is the purpose of this chapter to outline the accepted practices, facilities, and equipment that contribute to making freight operations safer and more efficient. Where necessary, reference is made to laws and standards that regulate operations.

TRUCK DOCK OPERATIONS

This section covers procedures that should be established in dock areas to process cargo safely and efficiently both manually and mechanically.

Dock Areas

The freight yard and dock area should be clean and well illuminated so that all vehicles can approach them safely. Employees should be instructed to stay away from areas in front of docks to avoid injuries. Trucks should be positioned flush against the dock to prevent personnel from falling through gaps. Truck wheels require constant chocking. Open dock edges, which are not used for truck mating, should be equipped with a suitable antiroll-off device. Fixed ladders should be provided between dock positions to enable truckers to gain easy access to docks.

Physical barriers should be positioned to prevent the public from entering work areas. Shippers and truckers should be restricted to the office area and not be allowed to wander around the airfreight terminal. Appropriate warning signs should be posted and the restrictions enforced.

Courtesy Federal Express.

Figure 6-1. Loading areas should be clear of all unauthorized vehicles. Equipment should be parked in designated areas a sufficient distance from service ramp to prevent damage to aircraft or vehicles.

Portable dock plates used as bridges between trucks and docks should be of a design and strength appropriate to that function. Standard plates have a device to prevent any movement. Whenever possible, plates should be moved by forklift trucks rather than manually, to prevent back and hand injuries to workers.

There should be a preventive maintenance program to ensure that all door mechanisms are serviceable and that doors are not likely to fall. To prevent damage, truckers whose vehicles have long, overhanging loads should be instructed to stay out of the dock wells until the door is opened.

Fire extinguishers should be provided to protect against truck engine fires, as required by the National Fire Protection Association (NFPA 10, see References). These extinguishers must be inspected periodically according to applicable laws.

Dock floors should be "broom clean" and free of any foreign material. Workers should be particularly alert for any items on floors which may damage freight or cause injuries. Cracks in floors should be filled with patching material to prevent tripping or catching crates that are slid over the surface.

Electrical outlets and equipment provided should meet applicable building codes; grounding should meet all regulations.

Checking Cargo

For both safety and service reasons, cargo should be carefully checked when received or delivered. Packaging should meet standard specifications. (In the United States, Department of Transportation (DOT) regulations apply. Following these is particularly important when hazardous materials are involved. See 49 CFR, 173.) If it is impractical to refuse such cargo, it should be repackaged before it is processed. Special care should be taken if restricted articles are involved. The condition of these shipments should be marked on the airbill for protection against claims.

High-density shipments should be provided with skids or pallets to spread the floor load and prevent damage to an aircraft floor. Workers should be alert for cargo with sharp projections or edges or with unnecessarily long bolts or nails.

When accepting livestock—particularly wild animals—workers should make sure cages are secure and will withstand rough handling. Employees should be cautioned to avoid allowing their hands to enter animal cages. Shipping animals capable of inflicting injury or damage during transit should be carried out in accord with the International Air Transport Association (IATA) standards. (See References.)

Some commodities require special packaging to protect them from damage during ordinary handling. Check governmental/local standards and company regulations or procedures to determine if packaging is acceptable. A commonly used reference in the United States is 49 CFR, 173.

Damaged inbound shipments should be repackaged before delivery to customers or truckers to prevent injury or loss by spillage or theft. A damage report should be prepared as required. In the United States, a Hazardous Materials Incident Report is required if restricted articles are involved. (Such forms may be obtained from state DOT offices or the Office of Policy Development and Information Systems Division, 400 7th St. SW, Mail Code DHM-63, Washington, D.C. 20590.)

Loading and Unloading Trucks

Cargo on trucks should be checked to see that it is stowed properly to prevent spilling or shifting in transport. Heavy packages and wooden crates should be placed on the bottom; light packages and cardboard containers, on the top. The height of storage racks should not be exceeded.

When cargo is hand-loaded from the truck to the dock, pallets or hand carts should be positioned as near as possible to the tailgates of the trucks. Only serviceable pallets, free of broken boards or projecting nails, should be used.

When forklifts enter a truck to unload large pieces of palletized cargo, drivers should make sure that truck brakes are set and that truck wheels are chocked on both sides to prevent movement of the truck away from the dock. Signs should inform truckers of these requirements. Forklifts should enter only those trucks with bed capacities well above the weight of the forklift. Airfreight terminal supervisors should check for compliance with this procedure.

Hand carts should be provided with brakes to prevent their rolling off a dock. Hand trucks, pallet jacks, and similar equipment without brakes shoud be kept away from the dock edge to prevent their rolling off. Forklift trucks and other self-propelled equipment should have brakes set when a driver dismounts.

Handling Cargo

A flow pattern should be planned to minimize the number of times cargo is handled. Whenever possible, cargo should be loaded on the pallet or cart on which it will be stored. Piles should be stacked evenly and "cross-tied" to bind the stack together, particularly in terminals where loads are stacked two or more tiers high. If possible, stacking pallets with loads not bound by wire or steel bands should be avoided.

Odd-sized or top-heavy shipments should be laid flat to prevent their falling over. Those that, by their nature, cannot be laid down should be secured to a base or pallet with the correct side up, as indicated by the imprinted arrows on the pallet. Small pieces should not be left on a floor where they will be a tripping hazard while building up a stack.

When manually moving cargo, workers should use extreme care to avoid injuries. Training in proper lifting methods is vital. (See the section on Manual Handling in Chapter 5.) For example, workers should be instructed to avoid twisting their backs; instead, they should move their feet in the direction of the lift. They should avoid sudden or jerky movements. When lifting heavy or awkward pieces, workers should keep their backs aligned with the natural posture curves and bend their knees. The load should be kept as close to the body as possible. Before handling any load, the worker should determine if help is needed. Two or more workers should be used, as required. When more than one person is lifting a load, all movements should be coordinated—they should lift or lower together to prevent one person from holding all of a load. Cargo should never be thrown from one employee to another.

Workers should wear gloves when handling wooden crates, metal parts, castings, or sheet metal. They should not pick up shipments by their bands or ropes. Safety shoes should be required for those dock workers who are exposed to toe and foot injuries.

Forklift Operations

Forklift operations can be hazardous, and they require careful supervision. Operators must be well trained. A set of rules for operating forklifts should be posted in the work area, and their use should be closely supervised. Workers in the area should stand clear when pallets are being moved by forklift trucks to avoid being crushed or having their feet caught. Drivers should also be careful when inserting tines in a pallet opening to avoid pushing a pallet. When loading pallets in racks or carts, workers should observe clearances on all sides to prevent damage to cargo or equipment.

Forklift tines should be spread as wide as possible to increase load stability. A load should be tilted back slightly before it is moved. Forklifts should move slowly in close quarters and avoid fast or sharp turns. Operators should also be on the alert for other employees who may not see or hear them approaching. When the load obstructs the operator's vision, the forklift should be driven in reverse. When placing pallet loads in racks or one on top of another, workers should make sure that the pallets are level or are resting on the cross members of a rack. When stacking one loaded pallet on another, workers should be guided by the weights involved, the rigidity of the packages, and the nature of the cargo. Internal combustion engines should not be operated in a confined space unless there is adequate ventilation to remove exhaust gases. Electrically run forklifts might be considered.

CARGO HANDLING SYSTEMS

Systems in airfreight terminals differ little from those in surface carriers' terminals. The principal difference is that in airfreight systems cargo is often sorted and stored in small lots for destinations that have little or inadequate mechanical handling equipment.

Live-Roller Conveyors

All electrical wiring on roller conveyors should be protected in thinwall or flexible metal sheathing and meet local building codes as well as the *National Electrical Code* (NFPA 70; see References). Belts, pulleys, sheaves, and drive systems should be guarded to prevent nip injuries.

When cargo is hand-sorted or transferred to carts or pallets, the conveyor should be at a convenient working height to reduce lifting (Figure 6-2). Conveyors should not be overloaded. Maximum weight limits for single pieces should be observed as specified by conveyor manufacturers. Signs that show maximum weights should be posted at the starting points on systems.

Signs stating WALKING ON ROLLERS IS PROHIBITED should be prominently posted, and the rule enforced.

Removable stops at the ends of all conveyors should be provided to prevent cargo from falling off. Employees working at these ends should be alert to prevent cargo from falling on them. Conveyors should be protected with curbing if mobile equipment is used alongside them.

Live rollers are driven by belts located below them. These belts are a hazard to anyone below the conveyor. Before maintenance is performed, or anyone is allowed to crawl under one to retrieve fallen items, the conveyor should be shut down and its power locked in the OFF position.

Tow Conveyors

There are three types of tow conveyors: overhead chain, in-the-floor, and magnetic track. The latter uses a battery-powered tractor and follows a track that can be moved at any time.

The first two are continuous chain conveyors and are mechanically driven. For both of these systems, there should be emergency shutoff controls strategically located around the terminal. The shutoffs should be prominently placarded, and all employees instructed in their use. A warning signal should be sounded before restarting.

Overhead Conveyors. For overhead conveyors, dragline paths should be painted on the floor to indicate the path of handcarts so that no obstruction will be in their way. Only standard handcarts designed for draglines should be used. No ordinary handcarts or dollies should be hooked-in. To prevent being caught and dragged, workers should stand clear of chains on overhead systems when the chains are not attached to carts. To prevent damage to the overhead conveyor, forklift trucks should not be allowed inside an area of a dragline.

In-the-Floor Conveyors. In-the-floor conveyor systems are more common than the overhead type. The freight terminal area should be kept clear of any material that may jam into a drag slot embedded in the floor. Again, only standard carts should be used and only a standard drop-rod should be used to connect carts to a chain.

Magnetic Track Conveyors. Magnetic track systems are most flexible; they can be moved by merely picking up the track or turning the track in another direction. These tracks should be moved only in accord with predetermined layouts so a new routing will not create a hazard. Only shift supervisors should have the authority to relocate the flow pattern. Consideration should also be given to the proximity of the track system to dock edges, fixed equipment, storage racks, and other hazards.

Standards for Conveyors. All handcarts should be provided with brakes to prevent their rolling when removed from draglines. There should also be a maintenance program to assure safe, reliable operation of all systems. This should include lubrication, battery charging, handcart repair, and periodic checks of drag chains. A positive lockout is also needed for repair work on these systems.

Storage Racks

There are numerous kinds of cargo-storage racks available. Lightweight racks with patented locking devices are frequently used because of their flexibility. These, on occasion, have not stood up under the usage common in airfreight terminals.

Wedge-locked devices should not be used. They can be unlocked simply by lifting the main supports and can collapse if locks are accidentally lifted by forklift trucks. Bolts or spring-loaded pins cost more but are far more reliable. Locking devices should be checked to ensure they are intact.

There should also be a sufficient number of cross braces to prevent racks from spreading. Cross braces should be placed to help support the pallets and prevent tipping. Rack width should be consistent with the pallets used. When pallets are stored in a rack, their bottom end boards should be outside the main frames to prevent the pallets from slipping. Rack weight limitations should be posted or stenciled on all racks. Rack members should not protrude beyond the front vertical supports.

Aisle width between racks should follow the recommendations of forklift truck manufacturers and applicable safety regulations. Aisles that are too narrow will result in accidents, damaged racks and cargo, and decreased efficiency. Convex mirrors should also be installed at blind intersections. Forklift truck drivers should be trained to operate in close quarters. Supervisors should periodically monitor forklift operators and correct their driving habits and their methods of pallet stowage.

Figure 6-2. Roller conveyors speed cargo handling in terminals. The conveyors should be at convenient working height to reduce lifting. Walking on the rollers should be prohibited.

A wide variety of forklift trucks is available. It is important that the right type for the terminal be purchased, since proper equipment is a key to a safe, efficient operation. Forklift trucks should have sufficient capacity to handle maximum pallet loads. The maximum lifting capacity of the truck (in relation to the load centers) should be displayed in view of the operator. Also, if the lift truck is operated in an area where falling pieces of freight are a hazard, overhead protection should be provided on the forklift.

Because of the hazard of falling cargo or collapsing racks, supervisors should constantly monitor pallet stacking, transporting, and stowing. Supervisors must also monitor vehicle operation in the terminal to make sure that correct driving practices are being followed. Speeding or other dangerous driving within a terminal area must not be tolerated. Indoor speeds should be walking speed.

LOADING AND UNLOADING PROCEDURES FOR AIRCRAFT

Cargo is transported in two kinds of flights: flights that carry cargo only or flights that carry cargo and passengers. The large passenger jets operated today by most carriers can accommodate loads in underfloor compartments greater than the gross weight of a DC-3. For this reason, the movement of cargo to and from gate areas has become one of the most important phases in cargo handling. A breakdown in loading cargo will affect the entire operation, passenger service as well as cargo service.

Assignment of aircraft space for cargo loads is a function of a dispatch group. Safety responsibilities of this group should include checking cargo for correct content, packaging, weight, size, condition (will not cause injury or damage to aircraft), and acceptability for air transport (see Chapter 8, Hazardous Materials and Processes).

It is important that only the freight recorded on the manifest be processed for loading. Sloppy loading can result in overgrossing an aircraft, incorrect balance, or possible injury to employees or passengers from unacceptable freight. Checkers must work closely with the load-makeup personnel to make sure that the correct freight is loaded in the correct carts and that freight requiring special handling receives it. Carts should be identified by flight number for correct loading at gate areas.

Cargo Carts

When loading cargo carts, the loading crew should stow freight evenly, with heavy pieces on the bottom and in the center to ensure stability. (To minimize lifting, the loaders might consider positioning heavy pieces next to the gate that will be used to unload.) They should make sure that the weight capacity of these carts is not exceeded. In addition, oversize pieces should not extend over the sides because they could endanger personnel or damage equipment. All doors, gates, and curtains on carts should be secured to prevent freight from falling out.

When hitching carts and tractors, workers should make sure hitches are serviceable and securely latched. Workers should straddle the tow bars when hitching, to prevent accidental drops. Connecting loaded carts should require the efforts of two employees.

Tractors should never be used to push carts when someone is in front of the cart. Carts must be under control at all times.

When towing cargo carts, drivers should slow down around corners to prevent cargo from shifting and overturning the carts. Most cargo cart trains tend to "drift in" (shorten the turning radius) when turning corners. For example, in a three-cart train, the last cart may hit the door frame even though the first clears it. Therefore, drivers should avoid turning prior to, or immediately after, passing an obstacle.

When turning a cart train, drivers should stay clear of trailing edges of wings or any projections. They should also be alert for fueling hoses and hydrant valves (Figure 6-3).

Management should determine the maximum number of carts to be towed in a train. Factors to consider in the decision are equipment specifications (i.e., tongue bolt strength, trailing characteristics, etc.) and prevailing operational conditions.

Empty cargo carts on ramps should be available to unload inbound cargo and thus to prevent double handling. Cargo carts should always be parked within designated parking lanes and their brakes set.

Ramp personnel should be made responsible for loading cargo correctly in the carts and securing all gates and doors on the carts. Drivers should be assisted in hitching carts to tractor trains. In some places, one group of drivers transfers cargo between terminals, while another group takes over operations on ramps. The ramp services group should be responsible for moving the carts to a staging area and for preventing exposure to jet blasts of nearby aircraft.

Freight terminal crews should exercise care when opening cart gates or curtains, because of the possibility that the ramp service crews may have loaded inbound cargo incorrectly into the carts. They should also check the stability of the stacking and make sure pieces are not leaning against cart gates. Cart gates should be lowered carefully. Workers should not turn their backs on a full cart, because serious injuries have resulted from freight tumbling out of carts. Workers should unload from the top down, without dislodging any "key" boxes.

Workers must be prohibited from walking on pallets when processing freight, because of the danger of sprained ankles from feet slipping between the deck boards. When moving freight from carts to pallets, workers should stand at a 45-degree (0.79-radian) angle to the load. They should pivot by moving their feet to avoid twisting. Pallets should be stacked carefully to prevent spilling.

Broken cartons should be repackaged at once. Damaged freight should never be placed in racks for transfer or delivery. Notify the freight service or sales group about shippers who consistently use poor packaging.

All cart gates should be closed when the carts are emptied, and the carts should be moved out to a parking area. Brakes should be set when the carts are parked. When towing in a terminal, drivers

Courtesy Federal Express.

Figure 6-3. Trains of loaded cargo carts should move at a maximum speed of 16 km/h (10 mph). Because most cargo trains "drift in" during turns, drivers should avoid turning immediately before or after an obstacle. They should also stay clear of the trailing edges of airplane wings or any other projections.

Figure 6-4. Cargo that is on a pallet may shift unless it is held in place by the right kind of net.

should follow the painted lanes and avoid short radius turns.

Cargo Pallets

Pallets are used in most cargo aircraft systems. These vary in size, according to carrier, but usually conform to industry-standard sizes. The most common size is 2.2 m × 3.2 m (88 in. × 125 in.). Pallets are made of aluminum or hardboard with a metal edge. Fixtures in the metal edge provide attachment points for tying down nets.

These pallets can be built up:

- By the shipper. The pallets are transported to the freight terminal by flatbed trucks or ramp equipment.
- By another carrier.
- At the dock, from trucks directly to pallets.
- From storage to pallets.

Whichever method is used, freight on pallets should be secured to withstand movement. These restraints are specified by government regulations (DOT in the United States) and apply equally to all carriers. Two means can be used to meet these requirements—nets or containers.

Restraint with nets is accomplished by lowering the net over the pile of freight and adjusting the length of the straps by buckles or hooks. Nets should be sufficiently tight to prevent freight from shifting (Figure 6-4). Pallet loads that shift can damage the interior of the cargoliner during loading and unloading, as well as during flight. Vertical and horizontal forces that may occur during takeoff, landing, or in flight as a result of turbulence must be considered when securing loads.

Containers may be closed on all sides or open on one side. The latter type is contoured to fit the fuselage and is referred to by trade names such as "huts" or "igloos." When loaded on an aircraft, the open sides of containers must be facing the same direction. Any unused space in the containers may be filled with inert dunnage to prevent the cargo from shifting while in flight (Figure 6-5).

All containers should be secured to pallets and meet the necessary restraint requirements. It is important that restraints be secured to a pallet at all attachment points to keep loads from shifting.

Some container bases have little rigid strength. Before handling them, determine whether they can be handled with a forklift truck. If container bases cannot be moved with a forklift truck, then they can be moved only on conveyor systems or on transporters equipped with conveyors. Lifting them with forklift trucks or allowing them to roll off conveyors will result in broken and distorted containers.

Loads should be distributed over an entire pallet; concentrating a heavy load in the center or in one small area will cause difficulty in loading the aircraft and may also damage the conveying system and prevent some of the locks from engaging the pallet. Improperly locked pallets have broken free during flight, inflicting major damage on aircraft cabins.

The maximum allowable weight for pallets specified by the manufacturer or company procedure should not be exceeded. Overloading could result in an incorrectly balanced aircraft. Therefore, for safety and efficiency, the entire pallet container and load should be weighed before dispatching.

Transporting Pallets

Pallets are usually transported between the airfreight terminal and the aircraft on a variety of vehicles. All have roller conveyor beds, some with power. It is most important, therefore, that end locks and side guides are installed on conveyors so that the load cannot roll off accidentally. The locks should be checked daily. Employees should be instructed that any mechanical cargo transporters with unserviceable parts must be tagged and immediately taken out of service. When overhead cranes are used to move pallet loads, the area should be restricted to authorized personnel only.

Transporter dollies are drawn by tractors or powered tow bars. Transfer by powered tow bars is a very simple operation, but has resulted in many injuries. Operators should be given a complete course of instruction by manufacturer's representatives or by company instructors. The most serious hazards are:

- Operators backing themselves against a wall
- Machines running over an employee's feet

Figure 6-5. The unused space between containers should be filled with foam rubber or plastic to prevent the cargo from shifting.

- Personnel falling under a power unit or dollie
- Controls being activated in the wrong direction
- Operators backing dollies into other employees
- Failure to stop in time
- Failure to allow sufficient clearance and striking other equipment or fixed installations.

Supervisors should periodically observe the operation of powered tow bars and take corrective action as needed. Operators must obey safe practices.

Batteries on tow bars should be charged in accord with governmental, local, and industrial standards. Only trained personnel should be allowed to do this work. Battery-charging areas should be isolated, if possible, to reduce potential damage to other equipment and should be inspected regularly. Smoking should be prohibited in the area.

Transporter trucks are basically flatbed trucks with conveying systems and mating devices to connect transporters to storage racks or aircraft loaders. Elevating trucks should have guardrails and fully covered decks. Trucks also require end stops, whether the rollers are powered or not. Trucks with any unserviceable controls should be immediately tagged OUT OF SERVICE.

Vehicles should be driven at low speed regardless of distance involved because of the height of the load and the method of restraint. Operators should be particularly alert for other personnel working in the area because a vehicle with a load is completely blind on one side.

Loading Cargo Planes

There are two basic loading systems for jet cargo planes: portable loaders that are driven to the aircraft and loading docks or bridges against which the aircraft parks (Figures 6-6 and, in Chapter 1, 1-6).

There are a number of portable loading units available; these recommendations apply to all loaders.

- Vehicles should have brakes capable of stopping or holding them under any operating conditions.
- Vehicles should operate at slow speed.
- A person acting as a guide is required when loaders are being positioned against airplanes.
- Operators should make sure that no part of a loader touches an aircraft, either when lowered or when raised to the door level.
- The following devices should be standard equipment on loaders: stabilizers, parking brakes, warning devices, automatic pallet stops, flow-control orifices (to prevent lifts from falling suddenly, if power fails), guardrails for employee protection, weatherproof controls, and placards on all controls.

When maintenance is being performed under an elevated loader bed, mechanical guards should be used to prevent accidental collapse of the bed.

Fixed bridges have certain unique hazards of their own. These procedures should be followed to ensure safe operation of fixed bridges:

- There must be docking aids and taxi guidelines so that aircraft can be positioned precisely.
- Bridges should be retracted all the way, which may also be necessary to prevent aircraft damage.
- Bridges must be extended carefully and accurately to provide correct mating with aircraft and to prevent damage.

Loading areas should be kept clear of all unauthorized equipment. No vehicles should be allowed outside equipment parking lanes. Employees meeting the aircraft must wear approved hearing protection.

When a portable loading system is used, equipment should be parked in a designated area that is a sufficient distance away from the service ramp to prevent the loader from being struck by improperly positioned aircraft.

Only after the aircraft has been parked and chocked, should the loader be allowed to approach. A basic rule: Prohibit all personnel and equipment from entering an area while aircraft are arriving and departing.

Service personnel should enter the aircraft and

Figure 6-6. Bridges must be extended carefully and accurately to provide correct mating with aircraft and to prevent damage.

open the main cargo door before a loader is positioned. The cargo door should be opened all the way and secured to prevent damage from wind. When a loader is operating, personnel should stand clear of the bed. In the event of a malfunction, the maintenance department should be notified immediately. Freight service personnel should not attempt any repairs.

Most loaders have numerous rollers or ball bearings on the deck. Workers must use care, therefore, to prevent falling or pinching their feet. Whenever possible, workers should stay on the walkway provided. Walks should have slip-resistant surfaces for better footing.

When pallets are pushed into an aircraft, enough personnel should be provided to keep the load under control and to prevent workers from overexerting themselves. Workers should position themselves to avoid jamming their hands or feet on door frames. When moving pallets into a stowing position, workers should monitor the shape of a load to make sure it does not damage the aircraft liner.

Pallets should be secured to the aircraft floor locks to prevent their shifting in flight. A pallet position checklist should be used by the lead person to ensure all locks are engaged as the aircraft is loaded. Workers should keep their fingers clear of locks. If locks are inoperative, a mechanic should be summoned immediately. After the last pallet has been put in place, all locks in the doorway should be secured before the door is closed. Upon completion of loading, space permitting, the lead person should make a final walk-through check of the cabin.

Unloading is essentially the reverse of loading. These general rules apply to both:

- Install a tail post as required during either operation to prevent the aircraft from "sitting on its tail."
- Keep carts and forklift trucks clear of the aircraft fuselage when belly compartments are being loaded.
- Report damage to interior liners in upper or lower compartments. The liners should be repaired to comply with governmental compartment classifications. (In the United States, see 49 CFR, 173.)
- When workers are pulling pallets toward the door of a plane, they should avoid catching their feet between the pallet and the floor hardware. Supervisors should make sure that employees wear safety shoes for this work, to avoid toe and foot injuries.

- Workers should be alert for pallet loads that have become deformed in flight. Handling such pallets specially will help prevent liner damage.

Traveling Lifts

Fixed docks or bridge systems utilize "traveling lifts" to move loaded pallets from storage to a bridge for loading in an aircraft. The lift operates on tracks similar to a railroad. To ensure safe operation, lifts should be designed so that the controls for operating them and those for operating roller conveyors are not too far apart to be operated by one person at the same time. The presence of two persons at the controls at any time should be forbidden.

The area in which a lift moves should be outlined with bold, painted lines, and a warning posted stating KEEP OUT OF LIFT AREAS. Flashing lights and horns should operate whenever lifts are moving. Lift operators should be responsible for seeing that tracks are clear before entering terminals. Warehouse or terminal doorways must be wide enough to provide safe entry, if the lifts operate within.

Operators should inspect their lifts daily to make sure that all controls, pallet stops, brakes, and other safety devices are operating. Pallet dollies or transporters should have brakes set when positioned at the traveling lift for off-loading. Braking prevents their being pushed, which would allow a pallet to fall. Operators should check to see that pallet stops are up before loading pallets on dollies.

Cargo Aircraft without Mechanical Loading Systems

While jet-powered aircraft have assumed the spotlight in present freight services, the piston aircraft is still the workhorse in some areas. Many carriers, scheduled as well as irregular, depend on them in their freight operation (Figure 6-7). Piston aircraft are generally loaded by forklift truck, rather than by mechanized systems.

Wooden pallets used for loading aircraft must be serviceable. They should have a sufficient number of bottom boards to hold a load even when off center. Three-sided pallets provide better stacking and keep freight from falling. They also provide a means of stacking one on another without danger of crushing a load. Unserviceable pallets should be removed from service and repaired or junked. This is particularly true of pallets with loose bottom boards. Fatal injuries have resulted from defective pallets that tilted and fell because boards were either missing or had pulled loose.

A pallet system depends on forklift trucks. The truck capacity required is determined by the maximum loads handled. All operators require special training before they qualify as aircraft loaders. Part of the training should convey an understanding of how the capacity of a truck is related to the distance of the center of the load from the front axle. An overloaded truck can drop its load or overturn. The maximum permissible load should be displayed in view of the forklift operator.

Drivers must make a full stop at least 3 m (10 ft) from an aircraft when loading. They should lift the load to just above doorsill height and move the pallet into a doorway slowly, making sure the loading crew is clear. They should also place pallets on the floor and then back straight out and not turn until the vehicle is past the wing tip or stabilizer. If there is insufficient room to leave a pallet in an aircraft, the leading board should at least be rested on the doorsill to stabilize the load while the forklift truck supports the load.

Wide-Body and Supersonic Aircraft

The "new generation" aircraft, such as the A-300 series, B-737, B-757, B-767; the well-established, wide-bodied B-747, DC-10, and L-1011; the supersonic and Concorde, present unique hazards to ramp workers. These aircraft are larger, their engines produce more thrust, and their cargo-loading drive systems are more complicated than earlier model aircraft.

These procedures and rules should be followed by those involved in cargo handling with the aircraft listed above:

- The size and shape of larger aircraft is such that a person in the tow vehicle or in the cockpit cannot see all parts of the aircraft. The area must be completely cleared of equipment and personnel during taxi and towing operations. The rule to follow is: They can't see you—stay clear!

- The aircraft are so much higher that falls can be fatal. Use barrier nets at open doors.

- Doors, flaps, and control surfaces operate very fast. Stay clear, and keep equipment clear also.

- Radio and radar antennas can radiate sufficient energy to cause physical injury. Stay at least 3 m (10 ft) from a transmitting antenna.

- The powered cargo system operates very rapidly, and workers can be trapped between moving containers. Make sure the area is clear before actuating power controls.

- The engine inlet and exhaust air velocity is much greater than that of older aircraft. For example, the B-747 exhaust velocity is three times that of the DC-8. Even at idle power, the area 150 m (500 ft) behind the B-747's engine contains exhaust gases with temperatures and velocities that are hazardous. The rule to follow is to remain clear of aircraft inlet and exhaust areas.

Loaders must use good lifting practices to avoid injuries. Large pieces should be pushed, slid, or moved with hand trucks, dollies, or heavy-duty pry bars. Off-balance pieces can be placed on the air-

Figure 6-7. The piston-engine aircraft, still the workhorse in air freight in some areas, is loaded by forklifts. Loaders and operators must be well trained in proper handling procedures.

craft floor or secured to the side with tie-down gear. Aircraft floor loading limits must be considered to avoid damaging the floor or structure under the floor. Heavy pieces may require dunnage to spread a load.

Cargo should be stowed neatly and interlocked when possible to prevent its shifting or falling on an unloading crew at the next stop. Instructions should be followed with particular attention to the weight and balance sheet. The load agent should be advised if any changes are made. Secure cargo by using nets or cables tied-down as required by company procedures. Apply these general rules:

- Install a tail post on the aircraft as required for loading or unloading.
- Forklift trucks should not move under wings or stabilizers. Positioning 3.6 m (12 ft) timbers, 0.15 by 0.2 m (6 in. by 8 in.) at the nose, along trailing edges of wings, and at the engine nacelles is effective as a guide for forklift trucks and helps to protect the aircraft while it is being loaded or unloaded.
- Personnel should not climb a forklift truck mast to enter an aircraft nor ride on forks or pallets. Riders on forklifts are not permitted.
- Floors should be kept clean at all times. Skid-resistant material should be applied to walking/working surfaces in the aircraft cabin, where possible. Workers should use caution when crossing over floor roller systems.
- Workers should keep their fingers out of animal cages. They should use the handles on the cages for moving and lifting. Animals should not be taken out of their cages.
- Cargo should not be thrown. It should be *handed* to the next person if brigade loading is used.

REFERENCES

International Air Transport Association, IATA Building, 2000 Peel Street, Montreal, PQ, Canada H3A 2R4.

Dangerous Goods Regulations.

In the United States: Cargo Network Services Corporation, 300 Garden City Plaza, Suite 400, Garden City, New York 11530.

Dangerous Goods Regulations.

National Fire Protection Association, Batterymarch Park, Quincy, MA 02269.

National Electrical Code, NFPA 70.

Portable Fire Extinguishers, NFPA 10, 1984.

National Safety Council, 444 N. Michigan Ave., Chicago, IL 60611.

Accident Prevention Manual for Industrial Operations, Engineering and Technology volume, 9th ed., 1988, Chapter 3, Manual Handling and Material Storage.

U.S. Department of Transportation, 400 Seventh St. SW, Washington, D.C. 20590.

Code of Federal Regulations, Title 49, Part 173.

American
CHICAGO FIRE DEPT.

O'HARE INTERNATIONAL AIRPORT
658

CHAPTER 7

Fire Prevention and Protection

Top: The first response fire team is answering an emergency call on the ramp.

Lower left: Standard turnout gear provides protection for fire fighters.

Lower right: An aircraft rescue fire-fighting vehicle is demonstrating dual hose capabilities.

Courtesy City of Chicago Fire Department; photos by Mike Sroka.

Fire prevention and protection starts in the planning of facilities when fire-resistive construction and fire-extinguishing equipment are incorporated into their design. The important principles for preventing fire loss are outlined in the National Fire Codes published by the National Fire Protection Association (NFPA), as well as in ordinances of government and other regulating bodies. Fire codes and legal requirements should always be met—and even exceeded where feasible.

This chapter presents basic information on the nature of fires and on fire protection programs. It also gives some standards for fire protection in aviation ground operations.

GENERAL INFORMATION ON FIRE PROTECTION

Fire Codes

The NFPA National Fire Codes have been developed over many years. They reflect current research and developments in fire-fighting methods and equipment. Widely adopted as the basis of good fire prevention and protection, the National Fire Codes cover the design, construction, and maintenance of structures, as well as safe operating methods in them. Some codes apply specifically to aviation facilities and operations while others cover facilities and equipment generally. (See References.) This chapter mentions only some of the fire protection considerations that are detailed in the codes.

The Fire Tetrahedron

To burn, fires require a supply of combustible material (fuel), oxygen, and sufficient heat. The fourth requirement for fire is that the chain reaction is continuous. This can be visualized as a four-sided figure or tetrahedron. Fire prevention and extinguishment aim to eliminate any of the four factors, and thus to destroy the "fire tetrahedron" (Figure 7-1). For example, fires can be prevented by eliminating heat, which would be a source of ignition. A practical application of this principle would be eliminating the use of open flames or any source of electrical sparks near combustible materials.

Eliminating any of the factors can help prevent or extinguish fires. A few examples are given here.

Controlling the Fuel. One way to control the fuel factor, which is needed for a fire to burn, is the use of fire-resistive construction materials. Other related ways to control the fuel factor are:

- Using fire-retardant coatings
- Limiting the amount of combustible materials stored in one unit
- Separating quantities of combustible materials with spaces that fire cannot cross
- Shutting off fuel supply; turning a valve
- Controlling or preventing fuel spills. (See Figure 7-2.)

Figure 7-1. Oxygen, heat, fuel, and a chain reaction are necessary for a fire. They form "the fire tetrahedron."

Courtesy United Airlines, photo by Mike Sroka.

Figure 7-2. A fuel spill cart containing emergency equipment should be positioned on the ramp.

Cooling. Cooling inhibits the spread of flames. Wetting combustible materials or covering them with foam lowers the heat and suppresses a fire.

Cutting off Oxygen. Placing materials in tight containers or covering them with noncombustible coatings would be ways to cut off oxygen. In the event of a fire, either carbon dioxide or foam will reduce the amount of oxygen that reaches the burning surface to slow down combustion.

Interrupting the Chain Reaction. Dry chemicals and Halons act to interrupt the chain reactions that are part of the fire tetrahedron.

Fire Precautions

Many of the fire precautions necessary for airport facilities have been covered in previous chapters.

- For information on incorporating fire prevention principles into the design of buildings (including airfreight terminals), see in particular Chapter 1, Airport Buildings and Fixed Facilities.
- For information on fire protection in ramp areas, see Chapter 3, Ramp Operations at Passenger Terminals. More detailed information on fire protection in ramp areas is given in the next section of this chapter.
- For a discussion of fire hazards in hangars and shops, see Chapter 5, Hangar and Shop Operations.

FIRE PROTECTION FOR RAMP OPERATIONS

Extinguisher Requirements

There should be at least two dry-chemical extinguishers with wheels for each commercial aircraft parked for servicing (including cabin and lavatory service, cargo service, fueling, or aircraft maintenance). Each extinguisher should be located no more than 75 m (250 ft) from the aircraft. These extinguishers are in addition to any portable extinguishers already provided in the ramp area.

The wheeled extinguishers near the aircraft must conform to the following standards:

- For parking locations used by wide-bodied aircraft, extinguishers should have an Underwriters Laboratories Inc. (or other nationally recognized approval agency) rating of at least 160B:C and contain a minimum charge of 136 kg (300 lb) of dry chemical. They should have a sufficient range to reach the highest aircraft engine.

- For parking locations used by aircraft other than wide-bodied ones, extinguishers should have an Underwriters Laboratories Inc. and/or Factory Mutual (FM) rating of at least 80B:C and contain a minimum of 57 kg (125 lb) of dry chemical.

Any commercial aircraft parked in a remote area where fueling is not normally conducted should be protected by a wheeled dry-chemical extinguisher. The distance from the extinguisher to the aircraft should not exceed 75 m (250 ft). This extinguisher is in addition to any portable extinguishers already in the area. For extinguishers to qualify for this service, they should have an Underwriters Laboratories (or other nationally recognized testing laboratory) rating of at least 80B:C and contain a minimum charge of 57 kg (125 lb) of dry chemical.

For extinguishers near aircraft, potassium bicarbonate-based chemical is preferred, though other approved agents may be used. Corrosive agents such as potassium chloride (super K) and monoammonium phosphate (ABC) should not be used. The unacceptable agent potassium chloride (super K) should not be confused with the acceptable agent purple K. Extinguisher maintenance, as well as maintenance records, are to be in compliance with the standards in NFPA 10, *Portable Fire Extinguishers* (see References).

Employees who work in the ramp area should be given training in the use of both hand and wheeled extinguishers. Such training would include how to extinguish the kinds of fires most likely to occur on ramps. Employees should be retrained on the use of extinguishers periodically.

Special Precautions For Ramp Areas

Fuel handling, outside storage of materials, and rubbish pose special fire hazards in ramp areas and require special fire protection measures. See NFPA codes on all three kinds of operations.

Fuel Handling. Gasoline and gasoline-blended fuels can ignite at extremely low temperatures if an ignition source is present. The temperature range in which it is possible to have flammable vapor-air mixtures is quite wide and covers the normal ambient temperature range. For example, at sea level in a gasoline storage tank, the temperature range could be from −46 C to +74 C (−50 F to +165 F). The temperature range for any one fuel, however, would be much narrower.

Autoignition temperature is the minimum temperature of a substance required to initiate or cause self-sustained combustion, independent of any sparks or other means of ignition. Under some conditions, the autoignition temperature of jet fuels has been measured at approximately 250 C (475 F). This temperature may exist for a considerable period in turbine engines after shutdown or on brake surfaces following hard use. (These figures were derived from laboratory tests; in field conditions, the ignition temperatures may be higher.)

Static discharge is one source of ignition, and jet fuels are more prone to acquire a static charge than aviation gasoline.

Fueling and defueling of aircraft should be according to procedures outlined in the NFPA codes. The procedures are designed to reduce static electricity and other sources of ignition and limit the opportunity for fuel to catch fire. (See References.)

Outdoor Storage of Materials. Outdoor storage of materials that are susceptible to ignition by sparks or flying brands requires special measures. The following points should be considered to reduce the hazards of materials stored outdoors:

- There should be adequate fire and police protection of the storage areas.

- Public water systems should be adequate, with hydrants suitably located.

- Well-maintained, all-weather roads should be available for fire apparatus.

- There should be sufficient clear space between any combustible buildings and the place where materials are stored, as well as between any roads and storage piles.

- The size and height of piles should be consistent with the stability of piles under normal as well as fire conditions.

- Clear aisles should be maintained between storage piles, as well as between the piles and buildings and between the piles and the boundary line of a storage site. Driveways in the storage areas should be of sufficient width to permit fire equipment to travel to all parts of the storage area, to remove material in an emergency.

- The storage area should be surrounded by a fence to reduce access by unauthorized personnel. There should, however, be an adequate number of gates in the fence to permit ready access by fire equipment.

- Any buildings in or near a storage area should be of noncombustible construction with adequate clearance to the nearest storage pile. Buildings that house hazardous operations such as paint spraying and fuel-control testing should be more than 15 m (50 ft) from the nearest pile. Explosion vents, blower outlets, or similar devices should not be directed toward the storage yard.

- Storage sites should be kept free of unnecessary combustible materials, weeds, and grass. Regular cleanup is essential.
- There should be adequate lighting, in conformance with the *National Electrical Code.* (See References.)
- Braziers, salamanders, portable heaters, or other open fires are not to be used in a storage yard.
- Tarpaulins, used for the protection of storage, should be of an approved flame-resistant fabric.
- Fire-extinguishing equipment meeting NFPA standards for size, placement, maintenance, and hazards encountered should be readily available.

Handling Rubbish. Rubbish should be collected around an airport. Waste materials may include paper, upholstery materials, wood, metal shavings, combustible dusts, and flammable liquids. This rubbish should be disposed of daily in a safe manner to avoid any possible fire hazard.

Types of rubbish should be segregated according to the degree of compatibility and method of disposal. Rubbish should be handled in an orderly manner and not be allowed to accumulate where it may expose buildings or piled stock to fire hazards.

Planned burning of rubbish outdoors is one method of disposal but, apart from the fire hazard, it creates a smoke nuisance in the vicinity of aircraft operations and to neighbors in the community. Burning rubbish in properly designed incinerations prevents the release of sparks and brands and reduces the danger. In many cases outdoor burning is being controlled or prohibited by laws because of air pollution restrictions. (All regulations covering disposal of refuse should be rigidly followed.)

FIRE INSPECTIONS

A fire inspection program should include provisions for periodic checks of buildings, outdoor facilities, installed systems, and shop and hangar equipment. In order for the program to be effective, there should be unannounced, random inspections, as well as periodic ones.

A thorough fire inspection program should go beyond mere checks of facilities: It should include plans for eliminating or reducing fire hazards. Someone trained in fire-inspection procedures should review potential hazards that occur in normal operations. Those engaged in routine operations, who may have production and schedules uppermost in their minds, may tend to accept hazards as an inherent part of the task. The person inspecting may find that some hazards can be eliminated or controlled. Some areas to consider are:

- Ways to improve housekeeping practices
- Better methods of handling flammable fluids
- Ways to reduce combustible material in storage
- Improvements in emergency handling procedures.

A designated person should conduct a fire inspection monthly. Use of an inspection checklist is often helpful (Figure 7-3). With the sample list, for each item the inspector merely checks YES, NO, NOT APPLICABLE. The inspector forwards the completed checklist to the airport fire marshal or a similar authority.

The airport fire marshal, insurance underwriters, and any governmental authorities having jurisdiction over the airport also undertake periodic inspections. Critical items, such as boilers and heating systems, electrical systems, pressure vessels, and flammable liquid storage, should be given careful attention to ensure compliance with applicable codes. It is desirable for an atmosphere of cooperation to develop between inspecting authorities and operators.

All fire-fighting equipment, both portable and fixed, should be inspected, tested, and maintained according to NFPA codes to ensure proper operation when needed.

FIRE TRAINING

The action taken in the first few minutes of a fire or other emergency is of critical importance. Therefore, all airport personnel should be trained in the procedures to follow before professional fire fighters arrive. In addition, designated personnel should be trained as fire-fighting teams which will take action in those early minutes before the professional fire fighters arrive.

Fire Instruction

Two kinds of fire instruction are necessary: (1) for general personnel and (2) for fire-fighting teams. General training should cover fire prevention and protection and include instruction on each of the following points:

- Fire prevention
- Fire detection
- Calling for assistance in the event of a fire
- Extinguishing fires
- Evacuation

FIRE INSPECTION CHECKLIST

Emergency Preparation

- ☐ Fire organization posted
- ☐ Fire drill held regularly
- ☐ Fire exits well marked and unobstructed
- ☐ Fire alarms well marked and unobstructed
- ☐ Aisles and stairs clear
- ☐ Evacuation procedures posted
- ☐ Procedures for handling fuel spills posted
- ☐ Emergency equipment well marked, in place and ready for use

Plant and Buildings

- ☐ Hydrants and water supply checked and serviceable
- ☐ Sprinkler system, checked and serviceable
- ☐ Foam and CO_2 systems, checked and serviceable
- ☐ Fire doors, checked and serviceable
- ☐ Fire extinguishers well marked, in place, checked and tagged
- ☐ Hose stations, checked and serviceable
- ☐ Electrical circuits identified, enclosed and provided with proper overload protection
- ☐ Gas systems, checked and serviceable
- ☐ Fuel pumping equipment, in good condition and free of leaks (extinguishing equipment adequate and available)

Production Equipment

- ☐ Spray booths, clean and properly ventilated and sprinkler heads protected from overspray
- ☐ Power tools and accessories, wiring in good condition
- ☐ Pressurized bottles, properly connected and secured
- ☐ Mobile equipment extinguishers well marked, in place and serviceable
- ☐ Powered equipment, properly grounded
- ☐ Test equipment, free of leaks, wiring in good condition.

Management

- ☐ General housekeeping, adequate
- ☐ Changes (alterations, processes, methods and procedures) cleared with Fire Marshal
- ☐ Floors, clean and free of flammable fluid spills
- ☐ Storage of material, orderly and in accordance with regulations*
- ☐ Aircraft fueling, in accordance with regulation*
- ☐ Spray painting, in accordance with regulations*
- ☐ Welding and other open flame operations, in accordance with regulations*
- ☐ Ramp and grounds, clean and free of debris
- ☐ Proper disposal of soiled shop towels and rags

* Separate checklists should be made for these operations.

Figure 7-3. To facilitate the process of fire inspection, the inspector can use a checklist like the one above.

Figure 7-4. Shown are fire fighters wearing heat protective fire proximity suits.

Courtesy City of Chicago Fire Department; photos by Mike Sroka.

- Rescue and first aid
- Salvage
- Disaster control.

All personnel, including the fire-fighting teams, should be trained and given periodic refresher courses in basic fire prevention and in emergency procedures. Fire prevention training should focus on the particular hazards of a location and on their control. Training should also cover what fire detection systems are in operation at a facility and what to do when emergency alarms are sounded.

Instruction on calling for assistance should include how to use a fire alarm, where alarms are located, and how and to whom to communicate additional information about an emergency. The mechanism of the fire alarm should be described and demonstrated. The importance of immediately calling for assistance should be stressed. A responsible person from each area should be designated to meet and give directions to the fire department.

Instruction on extinguishing fires should include the location and use of portable fire extinguishers and the correct type to use for each of the four classes of fire (ordinary materials, flammable liquids, electrical, combustible metals). The instruction should include demonstrations of how the fire extinguishers operate.

Evacuation routes should be carefully mapped and rehearsed, as should alternate routes in case of obstacles.

Fire-fighting teams should receive more extensive training than that outlined above, and they should receive frequent practice in techniques (Figure 7–4). Where fire-fighting brigades are responsible for the primary fire fighting at a facility, the NFPA *Fire Brigade Training Manual* should be consulted.

Fire Drills

Fire drills are a means of rehearsing what has been learned in training and of discovering weaknesses in current emergency procedures. Here are some practices to follow in conducting fire drills:

- Drills should be carefully planned so that an actual fire condition can be simulated.
- Observers should be posted at strategic points

throughout the area to review and time the actions of personnel and fire-fighting teams.

- The drill must be without warning to reproduce the conditions and reactions that are likely to exist in a real emergency.
- Drills should be held with sufficient frequency, preferably every quarter. Regular drills should serve to make employees' reactions to the alarm automatic and to make it possible to cover different emergency conditions in a reasonably short cycle.
- Weaknesses in existing procedures should be carefully recorded so that improvements can be made.
- For each drill, a potential hazard should be selected and how it affects emergency procedures analyzed. For example, observers can be posted in main corridors to warn people being evacuated that "this corridor is theoretically on fire and an alternate means of evacuation should be found."

REFERENCES

Department of the Air Force, The Pentagon, Washington, D.C. 20330.
Technical Manual 100-25-172, Ground Servicing of Aircraft and Static Ground/Bonding, December 1982.

Factory Mutual System, 1151 Boston-Providence Turnpike, Norwood, MA 02062.

Flight Safety Foundation, 5510 Columbia Pike, Arlington, VA 22204.
Aircraft Fueling Up-to-Date.

Industrial Risk Insurers, 85 Woodland St., Hartford, CT 06102.
Recommended Good Practice for Protection of High Piled Stock.

National Fire Protection Association, Batterymarch Park, Quincy, MA 02269.
Fire Brigade Training Manual.
NFPA Inspection Manual.

Standards
Aircraft Fueling Ramp Drainage, NFPA 415, 1983.
Aircraft Fueling Servicing, NFPA 407, 1985.
Aircraft Hand Fire Extinguishers, NFPA 408, 1984.
Aircraft Interior Fire Protection Systems, NFPA 421, 1973.
Aircraft Maintenance, NFPA 410, 1980.
Aircraft Rescue and Fire Fighting Operational Procedures, NFPA 402M, 1984.
Aircraft Rescue and Fire Fighting Services at Airports and Heliports, NFPA 403, 1978.
Aircraft Rescue and Fire Fighting Vehicles, NFPA 414, 1974.
Blower and Exhaust Systems for Dust, Stock, and Vapor Removal or Conveying, NFPA 91, 1983.
Construction and Protection of Aircraft Loading Walkways, NFPA 471, 1985.
Construction and Protection of Airport Terminal Buildings, NFPA 416, 1983.
Evaluating Foam Fire Fighting Equipment on Aircraft Rescue and Fire Fighting Vehicles, NFPA 412, 1974.
Fire Protection for Archives and Record Centers, NFPA 232AM, 1986.
Inspection, Testing, and Maintenance of Sprinkler Systems, NFPA 13A, 1987.
Installation of Air Conditioning and Ventilating Systems, NFPA 90A, 1985.
Life Safety Code, NFPA 101, 1985.
Low Expansion and Combined Agent Systems, NFPA 11, 1983.
Master Planning Airport Water Supply Systems for Fire Protection, NFPA 419, 1983.
Motor Freight Terminals, NFPA 513, 1984.
Portable Fire Extinguishers, NFPA 10, 1984.
Powered Industrial Trucks, Including Type Designations, Areas of Use, Maintenance, and Operation, NFPA 505, 1982.
National Electrical Code, NFPA 70.
Protection of Records, NFPA 232, 1986.
Rock Storage of Materials, NFPA 231C, 1986.
Repair Garages, NFPA 88B, 1985.
Removal of Smoke and Grease-Laden Vapors from Commercial Cooking Equipment, NFPA 96, 1984.
Roof-Top Heliport Construction and Protection, NFPA 418, 1979.
Safeguarding Building Construction and Demolition Operations, NFPA 241, 1986.

Seattle-Tacoma International Airport Fire Department, P.O. Box 6206, Riverton Heights Br., Washington 98188.
Standard Operating Procedures.
"Aircraft Salvaging Operations," "Airport Procedure Bulletin ST 4, Fire Department Inspections;" "Annual Report of Department Inspections;" "Code 19 Plan;" "Disaster Control Plan and Decontamination Teams;" "Inspection Report;" "Rules and Regulations;" "Training Classes, Class Outline."

658

O'HARE INTERNATIONAL AIRPORT
658

CHAPTER 8

Hazardous Materials and Processes

Top: The aircraft rescue fire-fighting vehicle performs an equipment check.

Bottom: This first response team is properly equipped for any emergency situation.

Courtesy City of Chicago Fire Department; photos by Mike Sroka.

Some of the common hazardous materials used at airport facilities and their possible harmful effects will be discussed in this chapter. Safety and health procedures that can be employed to avoid personal injury will be stressed. (See Chapter 6 regarding shipping hazardous materials.)

Hazards connected with materials and processes such as chemicals, solvents, compressed gases, and physical agents can be listed under four categories. These are listed in Table 8-A.

CHEMICAL HAZARDS

Potentially hazardous materials used in aviation ground operations include: paint strippers, cleaning solutions, brighteners, fluxes, insecticides, coating materials, resins, asbestos, solvents, and compressed gases. Processes such as plating, degreasing, stripping, cleaning, dipping, welding, plasma spray, soldering, aircraft skin repair, and auto body repair may generate toxic gases, vapors, mists, or dusts.

Potentially hazardous chemicals that may be used in airline operations are listed in Table 8-B.

Informing Employees about Hazardous Materials

Line management must ensure that workers are aware of the presence and the nature of any hazardous material in products they use. It is important that management find out and follow the manufacturer's recommendations for the storage, handling, and use of all hazardous substances. In the United States, the sample form shown in Figure 8-1, the Material Safety Data Sheet (MSDS), is used to request this information from suppliers, manufacturers, or distributors.

The Occupational Safety and Health Administration (OSHA) requires a written program establishing responsibilities for chemical labeling,

Table 8-A. Four Categories of Hazards

Health Hazards

Toxic effects from inhalation, ingestion, or absorption through skin
Oxyen deficiency
Dermatitis from repeated contact
Chemical burns from skin or eye contact with strong chemicals
Noise and vibration
Radiation effects, both ionizing and nonionizing
Biological effects from airborne or waterborne pathogens

Flammability Hazards

Materials that burn under specific conditions
Flammable and combustible liquids, gases, or vapors
Flammable solids
Cryogenic materials

Reactivity Hazards

Materials that may burn, explode, or produce hazardous gases on contact with other chemicals or when destabilized with heat or shock
Materials that may decompose and support combustion when heated

Special Hazards

Materials having unusual reactivity with water
Materials with oxidizing properties
Materials of radioactive character or having radioactive hazards

Source: NFPA 704.

proper employee training on health and safety hazards of chemicals, along with information on protective equipment, precautionary methods, and other controls. The United States Environmental Protection Agency (U.S. EPA) establishes standards for the control and disposition of hazardous materials and substances.

Some of the basic steps to follow in developing an internal program for the control of hazardous materials are listed below:

- Perform a chemical and hazardous substance inventory of every department.
- Request a Material Safety Data Sheet (MSDS) for every hazardous substance or material.
- Assess the needs of employees for training and the use of personal protective equipment.
- Analyze measures for the control of hazardous materials, along with the ventilation requirement for each area in which they are used.
- Order industrial hygiene surveys where required.
- Provide appropriate training for employees.
- Give all user departments current MSDSs.
- Provide for scheduled retraining of all users.
- Supplement training with periodic reviews and departmental safety meetings of hazards and reactions of various chemicals and substances.
- Maintain records indefinitely for those undergoing training.

Table 8-B. Chemicals, Flammables, Corrosives, Solvents

Chemicals

Acetone	1,2-Dichlorobenzene	Nitric Acid
Alcohols	Fluorides	Perchloroethylene
Amines	Hydrochloric Acid	Petroleum Distillates
Aromatic Hydrocarbons	Isocyanates	Phosphoric Acid
Benzene	Isopropanol	Styrene
Butyl Cellosolve	Methyl Ethyl Ketone	Sulfuric Acid
Chlorinates	Methyl Alcohol	Toluene
Chromic Acid	Methyl Butyl Ketone	1,1,1-Trichloroethane
Phenol and Cresylic Acid	Methylene Chloride	Trichloroethylene
Cyanides	Methyl Isobutyl Ketone	Xylene

Dusts and Mists

Aluminum	Cobalt	Titanium
Asbestos	Fibrous Glass	Wood
Cadmium	Lead	Zinc
Caustics	Nickel	Zirconium
Chromium	Silica	

- Provide any contractors whose employees will be exposed to hazardous materials or substances with appropriate MSDSs.
- Provide proper container labeling.

Where local, regional or other governmental laws provide for more stringent applications or controls, follow *those* standards or requirements.

Evaluating Hazardous Materials

In addition to the MSDS, several references are available on the toxicity and hazards of materials. (See, in References, National Safety Council *Fundamentals of Industrial Hygiene*, Hamilton and Hardy, Sax, American Industrial Hygiene Association, Chemical Manufacturers Association, *Patty's Industrial Hygiene.*)

Final determination of whether a material or process presents a hazard to employees should be left to qualified chemists, industrial hygienists, safety engineers, or fire prevention specialists. Such resource people may be available within an airline's organization. Other sources for this information include insurance carriers and private consultants. Governmental departments of health or labor may provide free occupational health consultation.

There are a number of direct-reading and air-sampling instruments for measuring concentrations of mists, vapors, or gases in ambient air or in confined spaces. The instruments can be used to determine whether an environment is safe or requires further evaluation and corrective action. With proper training by qualified specialists, personnel on site would be able to use them.

Such measuring instruments include color-indicator tubes for a large number of gases and solvents, combustible vapor detectors, oxygen meters, halogenated hydrocarbon meters, carbon monoxide meters, velocity meters, and dust collection and smoke tubes to evaluate exhaust systems.

Air-Sampling Instruments published by the American Conference of Governmental Industrial Hygienists provides an excellent discussion of instrumentation (see References). In addition, several professional periodicals provide information on such equipment, including *American Industrial Hygiene Association Journal*, *Safety and Health,* and others.

Control of Hazardous Materials

The following is the preferred order of approach to controlling hazardous materials or processes (this order is an OSHA recommendation and may not be accepted worldwide):

1. *Elimination:* Change processes to remove the hazard.
2. *Substitution:* Provide a less hazardous material or process for the one used.
3. *Engineering controls:* These include ventilation, noise control, enclosure of process.
4. *Administrative controls:* Alter the length of time and frequency of exposure.
5. *Personal protective equipment:* This includes respirators and earmuffs. This is the least desirable method and should only be used for temporary operations or where other methods are not feasible.

Asbestos and chemicals such as benzene and carbon tetrachloride ought to be prohibited from use. When their use cannot be eliminated, strict controls should be established. In most cases, satisfactory substitutes are available.

Personal Protective Equipment

When hazardous chemicals are handled, stored, or used, wearing personal protective equipment is necessary. Generally speaking, chemical safety goggles or face shields, acidproof aprons, rubber or nonreactive synthetic gloves, appropriate cartridge masks, or self-contained breathing units are the most common types used. Employees should be instructed in how and when to use this equipment as part of the training referred to earlier in the chapter. This equipment should be maintained in a clean and sanitary condition and inspected regularly for defects.

Personal protective equipment must conform to published standards. Its use should be under the control of someone knowledgeable in the subject. For more information on protective equipment, see, in References, American National Standards Institute (ANSI) *Practices for Respiratory Protection* and U.S. Department of Health and Human Resources *NIOSH-Certified Personal Protective Equipment.* See also Chapter 9, Personal Protective Equipment and Guarding, in this book.

Handling Chemicals

Chemicals come in bags, drums, cans, and bottles. The most dangerous kind of container is a glass bottle. Glass bottles of acid, for example, should be carried in a supporting container; acid carboys should be left in their wooden crates. Acid should be transferred from one container to another by a pump or carboy tilters. The mouth-siphoning technique should never be used.

Dangerous chemicals should be transferred from receiving to storage on flatbed hand trucks, special carboy trucks, or pallets that have sideboards. Good judgment in handling is necessary to prevent mechanical damage to packages containing hazardous chemicals. It is advisable to have chemicals placed on skids for storage to prevent contact with moisture or chemicals on the floor and, if necessary, to facilitate cleanup of spills.

Acid carboys, both full and empty, should be vented periodically to relieve internal pressures.

Figure 8-1, page 1. The Material Safety Data Sheet (MSDS) can be used to request technical information about a product. The form on these pages may be reproduced.

Material Safety Data Sheet May be used to comply with OSHA's Hazard Communication Standard, 29 CFR 1910.1200. Standard must be consulted for specific requirements.	**U.S. Department of Labor** Occupational Safety and Health Administration (Non-Mandatory Form) Form Approved OMB No. 1218-0072
IDENTITY *(As Used on Label and List)*	*Note: Blank spaces are not permitted. If any item is not applicable, or no information is available, the space must be marked to indicate that.*

Section I

Manufacturer's Name	Emergency Telephone Number
Address *(Number, Street, City, State, and ZIP Code)*	Telephone Number for Information
	Date Prepared
	Signature of Preparer *(optional)*

Section II — Hazardous Ingredients/Identity Information

Hazardous Components (Specific Chemical Identity; Common Name(s))	OSHA PEL	ACGIH TLV	Other Limits Recommended	% *(optional)*

Section III — Physical/Chemical Characteristics

Boiling Point		Specific Gravity (H_2O = 1)	
Vapor Pressure (mm Hg.)		Melting Point	
Vapor Density (AIR = 1)		Evaporation Rate (Butyl Acetate = 1)	
Solubility in Water			
Appearance and Odor			

Section IV — Fire and Explosion Hazard Data

Flash Point (Method Used)	Flammable Limits	LEL	UEL
Extinguishing Media			
Special Fire Fighting Procedures			
Unusual Fire and Explosion Hazards			

OSHA 174

Section V — Reactivity Data

Stability	Unstable		Conditions to Avoid
	Stable		

Incompatibility (*Materials to Avoid*)

Hazardous Decomposition or Byproducts

Hazardous Polymerization	May Occur		Conditions to Avoid
	Will Not Occur		

Section VI — Health Hazard Data

Route(s) of Entry:	Inhalation?	Skin?	Ingestion?

Health Hazards (*Acute and Chronic*)

Carcinogenicity:	NTP?	IARC Monographs?	OSHA Regulated?

Signs and Symptoms of Exposure

Medical Conditions
Generally Aggravated by Exposure

Emergency and First Aid Procedures

Section VII — Precautions for Safe Handling and Use

Steps to Be Taken in Case Material Is Released or Spilled

Waste Disposal Method

Precautions to Be Taken in Handling and Storing

Other Precautions

Section VIII — Control Measures

Respiratory Protection (*Specify Type*)

Ventilation	Local Exhaust	Special
	Mechanical (*General*)	Other

Protective Gloves	Eye Protection

Other Protective Clothing or Equipment

Work/Hygienic Practices

☆ U.S.G.P.O. 1986-491-529/45775

Hazardous chemicals should be mixed and used according to information provided by the manufacturer or as specified by written job procedures. Employees should be checked periodically to ensure they are following safe procedures. Engineering control equipment should also be checked periodically to ascertain that it is functioning properly.

Accidents sometimes occur when reactive chemicals or incompatible materials are mixed or improperly used. All containers used for hazardous materials must be properly handled, and must be correctly labeled. Proper labeling includes the name of the manufacturer, address, hazards, safety instructions, and other precautions. Procedures should be established to prevent the return of unused materials to the wrong containers. Combining or substituting chemicals should be prohibited, except as provided in written procedures or as under the control of qualified personnel.

Internal waste treatment and licensed disposal facilities are possible disposal methods. Among physical characteristics to consider are toxic vapors or fumes, corrosiveness, and oxidizing properties of chemicals and hazardous materials.

Flushing to storm sewers in any quantity exceeding "deminimus" amounts is illegal for wastes classified as hazardous under the United States Resource Conservation and Recovery Act (RCRA). Check also with local, city, and airport authorities for additional regulations that may prevail.

Spills

A spill or unintentional release of a toxic or hazardous substance into the environment may need to be reported to several agencies, depending on what was spilled, the quantity that was spilled, and other variables such as location, time, and effects of the spill itself. There may be several regulatory requirements in effect in an area. Management should research these regulations and prepare procedures accordingly, including a list of agencies that must be called under what circumstances. A form like the one in Figure 8-2 may be used to collect such information.

There are three methods for cleaning up spills: (1) flushing, (2) using absorbents or adsorbents, and (3) using fixants.

If moderate to large quantities of a spilled material are involved, some of the material might be recovered for reuse. Check with local authorities having jurisdiction regarding regulations that may apply. Then the remainder can be cleaned up by means of one of the three methods. (The factors to consider in deciding whether recovery is advisable are given later in this section.)

1. *Flushing*
   Small quantities of nonrecoverable residue can be "flushed" with excess amounts of diluting water. Flushing spills down the drain, however, is not always safe or appropriate. It definitely should not be attempted on large quantities of water-reactive materials since an explosion or fire could result. Before flushing is attempted, it is necessary to know that the material can be safely and legally cleaned up by this method.
2. *Using commercial absorbents or adsorbents*
   Small quantities of nonrecoverable residue can be cleaned up with commercial absorbent or adsorbent agents. Spill residues can be solidified with commercial batting materials, or with clays, kiln dust, fly ash, fuller's earth, soil, sand, or sawdust. Note that if the solidified waste is classified as hazardous, it cannot be legally dumped in a landfill; so, careless spills can result in very high costs to dispose of the residues.
3. *Using chemical fixants*
   Small quantities of nonrecoverable residue can be cleaned up with commercial fixant agents. Chemical fixation of spill residues can be achieved with certain commercial solidification products. Use of such products for minor spill residue cleanups may broaden the options for legal disposal and reduce costs.

The decision about whether to attempt spill recovery must take into account the potential risk of human exposure to hazardous materials during the recovery process. Factors that might eliminate the possibility of recovery would include proximity of a dangerous spill to a water supply or body of water, to a fire hazard, or to personnel or equipment.

These principles should be followed in spill handling programs:

- Plan methods that will allow recovery of materials to the maximum degree safely possible.
- Use cleanup agents that will not present disposal problems.
- Train employees in how to handle spills.
- In the United States monthly generation of more than 100 kg (45 lb) of spill cleanup residue and/or storage of more than 1,000 kg (453 lb) of such residue for more than 90 days is prohibited unless specifically permitted by the state regulatory agency for waste management or by the EPA under the Resource Conservation Recovery Act (RCRA).

Emergency Information

In the event of an emergency involving chemicals, call the Chemical Transportation Emergency Center, CHEMTREC, at 1-800-424-9300 in the United States. If outside the United States, call the U.S. Environmental Protection Agency (EPA) at 1-800-424-8802. *These telephone numbers are for emergencies only, not for information about routine handling and disposal of chemicals.*

These agencies will provide the caller with

HAZARDOUS MATERIAL SPILLAGE OR BREAKAGE REPORT

PLANE NO: ____________________ FLT. NO: __________________ DATE ______________

STATION STOPS: ____

PROPER NAME OF PRODUCT: ______________________________________

QUANTITY OF PRODUCT: PER UNIT: ________________________ UNITS PER PKS: _____

NO. OF PKGS CARRIED: ________________________

TYPE OF PRODUCT: LIQUID ____________ GAS ____________ SOLID _________

DUST ______________ GRANULAR ____________

EXACT LOCATION CARRIED ON AIRCRAFT: __________________________________

NAME OF CONSIGNEE: _________________________ CONSIGNOR: _________________

TYPE OF WARNING LABELS AFFIXED TO PACKAGE:

COLOR: ________________________________WORDING: ____________________

DESCRIPTION OF PACKAGING: ____

____

STATION DAMAGE OR SPILLAGE FOUND: ___________________ TIME AND DATE: _________

DESCRIPTION OF DAMAGE: ____

____

NUMBER OF PERSONS EXPOSED TO PRODUCT: ________________________________

WHO REPORTED INCIDENT: ____

WHAT GOVERNMENTAL AGENCIES HAVE BEEN NOTIFIED:

	NAME OF PERSON	PHONE NO.	TIME AND DATE
FAA:			
NRC:			
AIRPORT AUTHORITY:			
USPHS:			
OTHER:			

REPORT COMPLETED BY: ___________________________ DATE ______________________

Figure 8-2. When hazardous materials are spilled or their containers are broken, a checklist form such as this should be filled out in order to alert company safety personnel and the appropriate government agencies.

response/action information for the product and will give information on the first steps to take to control the emergency.

Water dilution of most chemicals reduces the harmful effects of them on the human body. Eyewash fountains, emergency showers, or water hoses should also be provided as required. Doctors and hospitals should have a list of hazardous chemicals and their antidotes so medical treatment, when necessary, can be given without delay.

Those chemicals requiring the same specific fire extinguishing agent should all be stored together. The fire extinguisher should be conspicuously mounted immediately adjacent to the storage area. Knowledge of chemicals used and proper handling will reduce the possibility of fire.

Additional information on storage and handling is available in Part 1910 of *Occupational and Safety Health Standards.* (See References under U.S. Department of Labor; see also Chemical Manufacturers Association in References.)

Solvent Storage

Some common solvents and their properties are given in Table 8-C. Bulk flammable solvents should be stored out of doors, in protected areas, or in well-ventilated rooms with explosion-proof electrical services, including light fixtures, intercoms, telephone accessories, and ventilation equipment. Storage facilities for bulk flammable solvents should be physically separated from other storage and operations. Construction of such facilities should be in accord with the National Fire Codes published by the National Fire Protection Association. (See References.) Additional information and requirements on construction and storage can be found in Part 1910 of *Occupational and Safety Health Standards* (see References, under U.S. Department of Labor).

Because of flammability hazards, leaking drums should be removed immediately from enclosed spaces to prevent the buildup of hazardous vapor concentrations.

The preferred liquid dispensing method is by hand pumps listed by Underwriters Laboratories Inc. (UL). If spigots are used, they should be a listed, self-closing type. Drip pans to catch spilled liquids should be avoided unless the pans drain into a closed container. Safety containers, with the name of the solvent clearly printed on the container along with other required labeling, should be used on the job. When flammable liquids are being dispensed, bonding and grounding are required to prevent static generation and explosion.

Spills should be wiped up immediately. Rags or absorbent compound used in the cleanup should be placed in listed waste containers. These containers should be disposed of only in a manner approved by the governmental authority having jurisdiction.

Housekeeping is a prime concern where flammable and volatile solvents are used. Hence, housekeeping measures should be regularly reviewed and upgrading should take place whenever indications are that housekeeping methods have deteriorated.

Table 8-C. Properties of Common Solvents

Solvent	Boiling Point (Deg. F)	Flash Point (Deg. F closed cup.)	Explosive Limits (% by vol. in air)		ACGIH '87/'88 Threshold Limit Values (Parts of vapor per million parts of air)
			Lower	Upper	
Acetone	133	1.4	2.6	12.8	750
Benzene	176.2	12	1.4	7.1	10*
Carbon tetrachloride	171	None	—	—	5*
Freon/(Trichloroflurometháne)	118	None	—	—	C 1000
Gasoline (Octane)	258	56	1	6.5	300
Isopropyl alcohol (99%)	181	53	2.0	12.0	400
Methanol	148.1	52	6.7	36	200
Methyl-ethyl ketone	176	21	2	11.5	200
Mineral spirits/Stoddard	220-300	100	.8	6	100
Perchlorethylene	250	None	—	—	50
Toluene	232	40	1.4	6.7	100
Trichloroethylene	189	None at B.P.	8	10.5	50
1,1,1 Trichloroethane/(Methyl chloroform)	165	None	8	10.5	350
Turpentine	302-356	95	0.8	—	100
m-Xylene	282	85	1.1	7	100

Source: 1987/1988 Threshold Limit Values from American Conference of Governmental Industrial Hygienists. Explosive Limits from *NIOSH Pocket Guide to Chemical Hazards,* Pub. No. 85-114, 1985, and NFPA 49, 1987.

*Listed as suspected human carcinogens.

C = Ceiling Value.

If possible, operations with volatile solvents should be isolated. Prolonged exposure to levels above the allowable limit should be avoided through methods discussed earlier and through administrative controls. Workers are to wear appropriate personal protective equipment when necessary.

If spills occur, workers should remove the exposed clothing quickly and thoroughly wash the exposed skin. Contaminated clothing should be laundered or discarded, depending on the contaminant material. Workers handling solvents should wash their hands before eating or drinking. Smoking should not be allowed around volatile chemicals as a matter of course. (For additional information, see, in References, Part 1910 of *Occupational and Safety Health Standards* listed under U.S. Department of Labor.)

Solvent Disposal

Flammable wastes should not be dumped into public sewage or drainage systems. In case of accidental spills into public sewage or drainage systems, copious amounts of water should be used to flush the system. The appropriate governing authority and the local department should be notified.

Solid flammable materials contaminated by flammable liquids should be placed in covered metal containers designed for this purpose and removed from work areas daily. Waste flammable liquids may also be saved and later burned in fire-fighting training exercises by the airport's private fire department *if* permitted by local regulations.

In any event, wastes should be disposed of properly. If not by burning in accord with local regulations, wastes should be disposed of by a reputable EPA-registered contractor. Wastes awaiting disposal should be stored properly.

Compressed Gases

The following gases are used in aviation:

- Acetylene, hydrogen, argon, and helium, used for welding
- Oxygen, for breathing and welding
- Nitrogen, for tire and strut inflation and as a fire-extinguishing propellant.

Other agents include:

- Carbon dioxide, a fire-extinguishing agent
- Refrigerant 12 (dichlorodifluoromethane), a refrigerant
- Refrigerant 1301 (bromotrifluoromethane), a fire-extinguishing agent
- Compressed air, for emergency equipment on aircraft and many other uses
- Liquified petroleum gas (butane and propane), a fuel used for motor vehicles, torches, burners, and heaters.

See Table 8-D for a list of common gases and their properties.

Pressurized cylinders may contain pressures up to 41,500 kPa (6,000 psi). A direct relationship exists between temperature and pressure. Most cylinders are designed and constructed according to U.S. Department of Transportation regulations and should bear the DOT, American Society of Mechanical Engineers (ASME), or equivalent cylinder stampings, found near the neck of the cylinder. Some cylinders have reinspection and hydrostatic testing dates stamped in the same place.

Cylinder contents should be legibly marked on each cylinder.

Table 8-D. Cylinder Data for Commonly Used Gases

Gas	Chemical Symbol	Usual Cylinder Pressure at 70 F psi	Capacity of Typical Cylinders		Calculated Density at 32 F (0 C) and atmospheric pressure (air = 1.00)	Fire Hazard
			cu ft	lb		
Acetylene	C_2H_2	250	300	22	0.91	Severe
Air, compressed	....	1600-3600	200	15	1.0	None
Argon	A	1600-2000	200	21	1.38	None
Butane	C_4H_{10}	19	780	122	1.87	Severe
Carbon dioxide	CO_2	830	440	50	1.53	None
Bromotrifluoromethane (Refrigerant 1301)	$CBrF_3$	200	26	10	4.77	None
Dichlorodifluoromethane (Refrigerant 12)	CCl_2F_2	70	435	145	4.17	None
Helium	He	1600-2000	200	2.2	0.138	None
Hydrogen	H_2	1600-2000	200	1.0	0.069	Severe
Nitrogen	N_2	1600-3600	225	16	0.97	None
Oxygen	O_2	1600-3000	245	20	1.11	Intensifies
Propane	C_3H_8	110	850	100	1.56	Severe

Serious accidents with compressed gases can generally be traced to misuse, abuse, or mishandling of the gas, cylinder, or related equipment.

Inside cylinder storage areas should be clean and free from excessive heat. Flammable gases should be stored separately from other gases, and oxygen should be stored separately from flammable gases.

Storage areas should have effective natural ventilation or listed mechanical ventilation appropriate to the exposure. The buoyancy of the gas in storage areas helps determine the proper ventilation. Gases lighter than air should be exhausted at the top while gases heavier than air should be exhausted at floor level.

In storage areas, cylinders of one type should not be mixed with other types of cylinders. Floors should be level and constructed of noncombustible materials.

Outside storage requires all the protection afforded by the inside storage facility, plus a noncombustible canopy to protect cylinders from weather.

Cylinders should stand upright, with the valve up, especially those of acetylene. Empty cylinders should be stored apart from full cylinders and the word EMPTY or the letters MT chalked in large letters on them. Valves should be closed and protective caps installed. Storage areas should be free of ignition sources, including smoking materials.

The authority having jurisdiction should be consulted about flammable gas storage. The storage area should be provided with chains (or similar devices) to keep cylinders from being knocked over. Areas near elevators, stairs, or ramps should not be used for storage. Storage of cylinders should facilitate their being used in the order which they are received.

Newly delivered cylinders should be checked for DOT or ASME stampings, condition, valve, and content labeling.

All compressed gas cylinders should be visually inspected for defects such as excessive rusting or dents. Cylinders with rust, dents, or missing protective caps should not be accepted from the supplier.

Valves or safety devices must not be tampered with. A leaking cylinder should be taken outside the building and tagged as defective. Leaking cylinders should never be accepted from a supplier.

Because of their shape and weight, most cylinders are difficult to handle manually. However, if such handling is necessary, they should be tipped slightly and rolled on the bottom edge—not dragged or slid across the floor. Mechanical handling generally requires carts or specially constructed skids. Using electromagnets or slings is not acceptable for mechanical handling. Inserting bars through the protective caps may damage valve assembly. *Bars should not be used.*

Cylinders should not be dropped or permitted to strike each other. They should not be used as rollers or for any purpose other than gas containers. A direct flame or arc must never be permitted to contact a cylinder.

Before compressed gas cylinders are connected to a system valve, outlets on all cylinders should be cleared, *except for cylinders containing hydrogen or toxic gases.* The valve should be pointed away from the body and away from other people, then opened slightly to release foreign material.

The compressed gas cylinder should never be used without a pressure-reducing regulator attached to the valve. If cylinders are in a manifold, the regulator should be attached to the manifold header. There are regulators and pressure gauges designed for use with a specific gas. Only those regulators and pressure gauges designed for the specific type of gas should be used. No one should attempt to force connections that do not fit easily. A Compressed Gas Association standard specifies various size threads for cylinders containing different gases; some have left-hand threads to frustrate any attempt to use a wrong regulator (see References). If a leak develops between the cylinder and regulator, the gas should be shut off at the bottle before attempting to tighten the union.

All compressed gas valves should be opened slowly to prevent sudden surges of pressure that may damage regulators. An oxygen valve, for example, should be opened slowly to prevent surge and possible fire, then opened fully to gain the sealing benefit of the double-seated valve. Valves on acetylene cylinders should be opened approximately one-and-one-half turns. The special tool recommended by the supplier should be the only tool used for these valves. The tool is to be left on the valve so that the gas can be quickly shut off in an emergency. Compressed gas cylinder valves should be closed when gas is not being withdrawn.

When high- and low-pressure taps are used on the same cylinder, hoses should be of different colors, and fittings on the hose ends should be of a different type and size.

Oil and grease should *never* be used as a lubricant for oxygen cylinders or appurtenances because an explosion may result. Oxygen cylinders and fittings should be kept away from oil and grease, and such cylinders or apparatus should not be handled with oily hands, gloves, or clothing. Workers should wash and thoroughly rinse their hands before handling oxygen cylinders or systems. Oxygen should never be used as a substitute for compressed air in pneumatic tools or for any unapproved purpose.

Cylinders must not be taken into tanks or other unventilated areas.

Manifolds for compressed gas cylinders should be a type approved by the gas supplier or the appropriate standards and specification group, such as the Compressed Gas Association or the NFPA.

Connections should be tested for tightness with conventional leak testing products. Testing for leaks by an open flame is prohibited.

Bottled oxygen and nitrogen are produced under rigid quality controls; however, as cylinders are rotated from one industry to another, contamination may result. Although such occurrences are rare, consequences are severe. If there is any suspicion of contamination, contact the supplier of the cylinder.

OTHER HAZARDOUS MATERIALS AND PROCESSES

Aviation employees may be exposed to other hazardous materials and processes, such as noise, poor lighting conditions, radiations, and explosive devices used to activate aircraft fire protection systems.

Noise

Noise can affect employees in several ways:

- Hearing loss
- Shift in hearing threshold
- Fatigue and irritability
- Communications interference
- Increased blood pressure.

Noise exposures are prevalent throughout the aircraft industry. Potentially damaging levels are common. All companies should install a hearing conservation program. The program should include at least the following:

- Sound level measurements to determine which areas exceed acceptable limits
- Medical surveillance—preplacement, periodic, and postemployment—by audiometric examination
- Noise control/reduction programs
- Administrative controls for employees in noise areas
- Personal hearing protection
- Employee training and education.

Noise control principles and techniques are varied and sophisticated. See Chapter 9, Personal Protective Equipment and Guarding, for more information on noise control. Also see, in References for this chapter, National Safety Council *Noise Control Manual,* American Industrial Hygiene Association *Noise and Hearing Conservation Manual,* NIOSH *Industrial Noise Control Manual* under U.S. Department of Health and Human Resources, and the American Petroleum Institute "Guidelines on Noise."

For severe noise control problems, a professional consultant might be engaged.

Nonionizing Radiation

Nonionizing radiation refers to that portion of the electromagnetic spectrum where energies of emitted photons are insufficient to disrupt absorbing molecules. Included in this portion of the spectrum are microwave energy, ultraviolet, visible, and infrared radiation. Sources of microwave radiation in the airline industry include radar, telecommunications, and high frequency heating. Ultraviolet, visible, and infrared sources include welding, plasma spray, lasers, and high temperature heated sources.

Depending on wavelength, the effects of nonionizing radiation (except for ordinary visible light) can be harmful: Microwave energy can cause thermal damage to eyes, testes, and the central nervous system; lasers can cause damage to the retina; infrared can cause heat stress; ultraviolet can result in photochemical effects to the eye and skin, skin cancer, and photosensitivity. (See Michaelson in References for a review of nonionizing radiation health problems and "Nonionizing Radiation," Chapter 11 in the National Safety Council *Fundamentals of Industrial Hygiene.)*

Microwave Ovens. Microwave oven use is well established. Depending upon their age and amount of use, ovens can leak microwave energy in excess of the 5 milliwatts per square centimeter (5 mW/cm^2) allowed as noted in ANSI C95.1. (See References.) It is good practice to check ovens periodically for leakage. Commercial instruments are available for this purpose. After a defective oven has been removed from service and repaired, another check for microwave leakage is recommended.

Lighting. Poor lighting (glare, low, or uneven light intensity) can cause eyestrain or low efficiency. (See *Illuminating Engineering Society Lighting Handbook*, listed in References, for detailed information on recommended lighting levels, lighting parameters, and equipment specifications.)

Ionizing Radiation

Some nondestructive testing operations use radioactive isotopes and x-radiographic equipment to examine critical aircraft parts. If the radioactive source is large enough, these operations must conform to requirements of the Nuclear Regulatory Commission (NRC) and/or other governmental regulations. A qualified safety officer should be assigned responsibility for radioactive materials and the handling and monitoring of x-ray-producing equipment.

Components like electron tubes, spark gaps, and luminescent signs contain radioactive material. The NRC and other authorities having jurisdiction have established standards for handling, storage, use, and disposition of radioactive materials. Local procedures should conform to these standards.

The quantity of radioactive materials contained in units like those previously mentioned is such that no significant external radiation hazard exists when handled singly or in small numbers. The most severe hazard would be encountered if one or more units broke down. For this reason, units should be stored in their packing containers. Units should remain in these containers until used as replacements, and then the replaced unit should be returned to the container. No radioactive component should be disassembled or discarded at random. Maintenance procedures must include instructions for returning units that need repair or maintenance to the supplier or distributor. Disposition of unserviceable units as well as those broken down should conform to governmental regulations.

Shipments of radioactive materials in airfreight present another potential source of exposure to ionizing radiation if breakage and spillage occur. Federal Aviation Administration and Department of Transportation regulations as detailed in *Dangerous Goods Regulations* must be complied with (see References).

A 1976 study of exposures from such shipments was performed by Harvard University under a contract from the NRC. (See U.S. Nuclear Regulatory Commission Report in References). A copy was provided all Air Transport Association of America member companies. A written procedure should be available detailing handling requirements and emergency procedures in the event that a spillage or suspected spillage occurs. (For additional information, see, in References, ANSI/NBS 114, EPA "The Effects on Populations . . . ," and Technical Operations *Isotope Radiography.*)

Explosive Devices

Presently there are two types of explosive devices used to activate aircraft fire protection systems. One device, commonly called an "initiator," is used to release the extinguishing system in the fuel tank's vents or wing surge tanks. These initiators resemble a blasting cap and, when not connected to an extinguisher, are subject to handling and storage procedures compatible with all laws and ordinances applicable to explosives and blasting devices.

Initiators must be packaged individually and the package certified to sustain and contain detonation of one initiator within an explosive atmosphere. All packages should be sealed with wires and/or lead seals or similar devices.

Initiators used or unused should remain packaged in the portable magazine while being stored and transported intraplant and interfield. Magazines should be painted red, the standard explosive label should be affixed to them, and the shelf life date marked on the container's exterior surface.

Provisions should be made to ensure safe disposition of units whose shelf life has expired. Shelf life should mean the period from date stamped on the unit or its nameplate.

Another explosive device is called a "squib." This unit has the force of a .45-caliber shell and is used for activating the engine fire-extinguishing system. Their shipping is governed by International Air Transport Association Regulation #1687, Note 200. (See References.) The units are packaged in quantities of one each for storage and issue purposes. When the shelf life of these units has expired, safe disposition is required. Often, local police authority will accept these units for safe disposition. They should not be disposed of with local trash.

REFERENCES

American Conference of Governmental Industrial Hygienists, 6500 Glenway Ave., Bldg. D-7, Cincinnati, OH 54211.
Industrial Ventilation.
Air Sampling Instruments.

American Industrial Hygiene Association, 475 Wolf Ledges Parkway, Akron, OH 44311.
Noise and Hearing Conservation Manual, 4th Ed., 1986.
Hygienic Guide Series.

American National Standards Institute, 1430 Broadway, New York, NY 10018.
Electromagnetic Fields, Safety Levels with Respect to Personnel Safety, ANSI C95.1-1982.
Installation Using Non-Medical X-ray and Sealed Gamma-Ray Sources, Energies Up to MeV, General Safety Standards for, ANSI/NBS 114.
Practices for Respiratory Protection, ANSI Z88.2-1980.

American Petroleum Institute, 1220 L St. N.W., Washington, D.C. 20005.
"Guidelines on Noise," Medical Research Report EA-7301.

Chemical Manufacturers Association, 1001 Connecticut N.W., Washington, D.C. 20036.

Compressed Gas Association, 1235 Jefferson Davis Hwy., Arlington, VA 22202.

Dangerous Goods Regulations, International Air Transport Association, 2000 Peel St., Montreal, Canada H3A 2R4, published annually.

Environmental Protection Agency, 401 M St. S.W., Washington, D.C. 20460.
"The Effects on Populations of Exposure to Low Levels of Ionizing Radiation" (BIER Report). Published by Office of Radiation Programs. Available from Criterion Standards Division AW-460.
"Toxic Substances Control Act."

Hamilton and Hardy, *Industrial Toxicology,* Publishing Sciences Group Inc., 1984.

Illuminating Engineering Society of North America, 345 E. 47th St., New York, NY 10017.
IES Lighting Handbook.

International Air Transport Association, IATA Building, 2000 Peel Street, Montreal, PQ, Canada H3A, 2R4.

Michaelson, Sol, "Standards for Protection of Personnel against Nonionizing Radiation," *American Industrial Hygiene Association Journal,* 35:766 (1974).

National Fire Protection Association, Batterymarch Park, Quincy, MA 02269.

National Loss Control Service Corporation, Long Grove, IL 60049.
Right to Know Compliance Manual.

National Safety Council, 444 N. Michigan Ave., Chicago, IL 60611.
Fundamentals of Industrial Hygiene, 3rd ed., 1988.
Noise Control Manual.

Patty's Industrial Hygiene and Toxicology: Toxicology, vol. 2A, 1981; vol. 2B, 1981; vol. 2C, 1982. John Wiley and Sons, Westport, CT.

Sax, Irving N., *Dangerous Properties of Industrial Materials,* 6th ed., Van Nostrand Reinhold, 1984.

"Suspected Carcinogens—Subfile of the Toxic Substances List," U.S. Government Printing Office, Washington, D.C. 20402.

Technical Operations, Inc., Radiation Products Division, Northwest Industrial Park, Burlington, MA 01803.

Isotope Radiography, Radiation Safety Handbook.

U.S. Department of Health and Human Resources, National Institute for Occupational Safety and Health (NIOSH), Cincinnati, OH 45226.

Industrial Noise Control Manual.

NIOSH-Certified Personal Protective Equipment.

U.S. Department of Labor, Occupational Safety and Health Administration (OSHA), Washington, D.C. 20212.

Occupational Safety and Health Standards in *Code of Federal Regulations,* Title 29, Part 1910.

U.S. Nuclear Regulatory Commission, Washington, D.C. 20555.

Exposure of Airport Workers to Radiation from Shipments of Radioactive Materials: A Review of Studies Conducted at Six Major Airports, Feb. 17, 1976.

N7015U
FLAMMABLE
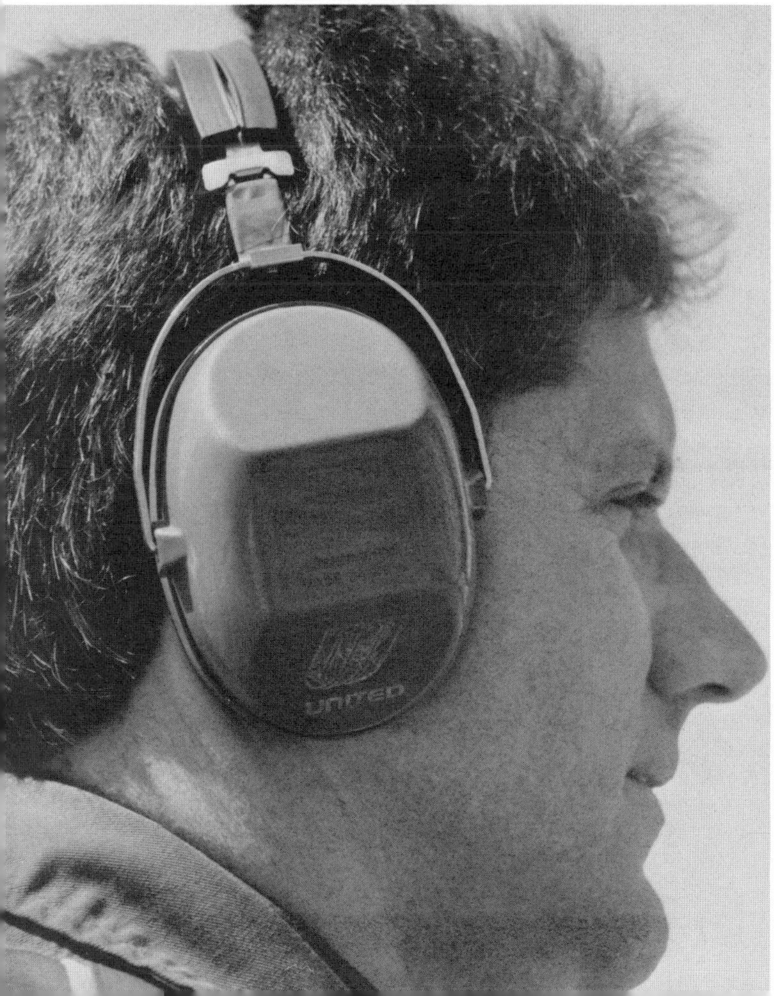
UNITED

CHAPTER 9

Personal Protective Equipment and Guarding

Top: A lift with side guardrails provides fall protection for a worker being raised to the aircraft wing.

Lower left: In areas where noise hazard exists, personnel must wear muffs or the type of hearing protection prescribed by management.

Lower right: A guardrail provides support for personnel who must mount the baggage conveyor ramp.

Courtesy United Airlines; photos by Mike Sroka.

Employees need and are required to use protective equipment when hazards or environmental conditions call for it. Chemical hazards, radiological hazards, and mechanical irritants are capable of causing injury or impairments to bodily function. They can affect the eyes, ears, respiratory system, head, face, hands, trunk, or feet through absorption, inhalation, or physical contact.

Directors, managers, and supervisors should evaluate their operations to determine what substances or operations are potentially hazardous. Correcting potential hazards may involve one or more of the following (the order of this list is an OSHA recommendation and may not be accepted worldwide):

1. Elimination
2. Substitution
3. Engineering control
4. Administrative controls
5. Personal protective equipment.

These control measures were discussed in Chapter 8, Hazardous Materials and Processes. This chapter focuses on personal protective equipment and guarding.

PERSONAL PROTECTIVE EQUIPMENT

Certain general principles should govern the selection of personal protective equipment. The equipment should be appropriate for the environment in which it is being used. For example, it would not be appropriate to provide acid handlers with the same kind of leather and asbestos apron worn by a welder. Nor would one furnish a welder with a rubber and plastic outfit suitable for acid handlers.

Personal protective equipment and clothing

should fit the user, do its job well, and cause minimum discomfort. All three factors should be considered if the equipment is to provide maximum effectiveness.

Eye and Face Protection

All work areas and specific jobs which create flying particles, harmful liquid splashes, or harmful rays should be identified. All persons exposed to these hazards should be required to wear proper eye or face protection (Figure 9-1).

In some cases, an entire work area (such as one in which a number of machine tools or chemical tanks are located) should be classified as a mandatory eye protection area. In other cases, eye protection may be required only for the employee performing a particular operation (such as deburring parts on a bench or pedestal-mounted belt sander).

Losing an eye may be costly under workers' compensation laws; and, losing a skilled worker's services can result in additional cost, but neither can compare to the cost to the injured employee.

If workers need corrective lenses, they may use prescription safety spectacles or goggles. Standard safety goggles that cover ordinary spectacles may also be worn, but they require cups that are deep and wide enough to accommodate the entire eyeglass area. Face shields are normally designed to provide protection for the face (that is, the front part of the head including forehead, cheeks, nose, mouth, chin and neck) but not for the eyes. Therefore, such devices should be worn over suitable, basic eye protection.

Applicable standards are in the ANSI *Occupational and Educational Eye and Face Protection.* (See References.) Note that occasionally inappropriate or deficient personal protective devices are sold as standard protective eyewear. To avoid mistakes in purchasing, be sure that the current ANSI standard is the one with which the manufacturer or supplier complies.

Figure 9-1. Employee protective eyewear should be suitable to the task being performed.

Hearing Protection

The use of hearing protection equipment is mandated in some countries, depending on employee exposure. In the United States, for example, employers are responsible for developing a hearing conservation program when worker exposure equals or exceeds an 8-hour time weighted average (TWA) sound level of 85 decibels, A scale (dBA), or an exposure of 50%.

In the United States, other OSHA requirements provide that employers:

- Monitor work environment noise exposure to identify exposure areas of 85 dBA or more.
- Make hearing protection available for all workers in exposure areas of 85–90 dBA.
- Enforce hearing protection use when worker exposure exceeds 90 dBA.
- Monitor additional noise exposure if a reasonable possibility exists that operational changes or employee exposures have increased to the point where other employees would need to be included in the hearing conservation program.
- Provide baseline audiograms for workers exposed to noise, as required for hearing conservation program development. (This includes workers transferred from a nonexposure area to an exposure area.)
- Notify each employee exposed at or above 85 dBA, preferably in writing.

Hearing conservation program development should include the items indicated above. In summary, include at least the following management considerations.:

- Sound level measurements to determine which areas exceed acceptable limits
- Medical surveillance—preplacement, periodic, and postemployment—by audiometric examination

- Noise control/reduction programs
- Administrative controls for employees in noise areas
- Personal hearing protection
- Employee training and education.

Guidelines for permissible noise exposures are standardized in Table 9-A.

Impact noise exposure should not exceed 140 dBA.

Daily noise exposure changes, with two or more noise exposure periods of different levels, can be calculated as follows: If the total of the following fractions

$$C_1/T_1 + C_2/T_2 + \dots C_n/T_n$$

is greater than one, the mixed exposures have exceeded the limit value.

C_n = total time of exposure at a designated noise level
T_n = total exposure time permitted
C_1, C_2 = individual sample exposure times
T_1, T_2 = exposure times permitted at the designated level

Where hearing protective devices are used, the degree of protection required must be the prime consideration, but employee acceptance and comfort versus cost should also be evaluated. Hearing protective devices, whether plugs or muffs, are available in and sold with a designated noise reduction rating (NRR). Obviously, the NRR is one more factor to be considered—exposure largely dictates selecting proper protection. Sometimes, in severe exposure areas, a worker may be required to wear both a plug and a muff.

Properly used, ear plugs and ear muffs individually may reduce noise reaching the ear by up to 29 dBA.

For additional information on the subject, refer to *Noise Control Manual,* 29 CFR, Part 1910, and *Principles and Techniques of Mechanical Guarding.* (See References). This information supplies basic knowledge on the subject of hearing protection and the effects and control of noise. For profound noise control problems, a professional consultant might be engaged.

Head Protection

Employees who work in areas where heavy objects are being handled overhead should be required to wear hard hats that comply with ANSI Z89.1. (See References.) Some operations permit the use of protective headgear known as a bump cap, a thin-shelled, lightweight plastic cap. Originally conceived for aircraft workers performing operations within the confines of a fuselage, it is not standard protective headgear. There are no specifications covering bump caps. Authorities warn that, although they are used for some applications, they are not a substitute for hard hats.

Table 9-A. Permissible Noise Exposure

Duration Per Day (Hours)	Sound Level dBA (Slow Response)
8	90
6	92
4	95
3	97
2	100
1½	102
1	105
½	110
¼ or less	115

Respiratory Protection

Engineering measures, such as ventilation, should be used to control occupational diseases caused by breathing air contaminants. Air may be fouled by harmful dusts, fogs, fumes, gases, smoke, sprays, or vapors. When engineering controls are not feasible, appropriate respirators should be used. Respiratory protective devices fall into three classes: air-purifying, air-supplied, and self-contained breathing apparatus. Only personal protective equipment that conforms to published standards should be used. Its use should be under control of someone knowledgeable on the subject. (See ANSI Z88.2 and the NIOSH standards in References.)

Air-Purifying Devices. Air-purifying devices remove contaminants from the atmosphere. They can be used only in atmospheres containing sufficient oxygen to sustain life (at least 16% of volume at sea level) and within the specified concentration limitations of the specific device. Air-purifying devices operate in one or both of these ways: Various chemicals remove specific gases and vapors, and/or mechanical filters remove particulate matter. The useful life of an air-purifying device is dependent upon contaminant concentration, wearer-breathing volume, and air-purifying-medium capacity.

Mechanical filter respirators provide respiratory protection against particulate matter such as nonvolatile dusts, mists, or metal fumes. Selecting the appropriate respirator is based on type, toxicity, and size of particulate matter.

Chemical cartridge respirators provide respiratory protection against certain gases and vapors in concentrations not in excess of 0.1%.

Combinations of chemical cartridge and mechanical filter respirators provide respiratory protection where exposure is both gaseous and particulate.

Gas masks provide respiratory protection against certain specific gases and vapors in concentrations up to 2% or as specified on the canister label, as well as against particulate matter.

Air-Supplied Devices. Air-supplied devices deliver breathing air through a supply hose connected to the wearer's facepiece. Air delivered must be free of contaminants (including oil from the compressor). The air source must be located in clean air and automatically monitored. With the exception of hose masks with blowers, these devices should be used only in atmospheres not immediately dangerous to life. Basic types of supplied-air devices are air-line respirators with constant flow or demand flow and hose masks with or without blower.

Self-Contained Breathing Apparatus. Self-contained breathing apparatus provide complete breathing protection for various periods of time based on the amount of breathing air or oxygen supplied and the breathing demand of the wearer. Basic self-contained breathing apparatus include the oxygen cylinder rebreathing type and the chemical oxygen rebreathing type (self-generating or oxygen-demand). Although proper selection depends upon the application and service time required, complete respiratory protection is provided and the problem of proper protection for a specified hazard is eliminated.

How and When to Use Each Type. Selecting proper respiratory equipment should be based on the following:

- Identify substance or substances that mandate protection.
- Know the hazards and significant properties of each substance, as related on the Material Safety Data Sheet (MSDS).
- Determine exposure conditions and air-contaminant levels.
- Ascertain whether any human capabilities and limitations are essential to safe use.
- Fit the respirator to each worker carefully and instruct workers in its use and upkeep.

One limitation applies to all respiratory protective equipment. Certain gases can harm the body by means other than through the respiratory tract. For example, ammonia, in concentrations of approximately 3% or higher, can cause skin burns (particularly on moist skin). To avoid that possibility, impervious clothing may be required in addition to proper respiratory protection.

Similarly, protective clothing should be worn when appreciable amounts of gases such as hydrocyanic acid are present. Hydrocyanic acid—a vapor at slightly above room temperature—is capable of penetrating skin and causing systemic poisoning. To do so, however, concentrations must be considerably higher than those required for poisoning through the respiratory tract.

There should be a continuous, documented program of respirator inspection, cleaning and disinfecting, repair, and storage, as well as training for all employees who use respiratory protective equipment.

Skin Protection

Employees exposed to skin irritants need to keep high standards of personal cleanliness. Good hygiene helps reduce dermatitis and should be monitored. Employees should be instructed as to how and when to wash. The type of soap they use is important, since even a generally mild soap may cause skin irritation. The choice of soap is best left to the medical department or others who are qualified.

Skin creams and lotions offer some protection against various chemicals, solvents, and fuels used in the aviation industry. However, their value is limited. If other protective devices can be used, creams and lotions should only be used to back up the basic protection. Water and soluble products should be used when workers handle aqueous solutions. Solvent and soluble protective barrier creams should be used when workers handle solvents. Sometimes emollient creams will be needed to replace natural oils and fats removed from the skin.

Special Work Clothing

Protection of the entire body or portions of the body is often required because of exposures to extremely high or low temperatures, corrosive chemicals, and other hazards. Basic types of protective clothing are listed below.

Gloves. There are many types of gloves that provide protection from a variety of hazards. The selection, use, and care of gloves depends entirely upon the type and degree of hazard. Workers should not wear gloves while working with drills, saws, grinders, or other rotating or moving machinery.

Cold Weather Clothing. Such clothing is to be selected and fitted to meet applicable working conditions and temperature extremes.

High Visibility and Night-Hazard Clothing. These garments are necessary and should be required for those employees exposed to traffic hazards (Figure 9-2).

Impervious Clothing. For protection against dusts, vapors, moisture, corrosive liquids (such as battery acid), impacts, cuts, and other hazards, impervious clothing appropriate to the specific hazard must be worn. Such clothing ranges from aprons and bibs to a garment that completely encloses the body.

Safety Shoes. Safety shoes should be worn by all employees where there is a reasonable probability of foot injury. Good judgment should also be exercised when selecting safety shoes. Some types will deteriorate rapidly when exposed to fire-resistant

Courtesy Federal Express.

Figure 9-2. Retro-reflective striping is recommended for the outerwear of ramp employees.

hydraulic fluids; others will not. Therefore, it is important to obtain manufacturer's specifications before buying. The sole and heel composition should be examined. Some shoes become slippery when exposed to fluids and rain.

PROTECTIVE GUARDING

Protective guarding for preventing injuries to employees who are using machinery or equipment falls into three basic categories:

- Point-of-operation guarding
- Power-transmission guarding
- Walking and working surface guarding.

Point of operation is defined as that area on a machine where the material is positioned for processing or change by the machine.

Power transmission is defined as mechanical components such as gears, cams, shafts, pulleys, belts, rods, and other parts that transmit energy and motion from the power source to the point of operation.

Effective guarding of machinery prevents accidents, whether to people or equipment, and thus facilitates production goals. One or more methods of guarding are usually provided to protect the operator and other employees from hazards such as those created by point of operation, ingoing nip points, shear points, rotating parts, flying objects, power transmission, and walking and working surfaces. (See the U.S. Department of Labor *Principles and Techniques of Mechanical Guarding* and the National Safety Council *Accident Prevention Manual for Industrial Operations* and *Safeguarding Concepts Illustrated* listed in the References.)

Machinery and Equipment Guarding

There are three accepted methods of preventing workers from contacting moving machinery parts or equipment that could cause physical harm. They are:

- Enclosure guarding
- Interlock guarding
- Automatic guarding.

Enclosure guarding prevents access to dangerous parts of machinery by enclosing the area of hazardous operations completely. The enclosure guards will admit stock but will not admit hands into the danger zone. Such guards also prevent user contact with rotating, reciprocating, and transverse motions of mechanical components.

Interlock guarding may be used when a fixed enclosure guard is not practical. This safeguard is not fixed and may be opened or removed as the operation requires. However, because of an electrical or mechanical interlocking connection with the operating mechanism, the machine cannot operate until the guard is returned to an operating position and the worker can no longer reach the point of danger.

When neither an enclosure guard nor an interlocking guard is practical, an automatic guard may be used. This safeguard acts independently of the operator and will repeat its cycle as long as the machine is in motion. Its purpose is to remove the operator's hands, arms, or any other part of the body from the danger zone created by the movement of the machine parts or the tooling at the point of operation.

Guarding of Walking and Working Surfaces

Open-sided floors, work platforms, walkways, and other surfaces located 1.2 m (4 ft) or more above the adjacent floor or ground level should be guarded by a standard railing and toeboard, except when there is an entrance to a ramp, stairway, or fixed ladder. In the United States, standard railing construction consists of a top rail, an intermediate rail, and posts. The top rail vertical height is 1.07 m (42 in.) nominal from the upper surface of the top rail to the floor. The intermediate rail is to be approximately halfway between the top rail and the floor. Various types and sizes of railing are acceptable if they are strong enough to withstand a pressure of at least 890 newtons (200 lb) applied to the top rail from any direction. Required floor openings such as those used at hatchways or chutes should be guarded either by hinged covers or removable railings. (See ANSI A12.1 in References.)

REFERENCES

American Industrial Hygiene Associaton, 475 Wolf Ledges Parkway, Akron, OH 44311.

Industrial Noise Manual.

American National Standards Institute, 1430 Broadway, New York, NY 10018.

Floor and Wall Openings, Railings, and Toeboards, ANSI A12.1-1973.

Industrial Workers, Protective Headwear for, ANSI Z89.1-1986.

Occupational and Educational Eye and Face Protection, ANSI Z87.1-1979.

Practices for Respiratory Protection, ANSI Z88.2-1980.

Safety-Toe Footwear, ANSI Z41.1-1983.

National Safety Council, 444 N. Michigan Ave., Chicago, IL 60611.

Accident Prevention Manual for Industrial Operations, 9th ed., 1988.

Fundamentals of Industrial Hygiene, 3rd ed., 1988.

Noise Control Manual.

Safeguarding Concepts Illustrated. 5th ed., 1987.

U.S. Department of Health and Human Resources, National Institute for Occupational Safety and Health (NIOSH), Cincinnati, OH 45226.

NIOSH-Certified Personal Protective Equipment.

U.S. Department of Labor, Occupational Safety and Health Administration (OSHA), Washington, D.C. 20212.

Occupational Safety and Health Standards in *Code of Federal Regulations,* Title 29, Part 1910.

Subpart G, Occupational Health and Environmental Control (1910.24-1910.1000)

Subpart I, Personal Protective Equipment (1910.132-1910.140).

Principles and Techniques of Mechanical Guarding, Publication No. 2057-1973.

NIGHT 9-911 NIGHT
1. Give Address
Floor
DAY
Floor Location
JOB SAFETY & HEALTH PROTECTION
The Occupational Safety and Health Act of 1970 provides job safety and health protection for workers by promoting safe and healthful working conditions throughout the Nation. Requirements of the Act include the following:
Employers
Employees
Inspection
Complaint
Citation
Proposed Penalty
Voluntary Activity
Consultation
More Information
U.S. Department of Labor

American
653
10

CHAPTER 10

Accident Investigations, Reports, and Records

Top: The OSHA 200 form should be posted on an employee bulletin board.

Bottom: All accidents should be investigated as soon as possible after the occurrence.

Bottom photo courtesy City of Chicago Fire Department; photo by Mike Sroka.

In any discussion of accident investigations, it is necessary to define the word *accident*. An accident is any unexpected event that interrupts an operation. Accidents do not necessarily result in injury or damage; they are always preceded by inadequate procedures, unsafe conditions, or both.

The purpose of an accident investigation is to determine the causes of an accident, develop corrective measures, and make recommendations for elimination of the causes.

ACCIDENT INVESTIGATION

Thorough accident investigation is crucial to a good safety program because it provides the necessary information for preventing similar accidents.

Gathering Information

One question often asked is, "Which accidents should be investigated?" Because *all* accidents are potentially serious, *all* should be investigated. Here are some other basic guidelines for accident investigation.

Who Should Make the Investigation? The person or persons investigating the accident should have some knowledge of all the circumstances surrounding the accident: the work process, the equipment, the employee involved in the accident, and accident sources and causes. The person who most completely meets this criterion is usually the immediate supervisor of the employee involved in the accident.

The health and safety director, the safety committee, or an insurance company representative may also assist in the investigation—or perform a supplementary investigation.

When Should the Investigation Be Made? The investigation should be made as soon as possible. Delays—even of only a few hours—can permit information or items of importance to be removed, destroyed, or forgotten.

If possible, every employee who is involved in, or is a witness to, the incident should be questioned. It is important that employees being questioned know that the purpose of the investigation is not to find fault or blame—it is to find the cause in order to prevent similar accidents.

The investigator should try to avoid jumping to conclusions: It is very important that he or she uncover the underlying or root causes of the accident. The investigator must ascertain *why* an unsafe condition existed or *why* the unsafe procedure occurred. Simply finding or identifying unsafe conditions is not enough. An apparently reasonable conclusion about the cause of an accident will often be changed when facts that did not first appear to be important are explored.

While gathering accident facts, the investigator should encourage employees to give their ideas on how the accident could have been prevented.

Preparing an Accident Report

Once the investigation of an accident has been performed, a report should be prepared that describes the findings in detail. The report should answer all questions pertinent to the accident and list the corrective actions to prevent a recurrence. The person preparing the report should follow these rules:

- Stick to the facts.
- Weigh the value of the facts.
- Reach justified conclusions.

The questions in the following section should be a helpful guideline to whoever writes the report:

Who Was Involved? Accidents usually involve more than just the injured person. Very often more than just a single person contributed to the cause of an accident. Therefore, the investigation should go beyond just the person or persons directly involved. It should also be determined who directed the employee to perform the particular job function, who trained the employee, and who failed to report an unsafe condition or procedure.

Where Did the Accident Occur? Again, the investigator must look beyond the obvious. The name of the department is not enough. A detailed description of the accident site should be included. Also, the investigator should determine if the people involved were supposed to be where they were. Was the equipment in its proper location?

What Happened? This question can be further broken down to uncover the following facts:

1. *What was being done?* The answer describes an action or procedure.
2. *What things were involved?* The answer could be a description of the tool, material, or equipment that was involved.
3. *What was the result?* This is answered by describing the actual injury, including the nature of injury and the part of the body injured, and/or detailing the equipment and property damage.

When Did the Accident Occur? The answer to this question requires more than just recording the date. The time of day and the day of the week can also be very important. Other questions that may be asked are: Did the accident occur at the beginning or end of a shift? Was it early or late in the day, and when did the employee start working? What were the light conditions or weather conditions (if applicable) at the time of the accident?

How Did the Accident Happen? The answer to this question brings together all the facts of the accident. The answer is a description of the people, things, places, and time as they all combine into a complete event. The exact sequence of events that led to the accident should be reported. The person preparing the report should write the step-by-step sequence of how the accident happened; the list should include everything that occurred.

Why Did the Accident Occur? In order to determine or recommend what corrective action should be taken, it must be determined exactly *why* the accident occurred.

The following questions should be answered: Why was the injured person inattentive? Why was he or she poorly trained? Why did someone fail to report an unsafe condition or procedure? Why did what happened produce an accident? Why did the combination of all the factors that made up the event result in an injury? Why did the event result in anything other than an ordinary, everyday occurrence? Were there any other conditions that contributed to the accident?

Recommended Corrective Action. After evaluating the facts, the investigator will most likely find that the accident was caused by a combination of unsafe conditions and inadequate job procedures. Recommendations to prevent a recurrence should pinpoint the unsafe condition or inadequate procedure. Recommendations should be designed to correct all contributing factors.

The report should now be submitted to top management. After the report has been submitted, it is very important to follow up to make sure that recommended changes are implemented correctly.

Summary. Here is a summary of the important steps in preparing an accident report: Remember, all accidents should be investigated *as soon after the accident as possible. All* people involved should be interviewed in an effort to determine exactly how the accident occurred. Once all the facts have been put together, a report should be submitted to top management. The report should answer the questions *who, where, when, what, how* and *why*. Further, no investigation is complete unless corrective action is suggested.

ACCIDENT RECORDS

The form of an accident investigation report may vary, but any report should contain all the essential information (as specified in the previous section.) This section contains examples of accident report forms (see Figures 10-1 through 10-4).

A well-designed safety program would seek to know not only the causes of accidents, but also their costs. From accident investigation reports and other company sources, a report can be produced that includes the following:

- Number of accidents by causes
- Cost of accidents by causes
- Accident causes by department and/or location
- Accident costs by department and/or location
- Accident summaries by shift.

Figures 10-1 through 10-4 show examples of report forms that can be used to aid in safety efforts. Often, the insurance carrier can assist in making accident investigation reports.

Accident information that is going to be computerized can be coded for ease of handling. Later in this section, examples are given of codings used by companies in producing reports.

Records on accidents can also be used to:

- Create interest in safety among members of management, supervisors, and safety committees by furnishing them with information about the accident experience of their departments.
- Help determine the principal sources of accidents so efforts can be focused in directions that will effect the largest reductions in accidents.
- Judge safety program effectiveness by showing whether accident experience is improving or getting worse.
- Make possible comparisons with other companies, industries, or groups.

Standard Classifications

The National Safety Council recommends that the ground accident experience of all airlines be recorded, using standardized employee classifications for the air transport industry. Preceding each group is a typical code number used for computer identification:

921 FLIGHT CREWS

924 Cockpit personnel—pilots, flight engineers, and navigators

925 Cabin attendants—stewards and cabin flight attendants

922 GROUND PERSONNEL

926 Overhaul base—includes all employees at the base (Does not include "station" personnel at the same airport or employees at the base who are not specifically a part of the overhaul base operation)

928 Food service—includes all personnel involved in passenger and employee meal preparation and related functions

929 Passenger handling—includes ticket counter, lost and found, skycap, load computation, flight clearance, communications, and other related terminal service activities

927 Other ground personnel—all except overhaul base and station employees

923 STATIONS

This category includes all of the following:

934 Ramp operations—includes cargo handling and cabin aircraft servicing

935 Cargo handling—includes receiving, loading, and delivery of cargo

936 Cabin servicing—includes loading cabin supplies and food, setup, and predeparture cleanup

937 Aircraft servicing—includes signaling, chocking, positioning passenger stands, electrical hookup, and fuel, oil, and water servicing

938 OTHER

This category includes anything not included above.

943 Aircraft maintenance—includes maintenance, cleaning, and stores

944 Maintenance—includes routine nonrouting maintenance of air frames, engines, radio, electric and electronic equipment, aircraft components, and related shops

945 Cleaning—major interior and exterior cleaning and refurnishing

946 STORES

939 Facility and equipment maintenance includes maintenance of buildings, equipment (fixed and mobile), carpenter shops, etc.

Standard reporting is useful because it enables each airline to compare accident experiences in any given classification of employees with a like group in another airline. For example, if one airline's problems are in an area in which another airline has had few accidents, the two companies could then discuss the area and perhaps develop meaningful ideas on how to make improvements.

The following format can serve as a guide in setting up a coding system for accident reports:

AGENCIES

1. Aircraft—other than aerotitis media (aviator's ear) and turbulence
2. Aircraft—aerotitis media
3. Aircraft—turbulence
4. Moving vehicles—including moving carts
5. Movable equipment—hangar, ramp, and office equipment, such as stands, parked vehicles, ladders, platforms, and furniture
6. Fixed objects and surfaces—stairways, floors, ramp area, and walls

ACCIDENT INVESTIGATION REPORT

CASE NUMBER

COMPANY ______ ADDRESS ______

DEPARTMENT ______ LOCATION (if different from mailing address) ______

1. NAME of INJURED	2. SOCIAL SECURITY NUMBER	3. SEX ☐ M ☐ F	4. AGE	5. DATE of ACCIDENT

6. HOME ADDRESS	7. EMPLOYEE'S USUAL OCCUPATION	8. OCCUPATION at TIME of ACCIDENT
	9. LENGTH of EMPLOYMENT ☐ Less than 1 mo. ☐ 6 mos. to 5 yrs. ☐ 1-5 mos. ☐ More than 5 yrs.	10. TIME in OCCUP. at TIME of ACCIDENT ☐ Less than 1 mo. ☐ 6 mos. to 5 yrs. ☐ 1-5 mos. ☐ More than 5 yrs.
11. EMPLOYMENT CATEGORY ☐ Regular, full-time ☐ Temporary ☐ Nonemployee ☐ Regular, part-time ☐ Seasonal	12. CASE NUMBERS and NAMES of OTHERS INJURED in SAME ACCIDENT	
13. NATURE of INJURY and PART of BODY		

14. NAME and ADDRESS of PHYSICIAN	16. TIME of INJURY A. ______ A.M. P.M. B. Time within shift C. Type of shift	17. SEVERITY of INJURY ☐ Fatality ☐ Lost workdays—days away from work ☐ Lost workdays—days of restricted activity ☐ Medical treatment ☐ First aid ☐ Other, specify ______
15. NAME and ADDRESS of HOSPITAL		

18. SPECIFIC LOCATION of ACCIDENT ON EMPLOYER'S PREMISES? ☐ Yes ☐ No	19. PHASE OF EMPLOYEE's WORKDAY at TIME of INJURY ☐ During rest period ☐ Entering or leaving plant ☐ During meal period ☐ Performing work duties ☐ Working overtime. ☐ Other ______

20. DESCRIBE HOW the ACCIDENT OCCURRED

______

21. ACCIDENT SEQUENCE. Describe in reverse order of occurrence events preceding the injury and accident. Starting with the injury and moving backward in time, reconstruct the sequence of events that led to the injury.

A. Injury Event ______

B. Accident Event ______

C. Preceding Event #1 ______

D. Preceding Event #2, #3, etc. ______

Figure 10-1. This form asks for the circumstances contributing to the accident, as well as for a recommendation for avoiding similar accidents.

22. TASK and ACTIVITY at TIME of ACCIDENT

A. General type of task ______

B. Specific activity ______

C. Employee was working:

☐ Alone ☐ With crew or fellow worker ☐ Other, specify ______

23. POSTURE of EMPLOYEE

______

24. SUPERVISION at TIME of ACCIDENT

☐ Directly supervised ☐ Not supervised

☐ Indirectly supervised ☐ Supervision not feasible

25. CAUSAL FACTORS. Events and conditions that contributed to the accident. Include those identified by use of the Guide for Identifying Causal Factors and Corrective Actions.

______

26. CORRECTIVE ACTIONS. Those that have been, or will be, taken to prevent recurrence. Include those indentified by use of the Guide for Identifying Causal Factors and Corrective Actions.

______

PREPARED BY ______

TITLE ______

DEPARTMENT ______ DATE ______

Developed by the National Safety Council

APPROVED ______

TITLE ______ DATE ______

APPROVED ______

TITLE ______ DATE ______

SUPERVISOR'S REPORT OF EMPLOYEE ACCIDENT/INJURY

PRINTED IN U.S.A.

This form shall be completed by Supervisors to report all mishaps in which there was a serious injury or damage potential, whether or not actual injury or damage was sustained. Its sole purpose is to aid in accident prevention – not to establish blame. Please report fully. Use other side or additional sheet(s) if necessary.

1. STATION/LOCATION/DEPARTMENT NUMBER	
2. DATE OF ACCIDENT	TIME
3. SITE OF ACCIDENT	

4. FULL NAME OF EMPLOYEE INVOLVED *(Last)* *(First)* *(Initial)*	5. POSITION/JOB TITLE		6. SHIFT
7. HOW LONG IN THIS POSITION?	8. COMPANY SENIORITY DATE	9. REGULAR DAYS OFF	
10. WHAT WAS EMPLOYEE DOING AND HOW DID THE ACCIDENT HAPPEN? *(Describe in detail)*			

11. IN YOUR OPINION, WHAT ACTUALLY CAUSED THIS ACCIDENT? CHECK ONE OF THE FOLLOWING CAUSES.

- ☐ UNSAFE PLANNING, LAYOUT OR METHOD
- ☐ UNSAFE EQUIPMENT OR FACILITY
- ☐ FAILURE TO PROVIDE ADEQUATE PROTECTIVE EQUIPMENT
- ☐ IMPROPER HOUSEKEEPING
- ☐ INADEQUATE MAINTENANCE
- ☐ INSUFFICIENT EMPLOYEE TRAINING
- ☐ POOR DISCIPLINE
- ☐ PERSONAL PHYSICAL CONDITION
- ☐ FAILURE TO USE PROTECTION AVAILABLE
- ☐ FAILURE TO OBTAIN HELP
- ☐ INFRACTION OF RULES
- ☐ HASTE *(unnecessary or unusual)*
- ☐ IMPROPER PROCEDURE *(includes improper use of equipment tools, or materials)*
- ☐ INATTENTION OR DISTRACTION
- ☐ ACTION OF ANOTHER PERSON
- ☐ OTHER *(Explain on reverse side – Be Specific)*

12. WHAT HAVE YOU DONE TO PREVENT OTHER INJURIES OR EQUIPMENT DAMAGE UNDER SIMILAR CONDITIONS?

13. SHOULD FURTHER PREVENTIVE ACTION BE TAKEN? IF SO, WHAT?

BY WHOM?

IF ACCIDENT RESULTED IN INJURY TO EMPLOYEE, FURNISH FOLLOWING ADDITIONAL INFORMATION

14. EXTENT OF INJURY *(May be described in layman's terms)*

15. DID EMPLOYEE RETURN TO DUTY ON HIS NEXT REGULAR SCHEDULED SHIFT?

- ☐ YES
- ☐ NO   IF "NO", INDICATE DOCTOR'S RECOMMENDATION

- ☐ ABSENCE
- ☐ RETURN TO LIMITED DUTY •
- ☐ RETURN TO REGULAR DUTY •

• IF EMPLOYEE DID NOT RETURN ON HIS NEXT SCHEDULED SHIFT AFTER DOCTOR RELEASED HIM FOR DUTY, EXPLAIN WHY EMPLOYEE DID NOT RETURN.

16. DOCTOR'S NAME

ADDRESS

17. HOSPITAL (NAME)

ADDRESS

IF, TO YOUR KNOWLEDGE OR IN YOUR OPINION, THERE IS ANY REASON TO BELIEVE THIS INJURY SHOULD NOT BE COVERED BY WORKER COMPENSATION, PLEASE GIVE DETAILS ON SEPARATE MEMO.

THIS IS A FULL AND ACCURATE REPORT OF THIS ACCIDENT/INJURY, BASED ON INFORMATION AVAILABLE AT THIS TIME.

NAME OF SUPERVISOR ______________________ *(Type or Print)*   SIGNATURE ______________________

TITLE ______________________   DATE ______________________

Figure 10-2. This form for making an accident report provides a checklist of accident causes.

SUPERVISOR'S INVESTIGATION REPORT

Name	Age	Time	Date

Department —Shift	Job	How long on this job?

WHAT HAPPENED?

Describe what took place or what caused you to make this investigation.

WHY DID IT HAPPEN?

Get all the facts by studying the job and situation involved.
Question by use of WHY — WHAT — WHERE — WHEN — WHO — HOW

WHAT SHOULD BE DONE?

Determine which of the 12 items under EMP require additional attention.

Equipment	Material	People
Select	Select	Select
Arrange	Place	Place
Use	Handle	Train
Maintain	Process	Lead

WHAT HAVE YOU DONE THUS FAR?

Take or recommend action, depending upon your authority.
Follow up – was action effective?

HOW WILL THIS IMPROVE OPERATIONS?

OBJECTIVE
Eliminate job hindrances

Investigated by	Date	Reviewed by	Date

Figure 10-3. This form for making an accident report focuses on the central qustions that an accident investigation should cover.

NOTE TO SUPERVISOR

REMEMBER, AN ACCIDENT INVESTIGATION IS NOT DESIGNED TO FIND FAULT OR BLAME. IT IS AN ANALYSIS TO DETERMINE CAUSES THAT CAN BE CONTROLLED OR ELIMINATED.

WHEN COMPLETING THE INVESTIGATION, TRY TO ANSWER THESE QUESTIONS

HOW DID THE ACCIDENT OCCUR?

WHERE DID IT HAPPEN?

WHAT MATERIALS, MACHINES, EQUIPMENT OR CONDITIONS WERE INVOLVED?

WHO WAS INJURED?

WHEN DID IT HAPPEN?

MAKE RECOMMENDATIONS!

NO INVESTIGATION IS COMPLETE UNLESS CORRECTIVE ACTION IS SUGGESTED.

FOLLOW-UP

DETERMINE WHAT ACTION IS BEING TAKEN ON YOUR RECOMMENDATIONS.

SUPERVISOR'S ACCIDENT INVESTIGATION REPORT

DATE: ____________ TIME ____________

EMPLOYEE INVOLVED ____________ AGE ____________

POSITION ____________ DATE EMPLOYED ____________

SUPERVISOR ____________ DEPARTMENT ____________

HOW LONG WAS EMPLOYEE PERFORMING THIS OPERATION? ____________

WAS THE EMPLOYEE INSTRUCTED ____________

DID THE ACCIDENT RESULT IN AN INJURY ____________

NATURE AND EXTENT OF INJURY ____________

DATE INJURY REPORTED ____________ WAS FIRST AID GIVEN? ____________

IF SO, WHEN, AND BY WHOM ____________

HOW DID ACCIDENT OCCUR? ____________

CAUSE OF ACCIDENT ____________

RECOMMENDATIONS TO PREVENT A RECURRENCE ____________

WHAT ACTION HAS BEEN TAKEN? ____________

SIGNED ____________ DEPT. ____________ DATE ____________

SAFETY COMMITTEE COMMENTS

RECOMMENDATIONS ____________

SIGNED ____________ DATE ____________

EXECUTIVE

SPECIAL ORDERS ____________

SIGNED ____________ DATE ____________

Figure 10-4. This is another form for making an accident report. Note that all the forms ask the supervisor to suggest corrective action.

7. Materials and parts—includes baggage and cargo
8. Machinery—shop and office machines
9. Hand tools or portable power tools
10. Natural calamities
11. Unclassified—not elsewhere classified

PERSONNEL CLASSIFICATIONS

1. Office employees—includes reservations agents
2. Porters and janitors
3. Transportation and ticket agents—includes transportation supervision
4. Cargo agents
5. Dining unit
6. Commissary unit
7. Mechanics and inspectors—includes supervisors
8. Fleet service and ground service helpers
9. Store clerks, progressmen, and leased truck drivers
10. Plant protection
11. Pilots
12. Flight engineers
13. Hostesses and pursers
14. Navigators
15. Outside contract employees

DISABILITY CLASS

1. Medical case—visit to first aid, physician, or hospital—(No Lost Time—NLT)
2. Temporary total
3. Permanent partial
4. Permanent total
5. Death
6. No injury
7. Reported minor injury—no doctor or lost time

ACCIDENT TYPE

1. Struck against
2. Struck by
3. Caught in, on, or between
4. Rubbed, abraded, and penetrated (nonimpact cases from handing materials or equipment; kneeling or sitting on sharp objects; foreign matter in eyes over a period of time)
5. Fall on same level
6. Fall from different level
7. Physical strain from lifting, pushing, pulling, jumping, and efforts to recover from slips and loss of balance (includes reflex actions of the body resulting from fright, surprise, or electrical shock)
8. Exposure to extreme temperature
9. Exposure to harmful noise
10. Pressure variations (aerotitis, etc.)
11. Occupational illness or disease (effects of fumes, chemicals, vapors, or dust)
12. Electrical shock
13. Crashes and collisions
14. Unclassified

PART OF THE BODY INJURED

1. Head (includes skull, scalp, and facial injuries not specifically covered next)
2. Mouth (includes teeth)
3. Eyes
4. Ears (internal as well as external)
5. Back
6. Chest
7. Arms, wrists, shoulders
8. Fingers, hands
9. Legs, knees, ankles
10. Feet, toes
11. Multiple
12. Respiratory system
13. Unclassified

TYPE OF INJURY

1. Bruises, contusions, abrasions
2. Auditory disturbances
3. Thermal injuries
4. Chemical reactions (dermatitis and chemical burns)
5. Concussions
6. Fractures
7. Hernias
8. Lacerations
9. Punctures and penetrations
10. Strains, sprains, and dislocations
11. Amputations
12. Respiratory disturbances
13. Infections due to delayed or inadequate medical attention
14. Death
15. Foreign bodies in eyes
16. Unclassified

Basic Causes of Accidents to Personnel

Figure 10-5 shows a lost-time accident analysis and 10-6 shows a lost-time injury report which provides basic data on the causes and nature of injuries.

How to use the form in Figure 10-5 is explained in this section. (The next section deals with reporting damage to equipment or facilities.)

Classifications 1 through 8. The following accident causes are attributable to management. They are used when the basic accident cause results from management failure.

1. *Unsafe planning, layout, or method.* Use where a faulty plan, layout, or procedure contributes to the accident, or where there is absence of a plan, layout, or method for good, safe operation.

2. *Unsafe equipment or facility.* Similar to 1, but use where dealing with faulty property rather than the plan, layout, or job procedure. It includes shortcomings in equipment or facility design that contribute to an accident.

LOST TIME ACCIDENT ANALYSIS

PERIOD __________ to __________

CODE NO.	BASIC ACCIDENT CAUSES	AGENCIES: AIRCRAFT	AIRCRAFT (Aerotitis)	AIRCRAFT (Turbulence)	MOVING VEHICLES	MOVABLE EQUIPMENT	FIXED OBJECTS AND SURFACES	MATERIALS AND PARTS	MACHINERY	HAND OR PORTABLE POWER TOOLS	ACTS OF GOD	UNCLASSIFIED	TOTALS
	CODE NO.	1	2	3	4	5	6	7	8	9	10	11	
1	UNSAFE PLANNING, LAYOUT OR METHOD												
2	UNSAFE EQUIPMENT OR FACILITY												
3	FAILURE TO PROVIDE ADEQUATE PROTECTIVE EQUIPMENT												
4	IMPROPER HOUSEKEEPING												
5	INADEQUATE MAINTENANCE												
6	INSUFFICIENT EMPLOYEE TRAINING												
7	POOR DISCIPLINE												
8	OTHER SUPERVISORY FAILURES												
11	PERSONAL PHYSICAL CONDITION												
12	FAILURE TO USE PROTECTION AVAILABLE												
13	FAILURE TO OBTAIN HELP												
14	POOR JUDGMENT												
15	INFRACTION OF RULES												
16	HASTE (UNNECESSARY OR UNUSUAL)												
17	IMPROPER PROCEDURE												
18	INATTENTION OR DISTRACTION												
19	ACTION OF OTHER PERSON												
20	INHERENT HAZARD (NOT POSSIBLE TO GUARD)												
30	UNABLE TO CLASSIFY												
	TOTALS												

Figure 10-5. This lost time analysis form is useful in analyzing and categorizing the causes of injuries. How to use it is explained in the text.

LOST TIME INJURY REPORT

STATION: ______________ EMPLOYEE: ______________ DEPT: ______________

DATE: ______________ TIME: ______________

NOTE: Check only one item in each category.

1. Place of Injury

- A/C Belly ☐
- Bag Room ☐
- Ticket Counter ☐
- Ramp ☐
- Maint. Shop ☐
- Other (specify) __________ ☐

2. Activity or Motion

- Kneeling/Crouching ☐
- Lifting ☐
- Pulling ☐
- Pushing ☐
- Reaching/Stretching ☐
- Fall from Elevation ☐
- Slipped/tripped ☐
- Struck Against ☐
- Struck By ☐
- Caught Between ☐
- Other (specify) __________ ☐

3. Part of Body

- Head ☐
- Face ☐
- Eyes ☐
- Ears ☐

Part of Body (cont.)

- Arm ☐
- Shoulder ☐
- Hand/Finger ☐
- Groin/Stomach ☐
- Back ☐
- Legs ☐
- Knees ☐
- Feet/Toes ☐
- Other (specify) ☐

4. Type of Injury

- Bruise ☐
- Burn/Scald ☐
- Cut/Abrasion ☐
- Sprain/Strain ☐
- Other (specify) ☐

5. Type of Aircraft
If Appropriate

____

6. Expected Lost-Time
Hrs. ______________
(Excl. scheduled days off)

7. Actual Lost-Time
Hrs. ______________
(Head Office use)

Figure 10-6. This is a form for gathering information on time lost because of injury.

3. *Failure to provide adequate protective equipment.* Use where there is inadequate personal protective equipment, machine guarding, safety interlocks, handrails, barricades, or other safeguards.

4. *Improper housekeeping.* Use where there are spills on floor or ramp, oily ladder rungs, ice patches, poor piling, or obstructions in aisles or work areas.

5. *Inadequate maintenance.* Use where design is good and protection is present and adequate, but where the condition of equipment or facility has deteriorated and has not been repaired, or where repairs that were made were inadequate.

6. *Insufficient employee training.* Use where the accident is caused because the employee was not taught either the job to which he or she was assigned or the hazards and the safety practices pertaining to his or her job.

7. *Poor discipline.* Use where there is failure to enforce established regulations and accepted safe practices.

8. *Other supervisory failures.* Use when there is loose supervision such as poor job instruction, failure to request obviously needed repairs or protective equipment, failure to correct employee performance deficiencies or poor work habits, and ignoring recognizable inadequate practices not specifically covered by regulations.

Classifications 11 through 19. These are attributable to the work force. These are used when the accident is caused by personal condition, attitude, or action of the person injured or by a second party employee, but where classifications 1 through 8 are not the basic causes.

11. *Personal physical condition.* Use where injury results from doing a regular job in a normal manner according to good procedure. Examples are "Stooped over and knee snapped," "Flying with a cold and ear hurt," "Lifted 7 kg (15 pound) box from bench and hurt back," "Turned ankle while walking—no obstruction or wet spot."

12. *Failure to use protection available.* Use where protection is furnished, but not used. For example, "Not wearing safety glasses," "Guardrail was not in place," "Machine guard had been removed by employee."

13. *Failure to obtain help.* Use when the employee should have obtained assistance in lifting, pushing, or pulling.

14. *Poor judgment.* Use only if another specific cause does not exist, and "poor judgment" is the only possible explanation. Applies in such cases as consciously taking obvious risks even though they do not violate any established rule or regulation.

15. *Infraction of rules.* Use in cases where it was clear that an existing rule, known to the employees, was broken. If an applicable rule exists but is not generally known, the cause would be "Insufficient training" (classification 6). If no rule exists but one should exist due to a general need for it, the cause would be "Unsafe planning" (classification 1).

16. *Haste (unnecessary or unusual).* Use where an employee rushes unnecessarily or uses shortcuts to get a job done. However, if undue hurrying is required as a routine way to do the job, the cause would be classification 1, "Unsafe method."

17. *Improper procedure.* This includes improper use of equipment, tools, or materials—applicable to speeding vehicles, towing with scooters, pushing with gas trucks, standing on boxes or stools instead of stands or ladders, hammering with wrenches, cleaning with gasoline or carbon tetrachloride, etc. Deliberate unauthorized use or substitution of equipment, tools, or supplies is to be charged to "Infraction of rules" (classification 15).

18. *Inattention or distraction.* Use when the accident is caused by distraction from any source, "daydreaming," or by inattention on the part of the injured.

19. *Action of another person.* Use when another person actually caused the accident, by deliberately distracting the victim (wantonly or otherwise), through horseplay or personal attack, moving an object against the victim, and the like.

20. *Inherent hazard (not possible to safeguard).* Care must be taken not to classify causes in this category just because the corrective action is not immediately apparent. Generally, "acts of God" may fall under "inherent hazard," but even, for example, windborne dust, where likely to occur, or icy ramp surfaces, where likely to occur, can be protected against. Air turbulence cannot be controlled, but loose objects in the airplane can be secured. Existing equipment may not be conducive to injury-free handling, but corrective action is possible with proper emphasis on training workers to use correct procedures. For these reasons, this classification should be used sparingly, and only after considerable analysis.

21. *Unable to classify.* Use only where complete investigation does not permit specific classification. If there is evidence that all facts have not been ascertained, consider the case open and subject to reclassification. If an undue number of "unable" classifications exist for any one station or personnel group, it is indicative of incomplete investigation, incomplete reporting, or both.

Basic Causes of Accidents to Aircraft and Ground Facilities

Figure 10-7 shows a form that can be used to make an accident analysis for damage to aircraft, ground equipment, or facilities. Note that the basic accident causes are, for the most part, the same as shown in Figure 10-5, Lost-Time Accident Analysis, used to analyze accidents to personnel.

Information needed to complete the accident analysis can be taken from a good accident investigation report (such as Figures 10-1 through 10-4). The wording and format can, of course, be changed to suit specific company requirements.

AIRCRAFT/GROUND EQUIPMENT-FACILITY ACCIDENT ANALYSIS PERIOD ______ TO ______		AGENCIES	AIRCRAFT (STD. BODY)	AIRCRAFT (WIDE BODY)	MOVING VEHICLES	MOVEABLE EQUIPMENT	FIXED OBJECTS & SURFACES	MATERIALS & PARTS	NATURAL CALAMITIES	UNCLASSIFIED				TOTALS
Code No.	BASIC ACCIDENT CAUSES	Code No.	1	2	3	4	5	6	7	8	9	10	11	
1	UNSAFE PLANNING, LAYOUT, OR METHOD													
2	UNSAFE EQUIPMENT OR FACILITY													
3	IMPROPER HOUSEKEEPING													
4	INADEQUATE MAINTENANCE													
5	INSUFFICIENT EMPLOYEE TRAINING													
6	POOR DISCIPLINE													
7	OTHER SUPERVISORY FAILURES													
8	FAILURE TO OBTAIN HELP													
9	POOR JUDGMENT													
10	INFRACTION OF RULES													
11	HASTE (UNNECESSARY OR UNUSUAL)													
12	IMPROPER PROCEDURE													
13	INATTENTION OR DISTRACTION													
14	ACTION OF OTHER PERSON													
15	INHERENT HAZARD (NOT POSSIBLE TO GUARD)													
16	UNABLE TO CLASSIFY													
	TOTALS													

Figure 10-7. This form is useful in analyzing accidents in which there is damage to aircraft, ground equipment, and/or facilities. How to use it is explained in the text.

The following format can serve as a guide to setting up a coding system. This format is based on Figure 10-7.

Agencies. The top portion of the form indicates the agency of the accident.

1. Aircraft—standard body
2. Aircraft—wide body
3. Moving vehicles (including moving carts)
4. Movable equipment (hangar equipment, ramp stands, parked vehicles, ladders, platforms, jetways)
5. Fixed objects and surfaces (buildings, fences, ramps, access roads)
6. Materials and parts (cargo)
7. Natural calamities
8. Unclassified

Accident type. This is a shortened list similar to that given earlier in this chapter for analysis of personal injuries and noninjury personal accidents:

1. Struck against
2. Struck by
3. Settled on
4. Failure to disconnect
5. Mechanical or structural (losing doors, fuel spills, shorted wires, poor maintenance)
6. Other (procedures not followed)

Basic accident causes. The vertical portion of the form indicates the basic accident cause(s). Classifications 1 through 7 are attributable to supervision (or failure of proper supervision).

1. *Unsafe planning, layout, or method.* Use where there is a faulty plan, layout, or procedure contributing to the accident, or where there is no plan, layout, or method for safe operation.

2. *Unsafe equipment or facility.* Similar to 1, but use where there is faulty property rather than a faulty plan, layout, or job procedure. It includes shortcomings in equipment or facility design that contribute to an accident.

3. *Improper housekeeping.* Use where there are spills on floor or ramp, oily ladder rungs, ice patches, poor piling, or obstructions in aisles or work areas.

4. *Inadequate maintenance.* Use where design is good and protection is present and adequate, but where the condition of the equipment or facility has deteriorated and has not been repaired, or where repairs that were made were inadequate.

5. *Insufficient employee training.* Use where the accident is caused because the employee was not taught either the job to which he or she was assigned, or the hazards and the safety practices pertaining to his or her job.

6. *Poor discipline.* Use where there is failure to enforce established regulations and accepted safe practices.

7. *Other supervisory failures.* Use where there is loose supervision such as poor job instruction, failure to request obviously needed repairs or protective equipment, failure to correct employee performance deficiencies or poor work habits, and failure to correct inadequate acts or practices not specifically covered by regulations.

Classifications 8 through 14 are attributable to the work force. These classifications are used when the accident is caused by personal condition, attitude, or action of the person injured or by a second party employee, but where classifications 1 through 7 are not the basic cause(s).

8. *Failure to obtain help.* Use when the employee should have obtained help in lifting, pushing, or pulling.

9. *Poor judgment.* Use only if another specific cause does not exist, and "poor judgment" is the only possible explanation. Applies in such cases as consciously taking obvious risks even though they are not in violation of any established rule or regulation.

10. *Infraction of rules.* Use in cases where it was clear that an existing rule, known to the employees, was broken. If an applicable rule exists but is not generally known, the cause would be "Insufficient training" (classification 5). If no rule exists but one should exist due to a general need for it, the cause would be "Unsafe planning" (classification 1).

11. *Haste (unnecessary or unusual).* Use where an employee rushes unnecessarily or uses shortcuts to get a job done. If, however, undue hurrying is required as a routine way of doing the job, the cause would be classification 1, "Unsafe method."

12. *Improper procedure.* This includes improper use of equipment, tools, or materials—applicable to speeding vehicles or pushing with unauthorized vehicles. Deliberate unauthorized use of substitution of equipment shall be recorded as "Infraction of rules" (classification 10).

13. *Inattention or distraction.* Use when the accident is caused by distraction from any source, "daydreaming," or by inattention on the part of the employee involved in the accident.

14. *Action of another person.* Use when another person actually and deliberately caused the accident by distracting the employees(s) involved in the operation, through horseplay, personal attack, or obstruction.

15. *Inherent hazard (not possible to safeguard).* Care must be taken not to classify causes under this category just because the corrective action is not immediately apparent. Generally, "acts of God" may fall under "Inherent hazard," but even, for example, windborne dust or icy ramps, where likely to occur, can be protected against. Existing equipment may not be conducive to injury-free operation, but corrective action is possible with proper emphasis on training workers to use correct procedures. For these reasons, this classification should be used sparingly, and then only after considerable analysis.

16. *Unable to classify.* Use only where complete investigation does not permit specific classification. If there is evidence that all facts have not

been ascertained, consider the case open but subject to reclassification. If an undue number of "unable" classifications exist for any one station or personnel group, it is indicative of incomplete investigation, incomplete reporting, or both.

REFERENCES

National Safety Council, 444 North Michigan Ave., Chicago, IL 60611.

Industrial Data Sheet: *Work Accident Records and Analysis,* 527.

Accident Investigation—A New Approach, 1983.

Accident Prevention Manual for Industrial Operations, Administration and Programs volume, 9th ed., 1988.

U.S. Department of Labor, Occupational Safety and Health Administration, (OSHA) Washington, D.C. 20212.

Recordkeeping Requirements under the Occupational Safety and Health Act of 1970. Revised 1978.

STOP

DURING
After

CHAPTER 11

Safety Program Organization

Cooperation between management and employees during safety committee meetings promotes a better safety program.

The organization of a safety program for aviation ground operations may be defined as follows: a method employed by management to share and to assign responsibility for accident prevention in ground operations and to ensure fulfillment of that responsibility. Safety must be built into every process or product design and into every operation. It must be an integral part of operations.

BASICS OF A SAFETY PROGRAM

Accident and injury prevention is basically achieved through control of the working environment and control of people's actions.

An effective ground safety program will have a working environment in which operations can be conducted economically, efficiently, and safely.

All successful safety programs invariably are built on six basic elements:

1. Management leadership (assumption of responsibility, declaration of policy)
2. Assignment of responsibility (to operating officials, safety professionals, supervisors, and committees)
3. Maintenance of safe working conditions (inspectors, engineering revisions, purchasing, and supervisors)
4. Establishment of safety training (for top management, for supervisors, and for workers)
5. An accident record system (including accident analysis, reports of injuries, first aid services, periodic health examinations, comprehensive safety inspection programs, and safety committees)
6. Acceptance of personal responsibility by employees (encouraged by training and maintenance of interest in safety).

Top management's attitude and approach toward accident prevention is typically reflected in the attitudes of the supervisory force. Similarly, the worker's attitude reflects that of the supervisors. Consequently, if top management is not genuinely interested in preventing accidents, few others in the organization will be. Because this basic fact applies to every level of management and supervision, an accident prevention program must result from top management's announced and demonstrated interest.

Details for carrying out an accident prevention program may be assigned, but responsibility for the basic policy cannot be delegated. The top executive officer of a company is responsible for overall safe performance. Senior management must regularly review safety performance—a task best performed through regular lines of supervision and those assigned specific safety responsibilities.

Safety Policy

A declaration of company policy must be established in the form of a written safety policy statement. The safety policy should be brief, clearly defining management's attitude. The policy must be signed or authorized by the top corporate official. Safety policies may vary considerably in scope: they may merely set forth company safety philosophy, or they may detail directives, responsibilities, and functions.

Once a safety policy statement is established, it should be publicized so that every employee becomes familiar with it, particularly with those aspects that apply directly to employees. Meetings, letters, pamphlets, and bulletin boards can be used to accomplish this. The safety policy should be posted in management offices to remind supervisors of their obligations in the area of safety.

Management Interest in Safety

Expressions of management interest in the safety program include:

- Enforcing policy and programs
- Recognizing good safety results
- Reviewing safety reports
- Participating in meetings, safety award programs, and other events that demonstrate their support for company safety efforts.

Management must take the lead in keeping interest alive by:

- Emphasizing that service, production, and safety go together in an efficient operation
- Setting a good example. For instance, if company rules require employees to wear eye protection or other personal protective equipment in particular areas, management must observe these regulations when they are in these areas.
- Attending safety meetings
- Reviewing and acting upon accident reports
- Reviewing departmental safety records through group conferences with department heads
- Motivating interest in safety through general letters, bulletin board announcements, and discussion of the department/company accident records.

ASSIGNMENT OF RESPONSIBILITY FOR SAFETY PROGRAMS

Although safety is ultimately the responsibility of management, authority to carry out a safety program is assigned down through all management levels.

The health and safety professional acts in a staff capacity to help administer policy, provide technical information, train other staff, and supply material for the safety program.

Heads of operating units can provide personal leadership. To achieve satisfactory protection against accidents in their areas, they can interpret company policy and actively support it. This sets an example and gives safety equal emphasis and weight with matters of production, cost, and quality. Top management should give prompt and fair consideration to recommendations for reducing accident potentials from heads of operating units.

The first-line supervisors should be responsible for seeing that:

- Each of their employees understands properties and hazards of material he or she handles or uses.
- Necessary precautions are observed when using equipment, including proper safeguards and personal protective equipment.
- Each employee understands and properly follows established work procedures for his/her safety.

Some supervisors have a strong interest in safety. Others must be trained by management to carry out the safety program.

Administration of the Safety Program

For advice and help in administering a safety policy and ensuring the continuity of the safety program, top management usually places the administration of the program in the hands of a health and safety department or a health and safety professional.

It is important that management formally assign full staff responsibility for safety administration to one responsible individual. The decision concerning proper placement of responsibility should be based upon the size of the company and the character of its operations.

Safety program administration depends on these factors:

- Size of organization
- Nature of operation (such as scheduled carrier, cargo carrier, supplemental carrier, fixed base operator, commuter airline, airport)
- Management interest in the type of safety program desired.

Generally, the following guidelines are suggested:

- Companies employing up to 500 people can place the program in the hands of an industrial relations manager, personnel manager, or other responsible member of the management staff who has some knowledge of safety procedures and standards.
- Companies employing 500 or more people should place the safety program in the hands of a full-time safety professional.

An important item that should not be overlooked or underemphasized is that an effective safety program requires money to operate—the safety professional's salary, the salary of the safety professional's staff, and the cost of safety equipment, safety training materials, awards, and meetings are just a few of the expenses connected with a good safety program.

The safety program under the direction of the assigned person should enjoy the same position as other established activities of the organization, such as operations, marketing, maintenance, and personnel.

Duties of the Health and Safety Professional

The duties of the health and safety professional ordinarily include:

- Formulating, administering, and making necessary changes in the accident prevention program
- Submitting, directly to the officer in charge, regular reports on the status of the accident prevention program
- Acting in an advisory capacity on all matters pertaining to safety as required for the guidance of management, the general manager, directors, managers, first-line supervisors, and such departments as marketing, purchasing, maintenance, and personnel
- Maintaining the accident record system, making necessary reports, investigating selected accidents, securing supervisor's accident reports, and auditing corrective action taken by supervisors to eliminate accident causes
- Supervising or closely cooperating with the training department in the safety training of employees
- Correlating safety work with the work of the medical department, including proper selection and placement of employees
- Completing periodic audits for the purpose of discovering and correcting unsafe conditions or unsafe work practices before they cause accidents
- Maintaining outside professional contacts to exchange information with others and to keep up to date
- Informing management of the requirements of federal, state, and local laws or orders bearing on ground industrial safety so that management can ensure compliance
- Securing necessary help or advice from professional safety organizations, governmental agencies, or insurance carriers on matters pertaining to safety and health
- Formulating and initiating activities that will stimulate and maintain employee interest in accident prevention
- Directing the activities of the safety staff so that the accident prevention program will be efficiently operated
- Administering fire prevention and fire-fighting activities when that function is not the responsibility of another department
- Administering industrial hygiene activities when that function is not the responsibility of another department
- Setting standards for safety equipment to be used by personnel
- Reviewing designs of new equipment to be used in work areas
- Recommending provisions for safety in plans and specifications of new building construction and repair or remodeling of existing structures.

ORGANIZATIONAL SETUPS FOR SAFETY PROGRAMS

The chain of command between the person charged with directing the health and safety program and the top company officer varies considerably. Free access between safety administration and executives ensures positive results.

The person responsible for administering the safety program should report to an officer of the company. The safety professional should have staff status and authority. The amount of staff required by the safety professional in order to discharge his or her task properly depends on the degree of responsibility, the size and operating policies of the company, and the type of operations.

A small company that is not in a position to hire a full-time safety professional can assign a person to the task part-time. In a small company, active management and control of the safety program may be vested in the chief executive, in the general manager, or in an experienced and qualified supervisor who has both authority and standing. It is neither fair nor productive to assign safety responsibility to someone, however, without giving the person specified time and facilities to carry out the responsibility. With a planned program, for which ample management time is allotted, a small company need not lack safety leadership.

SAFETY COMMITTEES

Safety committees of various types are found in many successful organizations. Although in themselves they should not be considered a "safety program," they do serve two basic functions. First, they help create and maintain an active interest in safety, and second, they serve as a channel for safety communication.

There are various types of safety committees:

- Management or central safety committee
- Departmental committee
- Labor committee
- Joint labor-management committee.

A large company may have all of these committees or more; a small company may use only one.

Safety committees can have positive or negative aspects. The negative aspect of safety committees results if management feels it has delegated its responsibility for safety to a committee. To avoid this, management should serve actively on a safety committee. The positive aspect of safety committees is that they permit employees to share in the work of accident prevention.

A point to be guarded against in safety committee operations, especially joint committees, is the tendency for some workers and some supervisors to neglect their own safety responsibilities if they feel that "the committee will handle the problem." Day-to-day safety matters should be handled at the supervisory level. The joint committee does not execute action; it simply recommends and should monitor the application and effectiveness of safety activity.

The work of a committee may be better accomplished in a prompt, effective, and orderly manner if a representative of top management serves as chairperson.

The safety professional can make a worthwhile contribution to meetings through preparing appropriate material and exhibits for presentation.

Even though safety committee meetings can vary considerably in the way they are conducted, one significant advantage results from conducting them on company time—it demonstrates to the employee that the company is just as interested in safety as it is in production matters. This is particularly true when employees are participating in the meeting.

SAFETY AUDITS

Safety audits are part of a safety program. Audits allow the safety professional to measure safety program procedures and performance against accepted standards. They fall into two broad categories:

1. Checking precautions against emergencies that cannot be observed in operation. Examples of these are location surveys of potential problem areas related to air contaminants, excessive noise, inadequate light, or flammable atmospheres. Safeguards must be in good operating condition. Other examples are emergency equipment: fire extinguishers, stretchers, fire blankets, medical kits, and rescue packs. Facilities and equipment inspections are made to determine compliance with specifications.

2. Legally-authorized safety inspections of an employer's premises. Because those assigned to maintain safety are not involved directly in day-to-day operation, and because they are more apt to have knowledge of safety codes, standards, and ordinances equal to that of the outside agency inspector, the employer's health and safety professional is the logical choice to accompany the agency inspector.

In matters of operational tools, equipment, and safety devices, the safety program does have an obligation to the inspecting organization to provide it with safety criteria to aid inspections. Such criteria, for example, could include special knowledge of an unusual work procedure, the particular part a piece of equipment played in an accident, or even a more stringent internally-developed requirement in a safety standard.

What the Safety Department Does Not Do

"Aviation in itself is not inherently dangerous, but, to an even greater extent than the sea, it is terribly unforgiving of any carelessness, incapacity, or neglect." Although no one remembers who in aviation first uttered these thoughts, this epigram does serve to emphasize that safety is not the sole responsibility of the safety department.

The safety department should no more be expected to hold prime responsibility for checking conditions of vehicles, hoists, slings, tank farms, loading stands, or conveyors, than it would be expected to inspect aircraft control cables, structure, or fuel system plumbing. Consequently, safety personnel's responsibility in checking operational equipment and facilities is a matter of "spot checking."

Routine audits of maintenance, service, and operations facilities are the responsibility of operating personnel.

Safety Audit Techniques

The safety audit must be conducted objectively and critically. It is not enough to look for things which have played parts in accident experience. It is prudent to also look for those things which could cause an "accident that hasn't happened yet."

A safety auditor must be vigilant for the unsafe condition. Discrepancies should be recorded so a meaningful report can be submitted to the responsible department head under whom the unsafe condition occurs. A safety auditor must be prepared to submit data to substantiate the recommendation for correction, if it becomes necessary to do so.

Procedures must be established to ensure that reported discrepancies and shortcomings are corrected. Follow-up review is required to ensure proper hazard elimination.

REFERENCES

National Safety Council, 444 N. Michigan Ave., Chicago, IL 60611.

Accident Prevention Manual for Industrial Operations, Administration and Programs volume, 9th ed., 1988.

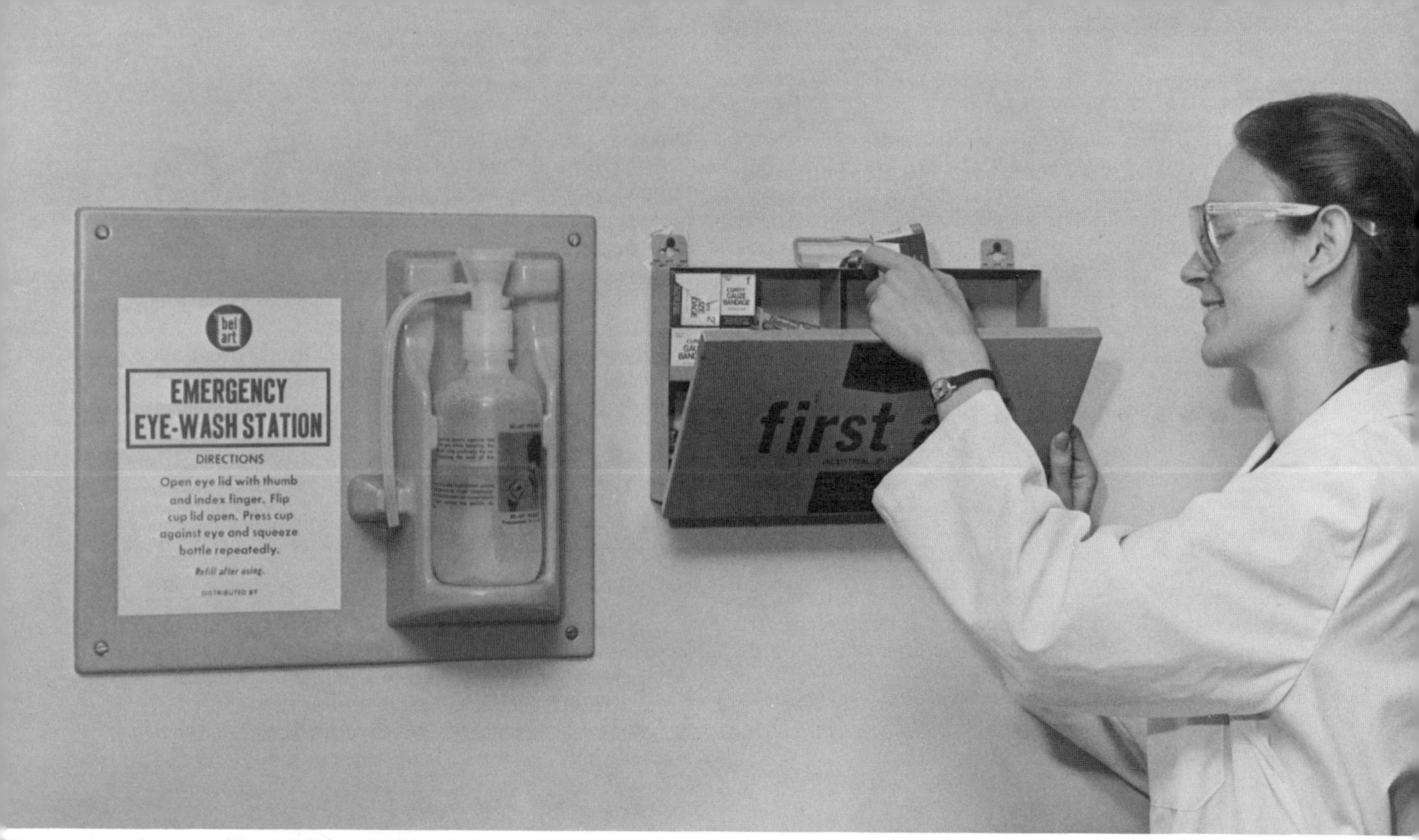
bel art
EMERGENCY EYE-WASH STATION
DIRECTIONS
Open eye lid with thumb and index finger. Flip cup lid open. Press cup against eye and squeeze bottle repeatedly.
Refill after using.
DISTRIBUTED BY
first

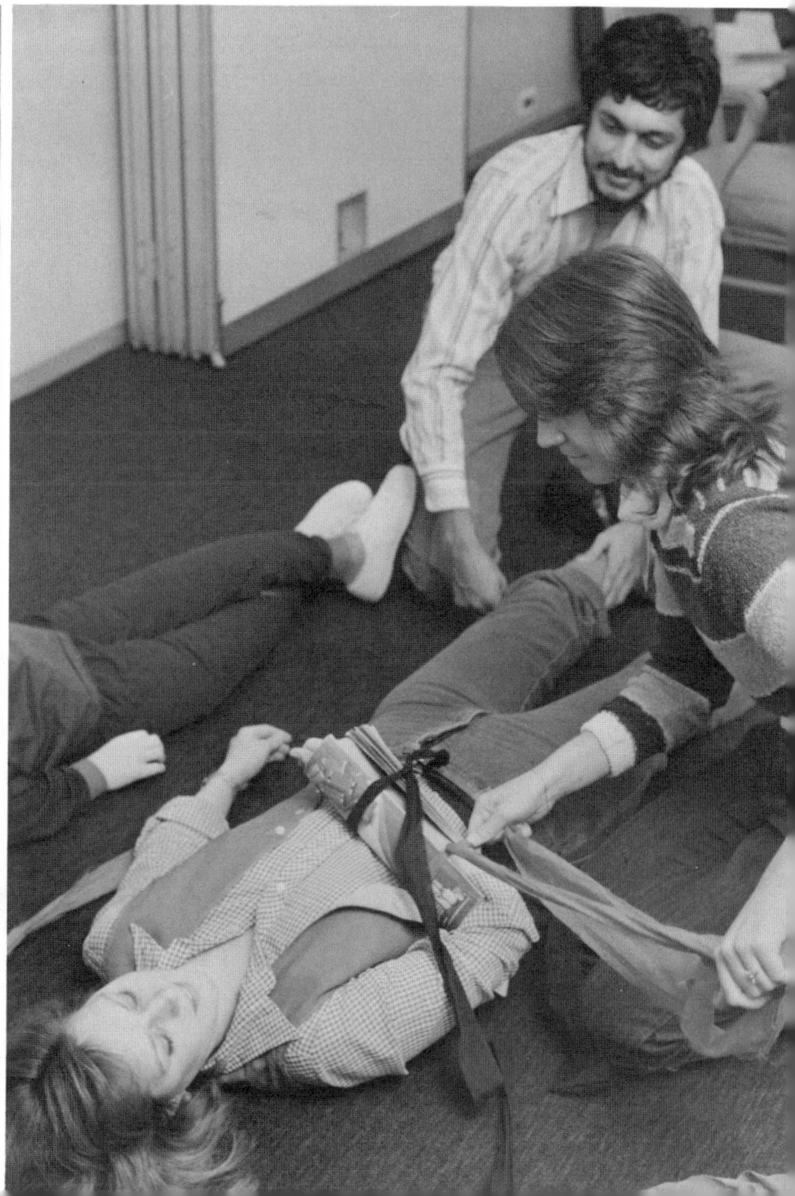

CHAPTER 12

Planning for Emergencies

Top: Periodic checks of the condition of equipment can prevent problems during emergencies.

Lower left: A positive action plan facilitates coordination of emergency evacuation procedures.

Lower right: Employees practice first aid techniques.

Emergencies in aviation operations include aircraft accidents, fuel spills, fires, hurricanes, tornadoes, floods, earthquakes, hijackings, bombs, bomb threats, and airport civil defense. Many of these emergencies require immediate response by specialized teams, such as the fire/rescue brigade or bomb and security team.

Regardless of the size or type of organization, management is responsible for developing, operating, and maintaining a flexible emergency action program that will provide:

- Maximum protection for passengers, employees, and the general public
- Maximum protection of equipment, facilities, and property
- Immediate and effective response to accidents or emergencies
- The ability to take prompt action in saving lives and preventing suffering or minimizing destruction or damage to property

This chapter provides basic information to help develop emergency action plans. Each area in an organization must prepare detailed operating procedures, which are to be part of the overall emergency action plan. The operating procedures could be in checklist form for ease in both instruction and use. These procedures must:

- Instruct how to notify key personnel in an emergency
- Assign responsibilities and/or tasks by position title
- Define operating locations
- Outline procedures/instructions on how each task will be accomplished. Instructions must be detailed enough to enable the individuals or unit to function properly.

All emergency programs should incorporate all or most of the following: a printed plan, company-wide planning, command headquarters, protection of records, personnel shelter areas, alarm systems, fire prevention and protection, property protection and security, first aid and medical, rescue and salvage, warden service and evacuation, transportation, mutual aid plans, local services, and program testing procedures. Training of personnel is extremely important.

Preparedness is insurance against sudden disaster. While it may not always be possible to prevent a disaster from happening, it is possible to minimize its effects by knowing just what to do and then doing it promptly.

AIRCRAFT ACCIDENTS/EMERGENCIES

Flight emergency conditions may be broken down into four categories:

- A major accident without warning where severe damage has occurred to an airplane and severe injury or death to passengers and crew
- A potentially serious accident where advance notice has been received (such as a severe fire aboard an aircraft, wheels-up landing, or structural damage in flight)
- A moderately serious situation involving such items as landing with an engine inoperative, hydraulic difficulties, and warning light irregularities
- A potentially serious accident where general cargo or hazardous materials are identified as toxic or flammable materials.

Ground mishaps involve situations such as:

- Aircraft equipment ground damages
- Cargo damage
- Fire resulting from fuel spills or other causes
- Personnel injuries/death
- Hijack and bomb threats.

Policy and Procedures

Regardless of the type of accident, the first priority is the rescue of all involved, and the second, the protection of aircraft, buildings, and equipment.

It is strongly recommended that each airport, air carrier, and corporate or fixed base operator have its own emergency plan(s) so that the procedures can be put into effect quickly. These plans should be coordinated with airport management to make sure that no conflicts exist. Although accidents and emergencies vary in nature, responses will be essentially the same.

Response to emergencies can be divided into phases to readily identify the actions required by each person in each phase. The phases are:

- *Notification.* Any agency or person receiving or having information of an actual or potential accident/incident or disaster will immediately relay this information to the predesignated communication center for appropriate action.
- *Response.* Each response agency must be prepared to act individually and should maintain contact with the communication center.
- *Recovery.* Recovery is a complex, time-consuming operation. Experience has shown that from one week to several months may be required to make a complete recovery following an accident or disaster. A recovery plan must be developed based on the requirements/findings of all response agencies.

Accident Plan. Items to be considered in an accident plan are:

- *A statement of management policy.* Accident response procedures should outline in broad detail the policy, action, organization, and responsibilities of individuals and groups who should govern the handling of all major accidents.
- *Periodic review.* Responsible individuals and groups should meet to review and update the accident procedures, as well as to discuss possible problems.
- *Coordinators.* These people would handle the following:
  - Communications
  - Medical assistance
  - Corporate liaison officers
  - Relative centers
  - Identification bases
  - Scene
  - Engineering and maintenance
  - Public relations
  - Security
  - Safety

Establishment of Notification/Communication Responsibilities. A detailed emergency plan would include provisions for notifying airline personnel, as well as outside agencies. Items in the plan might include:

- *Establishment of a central communication facility.* The overall assigned coordinator can keep in constant communication with all other coordinators as listed above.
- *Establishment of a notification list.* Principals assigned accident responsibilities are to be notified with a minimum of delay. The notification

listing should contain current names and telephone numbers (office and home) of individuals assigned specific tasks. Copies of the listing should be readily available in the communications center and included in the on-scene coordinators response kit.

- *Establishment of a method for notifying:*
  Civil Aeronautics Board (CAB), Federal Aviation Administration (FAA), Federal Bureau of Investigation (FBI), Royal Canadian Mounted Police (RCMP), Transport Canada (TC), International Police (Interpol), Scotland Yard, or other agencies having jurisdiction
  Medical assistance
  Post office department
  Package forwarding agencies
  Courier services (if agents are involved)
  Department of Defense (if security cargoes are involved)
  Appropriate military services (if service personnel are involved)

Establishment of Control Responsibilities.

- *Command/direction.* The airfield manager or fire chief (someone in complete charge) will direct and control all airfield operations relative to this plan. Persons having knowledge of an impending or actual disaster/major accident will immediately notify the appropriate designated individual (or position title).

- *Control* by sirens, loudspeaker, telephone, intercom, public address system, radio, or runners.

- *Establish a disaster response group* headed by the team chief/on-scene director described above. This group should consist of selected representatives from all airfield support activities who are qualified to take action in their respective functional areas and provide technical support to the team chief on particular facets of the situation. The disaster response group will include, but not be limited to, the following members:
  On-scene director
  Fire chief
  Security
  Medical
  Maintenance

Several USAF Air Rescue & Recovery and U.S. Army helicopter organizations are designated as Military Assistance to Safety and Traffic (MAST) units. These units have the responsibility of providing assistance during serious civilian medical emergencies (i.e., situations where an individual's condition requires air-evacuation to a medical care center as soon as possible to prevent death or aggravation of illness or injury). The decision to request a MAST helicopter is based solely on the judgment of the law enforcement officer, physician, or other responsible persons such as public safety officials at the scene of the emergency. Assistance may be provided only to the extent that it does not interfere with the performance of the military mission. The authority for the MAST program is contained in the Defense Appropriations Act, Public Law 93-155. When a MAST response capability (Air Force or Army helicopter operation) is located nearby, the basic plan should be coordinated with the unit commander.

Establishment of Specific Procedures. Establish procedures and designate individuals to secure and distribute the following information:

- Trip number (if air carrier)
- Date and time of accident
- Aircraft type (and plane number, both company and "N" numbers, if air carrier)
- Location of accident
- Crew names and domiciles
- Passenger lists
- Cargoes aboard such as mail, express, airfreight, baggage, company materials, and hazardous materials. Advise on-scene coordinator and identification coordinators immediately of any hazardous cargoes (radioactive, for example) or extremely valuable shipments.

Establish procedures and designate individuals to arrange for:

- Protection of aircraft, cargoes, passengers' belongings, and company equipment
- Crowd control
- Identification of authorized personnel
- Roadblocks as required
- Services of ambulances and hospitals
- Accommodations for personnel secured from other areas, relatives, etc.
- Transportation of personnel groups and equipment to the scene
- Food and special clothing
- Special equipment, such as bulldozers and cranes, for crash removal; coordination is especially important where USAF or Air National Guard units are located in the vicinity.
- Special personnel needs such as drivers, mountain climbers, water rescue personnel, etc. Where Army and Air National Guard units are located in the vicinity, coordination should be established for emergency use of security guards to prevent looting and provide safekeeping of wreckage; coordination should also be estab-

lished for possible usage of unit paramedics.

- Additional fire-fighting and rescue equipment
- Assistance to the injured
- Assembly point for the uninjured
- Center for relatives
- Identification of passengers and personal effects
- Disposition of bodies
- Temporary facilities to serve as hospitals and morgues
- Communication equipment (portable radios, transceivers and base station)
- Emergency lighting.

Availability of Nearby Facilities. The following contacts should be readily available. The type of assistance they can render should be determined in advance.

- Hospital
- Ambulances
- Fire-fighting and rescue vehicles
- State police and other enforcement agencies
- Maps and sketches for distribution to authorized individuals to use as guides to an accident scene
- Car and truck rentals
- Special equipment rentals
- Civil defense
- Government agencies (USAF, Coast Guard, etc.)

Emergency Salvage Kit. Consideration should also be given to establishing an emergency salvage kit if possible, or at least know the local source where the following items will be readily available:

- Supply of stationery items (paper, pencils, envelopes, carbon paper, folders, etc.)
- Rope, at least 300 m (1,000 ft), to be used in securing area, hoisting equipment, tying down tarps, and other tasks
- Miscellaneous: gloves (both rubberized and leather palm), hatchets, hammers, nails, hunting knives, blankets, flour or sugar sacks (for small items and personal effects), flashlights and spare batteries, tags with wire attached, block and tackle body bags, stretchers, axes, vacuum jugs, water cans, rakes, shovels and picks, coveralls, cameras and film, small hand tools, containers for fuel and oil samples, marking pencils, plastic bags, stakes for securing area, adequate footwear for area (boots, overshoes, etc.)
- Other items (such as cranes and barges) may be desirable and essential; the need is based on local terrain and conditions.

FUEL SPILLS AND FIRES

Spills of either gasoline or kerosene present a potentially serious fire hazard to personnel, aircraft, and equipment each time they occur. Therefore, every effort should be made to prevent them.

Controlling Spills

Following are recommendations to minimize the number of accidental spills:

- Develop a spill control procedure and establish a reporting protocol.
- Fuelservicing personnel should be thoroughly trained. They should observe proper grounding and bonding procedures. During overwing fueling, the fueler must never leave the hose nozzle unattended. The nozzle trigger is never to be wedged or tied in an open position. The fueler should also devote full attention to the job, making frequent checks of fuel level to prevent overfilling. During underwing fueling, the fueler must also understand the operation of the automatic shutoff in the aircraft fueling system and be able to monitor its operation at all times.
- All fueling equipment is to be properly maintained. It should be inspected daily and repaired as required.
- Every spill should be reported and investigated so that remedial action can be taken.
- If a fuel spill occurs, it should be treated as a potential fire source and the following action taken (note that if these are in conflict with local airport regulations, the local regulations take precedence):
- Stop fuel flow by closing the emergency shutoff valve immediately. Depending upon the nature of the spill it may be necessary to evacuate the aircraft.
- Notify the airport fire department (except for small spills as defined below). Supervisory personnel should be notified to determine whether operations in progress may either be continued safely or should be halted until corrective measures have been taken.

  Small spills of less than 0.5 m (20 in.) in any

direction are normally considered minor. Other than normal standby of ramp personnel with fire extinguishers, no other precautions are considered necessary.

Small spills (those not over 3.0 m (10 ft) in any dimension or not over 4.6 m^2 (50 sq ft) in area and not of a continuing nature) should have a fire guard posted with at least one fire extinguisher of a 20B rating, if fueling rate is not over 14 liter/sec (200 gal per min). (Extinguishers of higher rating are necessary if fueling rates are in excess of the above rate.) The spill should be cleaned up by using absorbent cleaning agents. The resulting residue should be considered a hazardous waste and handled according to local regulations.

Volatility of fuel is a major factor in spill hazard severity. Aviation gasoline and other low flash-point fuels at normal temperatures and pressures will give off vapors that are capable of forming ignitable mixtures with the air near the surface of the liquid. This condition does not normally exist with kerosene fuels. Each spill will have to be treated individually because of such variables as wind and weather conditions, equipment arrangement, personnel, and available emergency equipment.

Large spills, of over 3.0 m (10 ft) in any dimension and over 4.6 m^2 (50 sq ft) in area or of a continuing nature, are considered extremely hazardous. The airport fire department and regulatory agencies should be notified at once.

It may be necessary to evacuate the aircraft if it appears that the spill may present a serious fire exposure to the aircraft. Personnel should not walk through the spill area.

Motorized equipment within spill areas should not be started before a spill is cleaned up. However, if the engine is already running and the hazard to personnel is not judged too severe, the vehicle or vehicles may be driven out of the area.

Motorized equipment outside a spill area should be moved away or shut down as quickly as possible. If the fuel servicing equipment is moved, it should be determined that the fuel hose or pipe to the aircraft has been disconnected and stowed.

Large spills of fuel should be blanketed with foam. The spill should then be cleaned up and residues handled as hazardous waste in accord with local regulations. Fuel should not be washed down sewers or drains. If there is no alternative, the use of sewer or drains for elimination of fuel spills should be approved by authorities having jurisdiction and performed under their supervision. If this is done, the sewers should be flushed with large quantities of water.

Following a spill, depressed areas such as flap wells or wing sections of the aircraft involved should be inspected for accumulations of fuel or fuel vapors. Any fuel discovered should be removed.

All cargo should be inspected after a spill. If any cargo is contaminated with fuel, it should not be placed aboard until the fuel is removed or evaporated.

The aircraft should be removed from the fuel area before its engines are started, unless the spill has been completely eliminated.

Controlling Fires

If a fire does occur after a fuel spill, the following procedures are recommended and should be performed simultaneously (if sufficient personnel are available):

- The airport fire department and appropriate company management personnel should be called immediately.
- If an aircraft, fuel truck, or spilled fuel catch fire, the aircraft should be immediately evacuated. If fire prevents the use of the normal passenger loading stands, passengers should evacuate through the emergency exits.
- All equipment should be available to fight the fire. All members of a fueling crew in particular, and all ramp personnel in general, should be thoroughly trained in the use of fire extinguishers. Their training should include practice drills in extinguishing flammable liquid fires.
- If possible, the fuel truck should be moved from the fire area, following the precautions discussed above.

BOMB THREATS

Bomb threats are usually received in one of two ways:

- Casual remarks by passengers on aircraft or at terminals.
- Anonymous phone calls or letters.

Of the two, the latter is usually considered to be more serious. Both require investigation, however. The FBI or other cooperating agencies should be informed of all bomb threats.

Procedures

The following procedures are usually involved in bomb threat cases:

- Any person or agency receiving or having information regarding a bomb threat should record in detail all information concerning the threat and immediately pass it to the appropriate designated agency by the most expeditious means.
- The person receiving the call directly from the individual making the threat should solicit as much information as possible from the caller. If

possible, the person receiving the call should leave the line open and use another line to request the telephone operator to initiate tracer action. The person receiving the call should attempt to determine the following:

- Any accents or speech peculiarities of the caller
- Whether the caller is male or female
- Whether the call is local or long distance
- Any additional information that may assist authorities in their investigation
- Record the time the call was received
- Flights may be requested to return to the terminal. The aircraft may be removed to an isolated area. Passengers' baggage may then be removed and searched, usually by local authorities and the operating airline. Authorities or airline personnel will advise passengers on their course of action. The FBI normally interrogates all passengers.
- The aircraft may be thoroughly searched, usually by personnel of the operating airline.
- Certain military installations have dogs specially trained to sniff out most types of explosives. These dogs have been very effective. If a military installation is near, this possibility should be explored.
- Clearance for flight should be given only after all involved authorities have been satisfied that no bomb is on the aircraft.

NATURAL DISASTERS

Airline emergency procedures should include action plans for natural disasters such as hurricanes, tornadoes, floods, and earthquakes.

Weather bureaus are now able to detect and track hurricanes so that ample warning can generally be given for protection of property and for evacuation from threatened areas. Many airline weather units also can provide valuable warning information.

Establish severe weather warning procedures and checklists. Lead times for severe weather forecasts should be established and identified in order to complete required precautionary tasks. Lead times vary by locale so individual airports should establish times or distances for the following weather phenomena:

- Tornadoes/hurricanes/typhoons sighted within *x* kilometers or nautical miles of the airport
- Hail
- Surface winds 35 knots (18 m/s) or greater
- Freezing precipitation
- Heavy snow accumulation
- Thunderstorms

With tornadoes, however, it is usually not possible to provide as much advance warning or to anticipate the specific strike area as well as with other windstorms. Therefore, companies should be prepared with action plans that will protect their employees, passengers, and property.

In North America, many areas with seismic activities are found along the Pacific Coast. Earthquakes occur without warning. As with hurricanes and tornadoes, they generally affect the entire community or a large area. Therefore, assistance from community services may not be available; consequently, companies and/or airports may be solely dependent upon their own action plans.

Action Planning

Emergency action plans for all contingencies should consist essentially of three parts: (1) a thorough preparedness program developed in anticipation of an emergency condition, (2) a specific plan of action including definite assignments of responsibility during emergency conditions, and (3) a "clean-up" or salvage procedure to follow emergency conditions so that normal operations may be resumed as quickly as possible.

Copies of each response agency's action plan must be consolidated into one master document that is readily available to the command and control center.

Develop a procedure for evacuating personnel to a safe place. In the event of earthquake, evacuation should take place after the earthquake has subsided. During the earthquake, immediate protection under the nearest available cover should be sought. Personnel should avoid standing near windows or collapsible structures.

Some specific items to consider in developing the procedure are as follows:

- Designate shelter areas.
- Provide emergency lighting.
- Provide alarm systems.
- Provide for protection of aircraft; consider dispersal procedures and tie-down facilities.
- Provide an emergency water supply for fire-fighting services.
- Provide for protection of vital records (and duplication, if necessary).
- Design and construct buildings in accordance with all applicable codes so that they can better withstand destructive forces of nature.

- Establish procedures to shut down and restore service of utilities (such as steam, electricity, water, and gas).
- Assign and train specific crews for fire-fighting, rescue service, guard service, first aid and medical service, demolition and repair, transportation, investigation, public relations, communications, and warden services. Emphasize the need for panic control.

CIVIL DEFENSE

Procedures outlined in previous sections of this chapter cover most emergency situations that may develop; however, additional points of preparation should be considered in planning against the possibility of an enemy attack. Specific procedures that are developed should be based on information available from local Civil Defense offices and should be in accordance with current government regulations. Keep in mind that in the event of an enemy attack, industry may be completely dependent upon its own personnel and facilities to cope with an emergency. Because normal services may be wholly unavailable, management should, therefore, be prepared for self-sufficiency.

Specialized training in survival/nuclear warfare may be requested through the local or county Civil Defense Director.

Setting Up an Emergency Committee

An emergency committee should be appointed. This group is responsible for developing and publishing procedures and policies for handling emergency conditions. The emergency committee should be composed of senior personnel representatives from city and airport functions who will be responsible for the planning, execution, and support of the airfield operations outlined in the plan. The committee should meet at least semiannually to update plan functions, and review responsibilities and capabilities. As a minimum, committee membership should consist of the following:

Airfield manager	Chairperson
Fire chief	Member
Chief of security	Member
Civil defense director	Member
Medical representative	Member
Mortuary representative	Member
Airport tenants (airlines, fixed base operators, etc.)	

This group should have further responsibility for specifying preparation for an enemy attack. The following provisions are suggested.

- Blast and fallout protection
- Food and water supplies for a predetermined period
- Medical supplies for use by company doctors, first aiders, and others
- Emergency sanitation facilities in shelter areas
- Standby power units to provide power for pumping water, communications, lighting, and sewage disposal
- Emergency communication equipment such as appropriate radio to send and receive information concerning the attack
- Plan for evacuation, if considered an advisable course of action prior to or following the attack
- Radiation monitoring instruments to measure the radiation hazard
- Facilities for radiation decontamination.

Similar emergency plans should be drawn up by each airport tenant (airline, fixed base operator, etc.) to cover its own personnel and operations. This plan should be coordinated with airport management.

Setting Up an Action Committee

An action committee should also be appointed. This group is responsible for developing and executing all emergency activities that have been specified by the emergency committee.

A sufficient number of members should be appointed to the on-scene disaster control group to assure full coverage on a 24-hour operational basis. A typical on-scene disaster control group should consist of the following membership:

On-scene director	Chairperson
Fire/rescue	Member
Medical	Member
Security	Member
Public relations/news	Member
Maintenance/engineering	Member
Safety	Member
Photography	Member
Legal	Member

Additional representation as deemed necessary by the on-scene director.

The action committee is an "on-the-scene" committee that has the following responsibilities:

- *Police services.* These include espionage and sabotage control, prevention of panic and mass hysteria, traffic control to shelter areas plus evacuation of plant, policing after an attack to prevent looting and to protect company property generally, and plant security services.

- *Records control.* Important records at all plants should be protected in storage locations—such as vaults. Important company documents that are indispensable to company operations should be duplicated and stored in remote locations.

- *Health services.* First aid training should be given to selected company personnel. Facilities for transportation of the injured should be provided—both within the plant and from the plant to the hospital. First aid supplies should be provided as well as food and water supplies.

- *Personnel rescue, facilities rehabilitation, and salvage operations.* These functions would most logically be handled by the group normally responsible for routine maintenance of the facilities and equipment. Duties of this group would include releasing trapped and injured persons and transferring them to first aid; setting up a motor pool of all available equipment and providing drivers; shutting off broken gas lines, water mains, and powerlines, and restoring services as soon as possible, including the fire protection system; cleaning up buildings and grounds as soon as possible; working with the radiation monitoring crew in removing radioactive dust where necessary; and inspecting buildings and facilities for damage.

- *Personnel protection.* The safest areas (from blast and fallout) in the structures should be designated as shelter areas. Depending upon the nature of the emergency, personnel should either be directed to the shelters or ordered to evacuate the premises in accordance with prearranged plans. Wardens should be assigned to assist personnel.

- *Fire prevention and extinguishment.* Brigades trained in fire fighting and fire control should be established. After receiving an alarm, they should respond and attempt to extinguish fires using plant fire appliances. Other associated activities—closing fire doors, securing flammable liquids, and salvage operations—should be included in the activities of this group.

- *Radiation monitoring.* Proper instruments should be obtained and a crew trained to measure radioactivity following an enemy attack. Controls should be set up to protect employees from entering radioactive areas. (This crew would also work with the decontamination crew in cleaning up radioactive areas.)

- *Communications.* A means should be provided to receive alert messages signaling an impending attack and for transmitting this alert to plant personnel so appropriate action can be taken.

- *Protection of aircraft.* Consideration should be given to dispersal of aircraft, when possible, to protect against attack. (Hangars probably provide the best protection when they are available.) Following the attack, aircraft should be inspected and repaired as soon as possible.

REFERENCES

National Safety Council, 444 N. Michigan Ave., Chicago, IL 60611.

Accident Prevention Manual for Industrial Operations, Administration and Programs volume, 9th ed., 1988, Chapter 16, Planning for Emergencies.

INDEX